The Heart of Religion

The Heart of Religion

Spiritual Empowerment, Benevolence, and the Experience of God's Love

MATTHEW T. LEE,

MARGARET M. POLOMA,

AND STEPHEN G. POST

OXFORD
UNIVERSITY PRESS

OXFORD
UNIVERSITY PRESS

Oxford University Press is a department of the University of Oxford.
It furthers the University's objective of excellence in research,
scholarship, and education by publishing worldwide.

Oxford   New York

Auckland   Cape Town   Dar es Salaam   Hong Kong   Karachi
Kuala Lumpur   Madrid   Melbourne   Mexico City   Nairobi
New Delhi   Shanghai   Taipei   Toronto

With offices in

Argentina   Austria   Brazil   Chile   Czech Republic   France   Greece
Guatemala   Hungary   Italy   Japan   Poland   Portugal   Singapore
South Korea   Switzerland   Thailand   Turkey   Ukraine   Vietnam

Oxford is a registered trade mark of Oxford University Press
in the UK and certain other countries.

Published in the United States of America by
Oxford University Press
198 Madison Avenue, New York, NY 10016

Library of Congress Cataloging-in-Publication Data
Lee, Matthew T., 1972–
The heart of religion : spiritual empowerment, benevolence, and the experience
of God's love / Matthew T. Lee, Margaret M. Poloma, and Stephen G. Post.
p.   cm.
Includes bibliographical references and index.
ISBN 978-0-19-993188-0 (alk. paper)
1. Love—Religious aspects—Christianity.   2. Generosity.
3. Charity.   4. Benevolence.   5. Religion.
I. Poloma, Margaret M.   II. Post, Stephen Garrard, 1951–
III. Title.
BV4639.L386 2013   241'.4—dc23
2012012390

1 3 5 7 9 8 6 4 2

Printed in the United States of America
on acid-free paper

Belief in God has not gone away, no matter how secular society has become or how much effort reductionist science has exerted to banish Him. God has not gone away because people keep encountering Him, in unexplainable, intensely spiritual moments.

BARBARA BRADLEY HAGERTY, *Fingerprints of God*

If the outer mind hungers for status, money, and applause, the inner mind hungers for harmony and connection— those moments when self-consciousness fades away and a person is lost in a challenge, a cause, the love of another or the love of God.

DAVID BROOKS, *The Social Animal*

Contents

Acknowledgments

The Flame of Love Project, the research endeavor that supported this book, has been a journey—a research pilgrimage, if we may use the term—on which we have traveled for short and long distances with countless others. We would be remiss if we did not try to acknowledge the significant roles they played and to express our deep appreciation.

This project was made possible by a generous award from the John Templeton Foundation to the Department of Sociology at the University of Akron and the Institute for Research on Unlimited Love (IRUL) that provided funding for the national survey, the interviews, biannual meetings of our research team, five interdisciplinary subprojects funded through a competitive Request for Proposals, and a host of other activities. The scope of the Flame of Love Project allowed for serious dialogue between science and theology throughout the four years of active research and analysis, building relationships that are ongoing. Without a meaningful partnership with theologians, social scientists are left without a rich body of literature and expertise to interpret empirical findings, and theologians are at risk of developing their work dissociated from the lived experiences of real people. The dialogue is not always easy, just as interdisciplinary work more generally can be difficult. But we believe that our project has been greatly enriched by the conversations we have had with our research team over the past four years. To its great credit the Templeton Foundation continues to see the value of having serious dialogue between science and theology. For this we are most grateful.

Our work also benefited from the substantial international review process organized by the Templeton Foundation. Eleven external reviewers, in addition to the foundation's rigorous internal review process, critiqued our proposal. Although we were not able to satisfy all of the reviewer's requests, this process did sharpen our focus and helped us to clarify our goals, while strengthening our methods. We initially proposed a comparative study of the three Abrahamic faiths (Judaism, Christianity, Islam), but after constructive dialogue with the foundation we opted for a more restricted focus on Christianity, initially in the broadly defined pentecostal tradition (see chapter 2). More generally, throughout our funding cycle we received much constructive support and guidance from Kimon Sargeant (Vice President, Human Sciences), Christopher Stawski (Program Manager, Strategic Initiatives), and others at the Templeton Foundation. We remain grateful for their help and understanding as we modified important aspects of the project as it unfolded and developed.

Our initial research team of social scientists and theologians included Craig Boyd (Integration Professor of Theology and Science at Azusa Pacific University), Julie Exline (Associate Professor of Psychology at Case Western Reserve University), John Green (Distinguished Professor of Political Science and Director of the Ray C. Bliss Institute of Applied Politics at the University of Akron); Ralph W. Hood Jr. (Professor of Psychology at the University of Tennessee at Chattanooga), A. G. Miller (Davis Professor of Religion at Oberlin College), Thomas Jay Oord (Professor of Theology and Philosophy at Northwest Nazarene University), Clark Pinnock (Emeritus Professor at McMaster Divinity College), Arlene Sanchez Walsh (Associate Professor of Church History and Latino Church Studies at Azusa Pacific University), and Amos Yong (J. Rodman Williams Professor of Theology at Regent University).[1] Stephen contributed an additional theological voice, while Margaret and Matt approached the project from a sociological standpoint.

In the second year of the project, our research team expanded to twenty-two members as we added the principal investigators of the five subprojects funded through the Flame of Love Project. These individuals, and the titles of their projects, include Candy Gunther Brown (Associate Professor of Religious Studies at Indiana University) and Michael J. McClymond (Associate Professor of Theology at Saint Louis University), "Global Awakenings: An Ethnographic and Theological Study of Divine Healing in World Missions and Revivals as an Expression of Godly Love"; Donald E. Miller (Leonard K. Firestone Professor of Religion and Professor of Sociology at the University of Southern California) and Richard Flory (Associate Professor of Sociology at the University of Southern California), "The Dream Center: Love Embodied in Urban Social Ministry"; Kimberly Ervin Alexander (Associate Professor of Historical Theology at the Church of God Theological Seminary) and Mark J. Cartledge (Senior Lecturer in Pentecostal and Charismatic Theology and Director of the Centre for Pentecostal and Charismatic Studies at the University of Birmingham, UK), "Learning to Love and Loving to

Serve: A Study of the Socialization of Godly Love and Its Influence on Vocation"; Paul Alexander (Professor of Theology and Ethics at Azusa Pacific University) and Robert Welsh (Professor of Psychology at Azusa Pacific University), "Risking Death for the Love of God: A Theological and Psychological Study of Pentecostals Engaged in High Risk Social Action"; and Peter Althouse (Associate Professor of Religion at Southeastern University) and Michael Wilkinson (Professor of Sociology at Trinity Western University), "Charismatic Renewal as Mission: Godly Love and the Toronto Airport Christian Fellowship's Soaking Centers." Initial statements of these projects were published in a spring 2012 special issue devoted to the Flame of Love Project in the journal *PentecoStudies*. Matt and Margaret served as guest editors and we thank regular editor Mark Cartledge for inviting us to produce this issue.

The five subprojects added depth and diversity to our research initiative. The expanded research team served as a working group and think tank as individual investigators conceptualized and refined their research questions, methods, and data collection instruments. Our interviewees were selected with the help of the team, and our survey questions were developed with their assistance as well. We are grateful for their help and the wonderful dialogue we have had with them over the years.

Frank Macchia, an interviewee and a theologian at Vanguard University, has been especially supportive in this regard. Frank presented a keynote address at the Flame of Love Project's two-week summer seminar at Calvin College in 2009, as did Wayne Jacobsen, another interviewee and publisher of the best-selling novel *The Shack*. Both have been generous with their time, and their constructive criticism has helped us clarify our arguments. Our time at Calvin College was most productive, and we thank all of the participants in our summer seminar. Special thanks to Jong Hyun Jung, who took part in this event and subsequently promoted the project in Korea.

We also thank Roger Heuser (Professor of Leadership Studies at Vanguard University) and his assistants for their tireless work helping us to organize a public research seminar devoted to the Flame of Love Project in October 2010. The responses we received from the roughly one hundred people in attendance continue to shape our thinking. For more information on this seminar, see note 29 in chapter 7.

Cynthia Read at Oxford University Press provided helpful feedback on our manuscript, including the suggestion that we change the title to *The Heart of Religion*. We had made the argument that our work attempted to understand this topic, but Cynthia convinced us to tackle the subject directly. We also thank the five primary exemplars featured in the book and listed in table 3.2. We shared a draft of our book with them, and we appreciate their responses. In fact, throughout our research process we have sought out the opinions of those we interviewed, sharing parts of chapters with them or having follow-up conversations to explore with them the ideas and understandings that we were developing. Colleagues at Akron and elsewhere provided thoughtful reactions to drafts of our chapters. There are too many to list, but Becky Erickson, Kathy Feltey, Laura Harrison, and Vince Jeffries deserve special mention. Matt thanks the students in his classes, especially the Sociology of Love, for participating in dialogues that helped refine the ideas presented in this book. Research and teaching are enriched by this kind of reciprocal relationship. It should be clear by now that our debt to others is enormous. Our analytical perspectives have been broadened in important ways by our ongoing interactions with a large research team and the support of an even larger scholarly network. These good people challenged us to clarify our arguments and sharpen our analysis.

Last, but certainly not least, we need to thank our interviewees. Without their selfless giving of their time and willingness to share their lives with us, we could not have completed this book. Our national survey is informative, but in some ways it raises more questions than it answers. Our interviews help us to make sense of the descriptive patterns revealed by our survey.

This book emphasizes divine love as an overlooked component of contemporary Christian benevolence. We have endeavored to show how religious groups tend to see the world through different cultural grids, and we use accounts provided by our interviewees to demonstrate the process through which cultural grids are perpetuated and how they may change. When all is said and done, however, we must humbly confess that as scholars we too see only in part, as through a glass darkly. But we have seen the ways in which the experience of divine love matters in America. Our analytical approach grew out of a wide-ranging interdisciplinary dialogue about how we might shed more light on this important issue. We hope that our work advances this dialogue.

List of Tables and Figures

The Heart of Religion

Introduction

> The most dramatic stories about God came from Americans who felt that they were directly touched by God. In almost all cases, their divine encounters had powerful ramifications.
>
> PAUL FROESE AND CHRISTOPHER BADER, *America's Four Gods*

> All the world faiths insist that true spirituality must be expressed consistently in practical compassion.
>
> KAREN ARMSTRONG, *The Case for God*

THE BUDDHIST SCRIPTURES contain an apocryphal story of a religious leader who asked the Buddha whether he was a god. The Buddha is said to have denied this mantle, arguing instead that he had learned to transcend selfishness, with its illusions of pleasure. In the place of illusory and self-destructive paths, his daily practice cultivated an enlightened state of being that allowed him to live at peace in a suffering, conflict-ridden, and generally imperfect world. But more than this, it empowered him with the tools—emotional and physical—to make a positive difference in the lives of others. Enlightenment was not an end in itself; it had a practical application for the benefit of the larger world. The Buddha wished to be remembered, he said, not as a god but rather "as one who is awake."[1]

Through our research we have learned that millions of Americans are striving for this same goal, although their path generally travels through a Christian landscape rather than a Buddhist one. They are engaged in a never-ending struggle to wake up from the petty selfishness of an egotistic lifestyle to embrace and live out the values of the Kingdom of God: spiritual growth rather than the hedonistic exploitation of other people and natural resources; concrete acts of practical compassion instead of turning a blind eye to suffering. There are countervailing pressures at work in this process, as most of our actions reflect a combination of self-interest (enlightened or otherwise) and other-regard. But the struggle for spiritual enlightenment and the fruits of this struggle is a story worth telling. Cynics will decry as Pollyannaish any study of *spiritual empowerment*, *benevolence*, and the *experience of God's love*, as described by the subtitle of our book. And it is indeed important not to fix our gaze only on the bright side of life. After all, if the "spiritually empowered" are making a difference in the world, the difference that they make is not always universally acknowledged as beneficial. Some become active in politically conservative causes, others in liberal ones, in ways that may work at cross-purposes.[2] We do not gloss over such differences; instead, we seek under-standing by placing them into their social context.

What exactly is *benevolence*, and who gets to decide? This is an important question, and one for which there is a ready academic cop-out: it depends. Scholars are fond of qualifying almost everything, with good reason—human life is complicated in ways that resist glib generalizations. If our motives are always mixed, can there be any "pure" goal or unambiguously benevolent act? The answer depends on who is doing the judging. This point should not be lost on any Christian. After all, Jesus was tortured and put to death at the hands of religious leaders and government officials who saw him as a malevo-lent troublemaker rather than benevolent savior. Standpoints matter. And we can find plenty of contemporary examples of this kind of discord from our own research. To take just one example, consider Paul Alexander—whose interview serves as one of the five featured narratives of this book—and his struggle with his church-based employer and the larger denomination itself. Whereas his denomination has been overwhelmingly supportive of recent American military actions abroad, Paul has had a spiritual awakening that has put him at odds with his social context and his former self. This is because his new perspective precludes violence on the grounds that it is inconsistent with the life and teachings of Jesus. Who is right, old Paul or new Paul?

We will take up this question again, but we are getting ahead of the story. Paul, like the Buddha, has had a spiritual awakening (in fact, he has had several). This results in a *spiritual empowerment* that is a common experience among Americans and probably all human beings, even secular ones. That last point may sound counterintuitive, but those who have studied the issue care-fully would not be surprised.[3] Lots of runners, for example, and particularly ultra-marathoners (those who run races longer than fifty miles), talk about the transformative power of running—often in spiritual terms. Many argue that at some point they have had an awakening (some even use the phrase "born again") that ultimately increases their compassion. Matthew has noticed a culture of generosity among amateur runners that seems very different from other competitive sports. Perhaps there is something about spending many hours in a voluntary crucible of complete solitude and great physical pain that is purifying, that strips away the layers of selfishness that harden the heart. Dean Karnazes, an elite ultra-marathoner (he has run over two hundred miles without stopping, and he ran a marathon to the South Pole), describes what happened to him in the last mile of his first hundred-mile race. He went from crawling on the ground, to almost giving up after ninety-nine miles, to being able to stand again and finish the race as a runner:

> It struck me that in the space of a few steps that my past as I knew it had suddenly ceased to exist. Nothing would ever be the same from this point on. I'd been profoundly transformed by this journey.... My outlook became more expansive; my shortcomings less significant. Others were treated with greater compassion, increased tolerance, broader humility.[4]

The spiritual experiences associated with running long distances are analogous, not identical, with experiences of a deity. Both are personally transforming and capable of promoting greater concern for the welfare of others. More to the point, some of the people we interviewed for this book seem to be the religious equivalents of ultra-marathoners. They claim to have had dramatic encounters with God's love that gave them the strength to keep going during their darkest hours. The benevolent work of another of our five featured interviewees—Heidi Baker—has brought her into contact with the physical pain of contracting debilitating diseases as well as the emotional distress of having a child starve to death in her arms, among other nearly unbearable circumstances associated with living in the developing world. Yet she remains optimistic and full of hope. More importantly, she remains quite effective in organizing and motivating others to care for thousands of orphans in impoverished areas. Many follow her lead and adopt some of these children as their own.

Our focus is on Christian spiritual awakening, but we trust that readers of all backgrounds will find something in their own experience that helps them to identify with the transformative narratives that we will share. The latest book of one of the authors (Stephen), *The Hidden Gifts of Helping*, contains many examples of the power of generous giving itself—with or without a sense of spiritual empowerment—to evoke a deep, inner revolution within us all. He shares his own story of being uprooted from the community that he had called home for over two decades and "struggling to deal with feelings of displacement and loss."[5] But then he met a man named Jack on a train. Jack's wife had recently left him, he had lost his job, his money was running out, and he had recently been diagnosed with cancer. But Jack said that his work as a volunteer at a soup kitchen helped him keep going and that "some days I feel better than I ever have."[6] On hearing this, Stephen felt as if he had been "jolted awake from a deep sleep."[7]

This feeling of waking up to a new world is nearly universal, and it plays an important role in the processes we describe in this book. Recall the Buddha's wish to be remembered "as one who is awake." Religion, at its best, helps people transcend themselves and wake up to their true potential. There are corruptions, of course, and these have been well documented. There are also many ways of studying religion. Some examine how demographics affect church attendance and other religious behaviors; others explore the role of religious belief in shaping the outcomes of political elections. Recently scholars have helped us to better understand the role of social networks in organizing religious life. Demographics, creeds, denominations, social networks: these form the *structural shell* of religion. But our narrative is about how Americans wake up to the reality of divine love in a Christian context and then attempt to express that love to others through benevolent acts. This is the *heart of religion*. Our study focuses on the Christian tradition, but our findings may be applicable to religion more generally.

The "essence of religion," writes Karen Armstrong, is "transcendence," or "living beyond the confines of egotism."[8] This may seem like too lofty a goal to even imagine. But if you have ever been tempted to say something hurtful about another person and you refrained, you have experienced this state of being on a small scale. In her most recent book she concludes, "The point of religion was to live intensely and richly here and now. Truly religious people are ambitious. They want lives overflowing with significance."[9] What is the source of this significance? The sages of the Axial Age (900 to 200 BCE) who founded the bedrock religious traditions—Judaism, Hinduism, Buddhism, Confucianism, Daoism—that continue to shape our thoughts and actions today have left us an important legacy that speaks directly to this question. It is one that we overlook to our detriment. Whereas the modern era often seems preoccupied with doctrinal conformity, such that simply holding the "correct" set of beliefs has become the true test of faith in some circles, the Axial Age valued responsibility and practical, effective action. Religious leaders put "the abandonment of selfishness and the spirituality of compassion at the top of their agenda. For them, religion *was* the Golden Rule."[10] At the heart of this agenda was "love," which meant "being helpful, loyal, and giving practical support to our neighbor."[11] This is the standard by which religion was judged.

The people we interviewed have an intuitive grasp of this fundamental point. We found many pragmatists, but few dogmatists. There is an energy within people like Paul Alexander and Heidi Baker that is palpable. Others feel it, and it may be one reason they collaborate with them in their benevolent work. The energy comes from their experiences with divine love. Paul might prefer the phrase "divine justice," as he sees love and justice as inseparable, and at times possibly as synonymous. The image of God's warm, caring, all-enveloping love better reflects Heidi's experiences and understandings. Empowered by this self-transcending, divine loving energy, however it is understood, Paul and Heidi are better able to persist in their benevolence when the going gets tough and others might experience burnout. Why? The Christian tradition teaches that people who love others and who have done no wrong may find themselves under attack, rejected, disrespected, and even hated. They do not seek this, nor should they, as this would be pathological. But sometimes suffering finds them, and they accept it. They wish it were not so, yet they believe that if they continue to love unconditionally they will find eventual surprising results. This is because no matter how dark the scene in the drama of history, they tell us that they know (with a knowledge that "surpasses all understanding") that God is present in their lives.[12]

Paul, Heidi, and the others we interviewed are in touch with a sustaining love that revitalizes them when they feel like giving up and helps them see beyond their immediate circumstances to better understand how their lives fit into an overarching, loving plan for all. Their model is Jesus, who never became hurried, anxious, or distracted because he was engaged in an ongoing healing, loving, empowering prayer relationship with the Father and the Spirit. We explored with our interviewees how this experience of deep prayer helps prevent wrong decisions, reduces worry and anxiety, fosters inner healing and peacefulness, invites God into daily activity, produces confidence, sharpens discernment, increases energy for action, prevents distractions, and helps distinguish mere "busyness" from real fruitfulness.

If practical love born of an ongoing relationship with the divine is at the heart of religion, what about the third part of our subtitle: the *experience of God's love?* This relatively innocuous-sounding question begs many others. In *America's Four Gods*, sociologists Paul Froese and Christopher Bader document a contemporary "war over who God is" and a "deafening cacophony of descriptions of God."[13] Although they point out that 95 percent of Americans believe in "God," consensus about the meaning of this word quickly breaks down. For example, slightly more than half see God as sexless, while just under half believe God is male. Further complicating the matter, a large number of atheists claim to have spiritual or supernatural experiences (including feeling at "one with the universe"), which are indicative of the notion of "God" as a distant cosmic force rather than an identifiable deity with whom one can have a personal relationship.[14] Froese and Bader cite sociologist and Roman Catholic priest Andrew Greeley's view that religion is "the primary narrative of our lives" and "God is the foundation of our worldview," then immediately turn to a discussion of the "culture wars" and Americans' "fundamentally different understandings of reality."[15]

For the vast majority of people, God is indeed the lens through which the world—and the individual's place within it—is given meaning and order. But is this God loving and nurturing, or demanding and judgmental? Actively involved in the events of the world and individual lives, or disengaged and aloof? An impersonal force (e.g., the unknown and possibly unknowable "cause" of the Big Bang), or a being with whom one can relate, even in an intimate way? Americans are divided, and these divisions are closely related to social, moral, and political viewpoints. For some, stern judgment is itself a form of love, and all attempts at nurturing require the enforcement of clear moral boundaries. But the quote from Froese and Bader that opened this chapter—about "powerful ramifications" in people's lives resulting from being "directly touched by God"—raises an intriguing question: is a particular kind of religious experience especially important for *spiritual empowerment* and *benevolence*? Our research suggests that experiencing God's love is the key to these closely related outcomes. Froese and Bader note, "Nearly all Americans (85 percent) feel that the term 'loving' describes God well. In fact, the term 'God' is almost synonymous with the idea of a loving deity."[16] Perhaps by paying more attention to the experience of God's *love* we might reduce the "deafening cacophony" that seems to obscure our collective image of God. Yet we have relatively little systematically collected empirical data about how this love is experienced. Our study represents a starting point for remedying this gap.

If better than eight out of ten Americans use the word "loving" to describe God, it would seem that this variable holds little promise because of a lack of variation. But our work does not stop with this single measure. Instead, we employ a national survey to better understand variations in the extent to which some people *feel* God's love and whether they feel this directly, through others, or as the greatest power in the universe. We also asked whether this experience impacts their compassion for others in a variety of ways. Never before has this level of detail about the experience and expression of divine love been collected. If, controlling for other factors, those who claim to experience God's love most often or most intensely are the ones who are most generous with their time and money and most extensive in their benevolent service to others (beyond the near and dear), then it behooves us to explore the reasons why. This we accomplish through in-depth interviews with Christians known for their benevolent work.

We were not sure when we began this study exactly what we might find. And as scientists we are frequently reminded that this kind of research is fraught with difficulty. As a recent example, a best-selling book by Arthur Brooks claiming that religious conservatives were the most generous group in America was rightly unmasked as based on "an elementary statistical mistake."[17] One of the virtues of science is that other researchers eventually reveal such mistakes. We wanted to be certain that we had solid empirical foundations—both quantitative and qualitative—for the story that we relate in this book. After the data were collected and analyzed, we were relieved to find that we had something to say.

This is not to suggest that we have the final word on the topic. We shared drafts of our chapters with a diverse cross-section of readers. As we aim for a broad audience, this group included academics in a variety of social scientific disciplines and theologians, as well as laypersons. Some were religious; others were not. Their comments indicated that some of them liked what they read more than others, but the overwhelming reaction was a desire to read the rest of the book. We were clearly on to something that people cared about and had not seen systematically explored in previous works. Of course the scholars would have preferred to see more tables and methodological details, the laypersons less. Those looking for a uniformly "inspirational" book about religion were disappointed with our nuanced and qualified (read: academic) presentation. On the other hand, secular readers felt that more caveats were needed, lest it appear that their viewpoint came across—through omission—as less important than religious ways of seeing and being. We did interview some secular people engaged in benevolence for comparative purposes, but that is not our primary focus. And of course we could not accommodate all of the conflicting suggestions. Our aim was to investigate the relationship between spiritual empowerment, benevolence, and the experience of God's love in America and to write about it in a way that would satisfy scholars but also reach beyond the academy.

This work is the product of an ongoing dialogue between a theologian and two social scientists. We were informed by a larger research team also composed of social scientists and theologians, as well as a variety of different theologies, in developing our research questions, in designing our research instruments, and in conducting our interviews. Although sensitized by theological insights, in the final analysis this book is an empirical work guided by the rules and methods of social science. We believe that our interviewees were so open about the details of their lives and their innermost thoughts because we took their (lay) theologies seriously and created a safe space for them to express themselves freely. If previous studies have not picked up on the centrality of a loving God in the lives of benevolent people, this might reflect a more general bias against plumbing the depths of religious experience (as opposed to belief) in the academy.

Altruism or Benevolence?

We have avoided the term "altruism" in this book, preferring instead to focus on benevolence. This is partly because the people we interviewed overwhelmingly reject the cost/benefit distinction implied by altruism and prefer to see their benevolent work as a win/win effort, one that benefits themselves as well as others.[18] In a sense, this book stands outside the interpretive communities of scholars across disciplines who are focused on altruism, although it should be of great interest to these groups. A recent sociological review of the relationship between religion and altruism exemplifies the broad definition of altruism that has come to be taken for granted. It asks the question "Are religious people nicer people?"[19] This is no doubt a "leading-edge question in social science," as the authors contend, but it may be a distraction to equate altruism with being "nice." The prophets of the wisdom traditions of the world's religions were often not nice at all in their confrontations with social orders that they felt were contrary to the Kingdom of God. Such people were sometimes hated and persecuted, even to the point of being put to death. Importantly, for most of human history altruism was "associated with an absolute, transcendent, or cosmic sense of moral order…a fundamental shift in orientation away from ordinary life toward a higher conception of value, not simply doing good or having an other-directed orientation."[20] This conception can be found in early texts of the major world religions, such as the Sermon on the Mount, with its "language of excess." This sermon is "excessive" because it argues that it is not enough to conform to conventional norms (love your neighbor); rather, you must break with convention and behave according to the "radical polar alternative" (love your enemy).[21] The concept of altruism in contemporary parlance has lost this critical edge, as it has become the purview of the reductionist, cost-benefit analysis models of "sociobiology, psychology, and rational-choice economics."[22]

The people we interviewed would be more comfortable with classical understandings of altruism, which were predicated on a pre-Enlightenment belief in an "absolute, transcendent, or cosmic sense of moral order," and the notion of benevolence as a way of life, rather than one social role among many. Consider these remarks by sociologist Robert Wuthnow:

> Altruism still serves as a mode of cultural criticism offering a transformative vision of something higher.... Doing good, engaging in prosocial behavior, volunteering, helping our neighbors, constructing accounts of the worth of such actions—these are not examples of altruism; they are only made possible by the idea of altruism, by our conception of it as a more pure, higher existence to which we can only aspire.[23]

For most of us, this higher notion of altruism is not at the core of our self-identity. But it is for many of those we interviewed. In fact, the sociological review of altruism and religion cited above is explicitly dismissive of the "religious virtuosi" and "the extreme self-sacrificial demands of the Christian concept of love" as a foundation for defining altruism because this "may be too hard for the average person to practice."[24] It is little wonder that Wuthnow offers this conclusion about altruism in America:

> We make compassion culturally contingent. It ceases being an absolute and becomes relative to our values. In a society that doles out good deeds in small doses through volunteer agencies, voluntarism becomes compassion.... We do not believe in self-sacrifice; we do not believe in sharing too deeply in the suffering of others. Our individual autonomy is too important.... Some of the work—the work that can be divided into limited commitments—is accomplished. Much of it remains undone.[25]

This conclusion does not apply to many of those we have interviewed. The social, political, and psychological forces that shape participation in garden-variety prosocial behavior and volunteerism (e.g., donating blood), which is the topic of many studies of altruism, may not help us understand those who, like Heidi Baker, have devoted their lives to a sacred calling. We employ the term "benevolence" because it is less loaded with conceptual baggage and hopefully less distracting to readers with strong opinions about "altruism."

Caveat Emptor

The focus of our study is Christianity. This is not because we have evidence or make any assumptions that Christians are more compassionate, more benevolent, more religious, or more spiritual than other groups. We do not have the data to make such comparisons. Being well aware of the increasing religious diversity found in the American population and projections of what the American religious mosaic will look like in the future, we recognize that other faiths and those with no religious faith also have stories to tell. But research studies, taking place as they do at a specific time, are not crystal balls that describe the future but rather are limited by the era in which they occurred. In other words, most Americans self-identify as Christian, and our national survey reflects this fact: 78 percent claim Christian identity. Even 30 percent of those for whom religion and spirituality are not important accept the Christian label, which implies that they are cultural Christians, while virtually all (92 percent) of Americans who are both very religious and very spiritual also claim to be Christian.

Furthermore, although our survey is highly representative of the American population, its size does not provide the information that would allow comparisons of the smaller religious groups, some of which may become increasingly important in the religious mosaic of the future. For example, it would have been interesting to explore whether the other two Abrahamic faiths (Judaism and Islam) produce findings similar to those we found for Christianity. With a general sample of 1,208 cases across the United States, only 1.5 percent of the sample is Jewish and 0.7 percent is Muslim, making any meaningful comparison of the three Abrahamic faiths impossible. Buddhism (0.5 percent), Hinduism (0.3 percent), atheism (1.7 percent), and agnosticism (3.0 percent) represent other self-referenced religious identities too few in number to make valid statistical comparisons.

Our findings hopefully will lead other researchers to make comparisons of the patterns outlined here with those in religions for which we do not have adequate information. We have good reasons to believe that the traditions that developed from the foundations of the Axial Age (i.e., all of the major world faiths) will have much to teach us about the experience of God's love and the consequences of this experience. Most idealize *kenosis*: the concept of "self-emptying" by which one's will is subordinated to the perfect will of God.

Jesus, of course, is an archetype. According to Christian theology, he suffered a "humiliating 'descent'" in order to redeem the world.[26] In other words, he made himself nothing, to the point of crucifixion, in order to benevolently serve all humanity. Similarly, the apostle Paul claimed in Galatians 2:20, "I have been crucified with Christ; it is no longer I who live, but Christ lives in me." The ideal of selfless service to others is found in all traditions. In Hinduism, "Vishnu gave up the bliss of heaven to save the world," and "self-surrender was the central act of *bhakti*; it was an act of kenosis that transformed the person into a *bhakta*."[27] In Buddhism there is the hero figure of the *bodhisattva*, a person who forgoes the bliss of nirvana in order to help others find enlightenment. And the word "Islam" itself translates as "surrender" and requires "transcendence of the ego" in obedience to the will of Allah.[28] The list could go on.

Although we cannot explore these comparisons with our data, we do wish to note that our survey is able to identify and analyze differences among the various families of Protestantism, including mainline, evangelical, Pentecostal, black, Hispanic, nondenominational Protestants, and Roman Catholics, including charismatic Catholics and Hispanic Catholics. Moving beyond the numerical patterns revealed by our survey, we present some truly remarkable narratives from our interviews. Many of the people we have interviewed feel incredibly empowered by an intense, affective love relationship with God; others seem energized by less intense divine-human encounters. Some operate in a milieu that offers little support for supernatural experiences, while others are embedded in cultures that encourage the interconnections between such experiences and benevolent service. Some specialize in personal acts of benevolence that focus on families and friends; others are engaged in exemplary acts of service to church, local communities, and/or the worldwide human family. Some of the narratives that we present might seem unbelievable to some readers. We have chosen not to exclude accounts of events that seem impossible because perceived experiences of the miraculous are important to the biographies of our interviewees. They have become who they are because of their experiences and their reactions to these experiences. People claim to dialogue with God and they claim that this matters to them and shapes their behavior. Therefore, we must accurately represent their life *as they understand it*, rather than trying to sanitize or revise it to make it more palatable to some groups of readers who might feel uncomfortable with their claims. We are well aware of the "feet of clay" that some supposed saints turn out to have—indeed, Margaret has written a book on this topic.[29]

Our goal is not the creation of hagiography, and in fact the people we interviewed would be the first to point out that they are not saints and have important limitations.[30] Through their stories, we can grasp their humanity *and* their attempt to grapple with the mystery of divinity as they strive toward acts of practical compassion. If you find this idea intriguing, we invite you to join us as we document the widespread and life-changing phenomenon we refer to as *the heart of religion*.

I

Why Should We Care about Godly Love?

ENCOUNTERS WITH GOD'S love are quite common in America. They can be transformative, both for individuals and their communities. At times the effects reverberate throughout the world. Our national survey reveals that eight out of ten Americans claim to have had such experiences, at least on occasion. Eighty-one percent of respondents acknowledged that they "experience God's love as the greatest power in the universe," and 83 percent said they "feel God's love increasing their compassion for others." In order to better understand these broad patterns, we interviewed over one hundred Christian men and women from all walks of life across the country who provided us with countless examples of how their experience of participating in God's love, loving God, and expressing this love to other people has impacted their life and the lives of others. In this book and in a number of previous works, we have called this set of dynamic interactions *godly love*.[1] Godly love is a scholarly concept and is related to the Christian "Great Commandment" of loving God above all and loving neighbor as oneself, but it also includes the additional elements of receiving God's love and working with others in benevolent ways.

The twofold Great Commandment (see Matthew 22:36–40) directs Christians to love God and to love their neighbors as they love themselves. Godly love incorporates this but goes further, adding two additional components. First, one must experience God's love in order to love others properly. This is the "New Commandment" articulated by Jesus in John 13:34–35: "A new command I give you: Love one another. As I have loved you, so you must love one another. By this everyone will know that you are my disciples, if you love one another."[2] This aspect has been a major focus of some recent Christian teachings, which have replaced the image of God as an impassive, unmoved mover with the image of God as one who desires deep relationships and who suffers with people while lavishing an extravagant love upon them.³ The fourth component of godly love involves interacting with other people to realize not just one's own vision of benevolence, but to work together to establish the Kingdom of God (as collectively defined) on earth. To illustrate this somewhat complicated concept, we begin with a simple story.

Love Can Change the World—or at Least a Piece of It

When we conducted an interview with German missionary Klaus Kugler, we were not aware that he was one of the unnamed "missionary friends" cited by Jared Diamond in his Pulitzer Prize–winning book *Guns, Germs, and Steel*.⁴ Diamond described the Fayu of New Guinea much as Klaus had during his interview: at that time they consisted of about four hundred hunter-gathers who had formerly numbered about two thousand, "but their population had been greatly reduced as a result of Fayu killing Fayu." Diamond also mentioned that "one group of Fayu invited a courageous husband-and-wife missionary couple to live with them. The couple has now resided there for a dozen years and gradually persuaded the Fayu to renounce violence." Diamond's account of New Guinea was undoubtedly enriched by Klaus and his wife's knowledge about the Fayu, and he probably saw no cause to mention the details that Klaus shared with us. Different people tell the same story differently and for varying purposes. But the details not presented in Diamond's report of how peace came to the Fayu provide a good illustration of how godly love unfolds in the real world. It demonstrates how this love can change the world—or at least a piece of it. Klaus began his interview with the same story he had told earlier in the day at a local church in northeastern Ohio one November morning as we—Matthew, Margaret, and Stephen—were beginning to write this book.

> At one point in the 1980s when we had first come to Irian Jaya [West Papua New Guinea], members of the local tribe were breaking into our household while we would go shopping for supplies. They would break in with their stone axes and steal all kinds of stuff—like children's clothing. I don't know what they would do with it; they would just take it. Finally we said, "Lord, we have to come to you; we don't know what else to do. They are breaking into our house. What should we do?" And he said to us, "When they take your cloak, give them your coat also; if they take your goods, do not ask for them back." I could not believe it. Everything in me said "*No!* No!" You see, our Father is

never pushing us. You asked the question; that is the answer. You make the decision.

Then one day we made the decision. We said, "We want to do it." So I went to a boy who I knew was stealing. I didn't want to scare or frighten him; he was testing me with his bow and arrow. I said, "I know you have broken into my house, and I am here to tell you that I love you. I am not angry with you. And because you have broken into my house, I will give you this knife on top of all you have taken." He looked at me and then looked at the knife. He didn't understand it; but honestly, I didn't understand it either. But that is it—to show them that your love is not centered around material things but it is centered somewhere else.

Margaret heard Klaus share with the Sunday morning congregation details about his recent return visit with the Fayu, after having left Irian Jaya some years earlier. She decided to return for the evening service to learn more. She was struck by Klaus's account that demonstrated how one person's "hearing" from God can have dramatic social effects in a community—effects of spiritual experiences on the natural world that the research team had been studying for nearly three years. In response to a request Margaret made to the church member who was hosting Klaus, the missionary agreed to an interview with her. As Margaret and Klaus shared a late-night meal at a local restaurant, Klaus would further develop his story. This opening account, he went on to say, "was only the beginning"; the main breakthrough would come a few months later.

The chief's teenage son came by, and I had a big chunk of crocodile meat over the fire. He was hungry, and he was just about to take the meat to run. But I caught him in the nick of time and said, "Young man, this is my meat. Put it back on the fire" (which he did). But his father was so angry with him that I could hear him yelling for miles against his son—because he didn't know what I might want to do with him. When they steal among themselves, you get shot with an arrow. So we [Klaus and his wife] were talking—what would we do? Obviously he is afraid of me. My wife then wrapped a big chunk of meat in a piece of paper and said, "Go over there and give it to him." And I did. He was at first hiding in the jungle (he was afraid), but then he came out. And I was able to say in his language [Klaus spoke in the indigenous tongue]—that means, "My heart is not angry with you. I love you;

I have forgiven you; and I want you to receive this piece of meat—only for you." And I gave him the meat. He looked at me and then looked at his dad—and it was so (how shall I say it) so outside the normal experience because in these moments something significant happened. Something penetrated their culture—the principle of love and forgiveness.

And then the Holy Spirit spoke to me. He said, "Klaus, you want to translate my word (the Bible) and you think it takes twenty years." And I thought, "Yes, that is what all the linguistics books say." And the Lord said, "No. From the first day you were here you were translating it." And I said, "But, Lord, I can hardly speak the language." And he said, "You don't need to. You are translating my word through your life."[5]

This short narrative illustrates how godly love might inform the ways in which people respond to life's biggest questions:

- What is my purpose in life?
- How should I respond to those who harm me?
- What are my responsibilities to others?
- How am I to live in a conflict-ridden world?
- Who is my neighbor?
- Where can I turn for support in my hour of desperation, when circumstances seem to make little sense?

Perhaps the most important question is this: do experiences of God's love actually move a person to have a truly helpful effect on the lives of others? Plenty of evil has been done in the name of God and religion—one need only conjure a mental image of suicide bombers or what some have called "toxic churches" to grasp this obvious point—so what good is religious experience for making the world a better place? Is there a true religion of love to be contrasted with a false religion of hate?

We learned a great deal about how deeply spiritual people respond to such questions through the rich interview narratives we collected from over one hundred exemplars of notably self-giving lives. The wisdom we gained from these interviews helped us to develop a national survey on the relationship between religious experience and benevolence. These two sources of data, along with previous research, provide the empirical foundation for the central arguments of this book—a book that is less concerned with the external shell of "religion" (social networks, religious organizations, denominational creeds) and more focused on the inner experience of lived religion.[6] This is what we have called the "heart" of religion: the dynamic and emotionally powerful experience of a radically loving, radically accepting God that provides the energy for religious social networks and institutions. Ongoing encounters with divine love motivate many people to engage in the benevolent service of others, with the help of other people. This is not often recognized in contemporary discourse on benevolence, or even religion.[7] Our book seeks to establish a new dialogue on this neglected topic.

Consider the words of Klaus Kugler that you just read. How would you have responded to a thief in a similar circumstance? Would you have responded in anger or love? Would you have acted on a desire for retribution, or would you have also given more of your possessions to the thief as an expression of unconditional love? Klaus was not fully certain at the time why he responded the way he did. His generosity seems like a reflex. He was clearly influenced by his wife, who suggested to Klaus that he offer the chief's son more meat, in addition to what he had attempted to steal, as an act of radical love. Perhaps Klaus also had experiences with God and other people earlier in his life that might have conditioned his spontaneous expression of a love that, in his words, "is not centered around material things but it is centered somewhere else." In our overly cognitive social discourse, we do not talk about people like Klaus very often. Nor do we try to deeply understand why they engage in such counterintuitive actions. In *The Social Animal: The Hidden Sources of Love, Character, and Achievement*, David Brooks has written about the "intellectual revolution" currently occurring in some segments of the scientific community. This revolution has dethroned the "conscious mind from its privileged place at the center of human behavior"—a shift in thinking equivalent to the one that occurred after Galileo demonstrated that the earth was not the center of the universe.[8] This is not to suggest that rational thought, or the more general external approach to understanding religion, is unimportant. Both are essential. But there is more to the story.

As a German missionary to an exceptionally violent and isolated tribe in a remote part of New Guinea, Klaus, his wife, and their young children had the explicit intention of sharing God's love with a group of people who had had virtually no contact with the outside world for thousands of years. This group of people had escaped the seemingly ubiquitous reach of globalization and maintained a prehistoric lifestyle. At first Klaus did not understand their language or customs and given their violent ways this could have proved fatal. In an early encounter, Klaus watched in horror as men from two rival tribes engaged in a war dance which put them in a trancelike state that escalated into violence and ultimately culminated in brutal killings on both sides. As weeks turned to months, Klaus tried in vain to prevent the tribe from routinely stealing from his family. Catching the boy stealing a piece of meat, described above, provided an opportunity to solve this previously intractable problem. The boy's father expected Klaus to exact the appropriate penalty for stealing: death. Instead, despite his anger and not feeling fully in control of his actions, Klaus took a page from Jesus's playbook and—at the suggestion of his wife—responded by giving the boy an additional piece of meat. This display of unconditional love bewildered the tribe and served as a turning point in their relationship. According to Klaus, the tribe became eager to know more about the God who inspired such selfless giving. The horrors of the traditional war dance were replaced by an unexpected dance with the divine; peace now reigns among the members of this tribe.

As our study of godly love has continued to unfold over the past five years, we have been continually astonished by the ways that our findings revealed dimensions of the relationship between religious experience and benevolent service that have largely escaped sustained scholarly and popular attention up to this point. The reader might also be surprised by the following findings:

- "Prayer" is a richly textured religious phenomenon that has been largely overlooked by social scientists. Although nearly nine out of ten Americans say they pray (a figure that has not changed much over the past sixty years for which data exist), some forms of prayer (devotional, prophetic, mystical) are more empowering than others. A few virtuoso pray-ers have integrated multiple forms of prayer to great effect, and benevolence might be better served by this holistic approach.
- A spiritual transformation rooted in divine love is often intertwined with significant suffering. Both appear important as an individual makes the switch from self-interested goals to a life of serving others. In the process, the meaning of "well-being" is fundamentally redefined and enhanced. Suffering often persists after the transformation and continues to play an important role in benevolence. Although some religious subcultures have avoided or downplayed the centrality of suffering to the human condition, many of our interviewees continue to unflinchingly—and constructively—confront this issue.
- Anger at God is a normal part of the process of experiencing divine love and engaging in benevolence. Far from indicating lack of health in the human/divine relationship, anger—at a certain dose—is a signal that a deep relationship exists and is worth fighting for.

- Discussion of religion and spirituality often turns on the issue of belief. Cognitions are important, but the affective side of the human condition is often ignored. Our work shows that emotionally powerful experiences are key, and they often reshape beliefs. Our interviewees generally moved in one direction: discarding a judgmental image of God picked up during childhood socialization in favor of a loving and accepting representation of God that is more consistent with their direct, personal, and affectively intense experiences. Creeds evolve as people repeatedly encounter the loving presence of God in the midst of a suffering world.

- But perhaps *our single, most important finding concerns the extent to which experiences of divine love are related to a life of benevolent service.* For many Americans, the two are inseparable. And indeed, repeated experiences of divine love can provide the energy for a "virtuous circle" in which a positive feedback loop fosters increasingly intense or effective acts of benevolence. This holds across religious and social groups. Whether liberal or conservative; male or female; young or old; black, white, or Latino; or Amish, Episcopal, or Pentecostal, powerful experiences of God's love motivate, sustain, and expand benevolence.

Our approach was to collect diverse narratives from across the political, social, and religious spectrum, and our national survey was open to all Americans whether or not they were religious. From this initial diversity, some group differences turned out to be especially important in shaping the nature of godly love. A major purpose of this book is to better understand these differences while not losing sight of the common finding that unites these groups.

Rumors of Angels?

In much of American society there is a reluctance to share personal experiences of God's love. Much like sex in the early half of the twentieth century—before Alfred Kinsey released his two books on human sexuality—talking about personal experiences of the divine is off limits. It appears that many media producers—journalists, authors, playwrights, and scholars alike—may themselves be uncomfortable with the topic, so few have sought to explore the depths of American spirituality and the effects it can have on society. We are not talking about the taboo that instructs us to refrain from talking about religion and politics in polite company, but rather about the silence that seems to encompass sharing details about an affectively intense, personal relationship with God.

Debates about deity are hardly new to human history, but they have intensified with the development of modernity with its focus on scientific rationality as a foundation of all knowledge. This is a common trope in modern literature. Leo Tolstoy's classic nineteenth-century novel *Anna Karenina* (made popular for a new generation through Oprah's Book Club in 2004) provides one example. Konstantin Levin, a main character in the novel, and often regarded as Tolstoy's fictional alter ego, received "unquestionable knowledge," which was "revealed, inconceivable to reason," directly to his "heart" by God.[9] The Russian peasants Tolstoy so admired were quite familiar with this heart knowledge; aristocrats like Levin (and a young Tolstoy) found it harder to accept.

Four years after *Anna Karenina* made the *New York Times* best-seller list and as we began working on our research project, a cultural phenomenon known as *The Shack* was exploding. As we write these lines in May 2011, this novel has sold over 10 million copies in thirty-four languages. It has been on the *New York Times* best-seller list for 138 consecutive weeks (52 at number one) and was ranked as the best-selling book of 2008 by Nielsen.[10] Written over a century after *Anna Karenina*—and in much more prosaic prose, to put it mildly—*The Shack* has resonated with the people of Main Street while remaining virtually unknown to most scholars in the Ivory Tower.

Part of the appeal of *The Shack* is that it depicts God the Father as a black matronly woman, simultaneously compassionate, loving, and wise, an image that has connected in a deeply personal way with millions of readers around the globe. Through this fictional account many were able to reconcile the idea of a loving God with the undeniable reality of evil in the world. It achieved this goal, not through theological exegesis, but by imagining how a loving God might be a co-participant in suffering with people. In short, the book focused on relationships—a deep, committed, and emotionally intense relationship between a compassionate God and, in the case of the novel, a suffering father whose daughter was brutally murdered by a serial killer. By the end of the novel, the father has compassion for the killer and knows that God is not absent during his worst experiences. Therein lies hope. *Shack* author W. Paul Young, a son of missionaries and a former janitor, found such hope himself and shared it through his best-selling fictional account.

As a young child Paul was raised by his Canadian missionary parents among a Stone Age tribe near the part of what was New Guinea (West Papua) where Klaus Kugler would later follow his calling. Paul's life was scarred by sexual abuse, and he himself became an abuser while attending a Christian boarding school. Although always religious (he even founded a small church), he was haunted by his past. His spiritual awakening that brought the healing of a loving God to his tortured soul paralleled that of the main character in *The Shack*. An interviewer summarized Paul Young's awakening to God's love as follows: "[Young] found healing through relationships—with people and with God. But he said his religion failed him. 'Religion won't heal us. Religion can't.'"[11] Loving relationships with people and with God rather than religion—this is the theme of *The Heart of Religion*. Like *The Shack*, this book reflects the spiritual revolution that has occurred in American culture as the dominant image of God has shifted from a divinity who is the creator of hellfire and brimstone to a God who is love.[12] *The Heart of Religion* lifts the shroud around common religious experiences that are both personally life-changing and deeply transforming for some communities.

In the Beginning: Studying Godly Love

With orange, red, and yellow leaves dancing in the gentle sunlit breeze, Margaret made the familiar drive to the bucolic village of Hudson, Ohio, on a beautiful autumn afternoon. Stephen and Margaret often chose to meet at a coffee shop conveniently located between their homes in Cleveland and Akron, one with big windows to frame the beauty of the day and an ambiance hospitable to intense discussion. They had met there a couple of times before to talk about doing research together on "nature and grace," a shorthand phrase Stephen used to describe how God's unlimited love might affect human behavior. In many ways, Stephen and Margaret were an odd couple, with his theologically trained mind ever soaring toward the big questions of life and Margaret's sociological training forcing her feet to remain planted in a ground more amenable to scientific assessment. She would soon catch his vision, as each recognized the complementary gifts the other brought to the proposed project.

But something was still missing. Both were senior scholars and closer to the end of their careers than the beginning; the project needed the energy and insight from a member of a younger generation. For Margaret, Matthew seemed to be the perfect person, and he would be meeting Stephen for the first time this afternoon. Margaret had many intellectually stimulating exchanges with Matt, a sociologist who joined the faculty at the University of Akron as a specialist in criminology and whose office was across the hall from hers. Despite their dissimilar specialties—hers in religion and his in crime—they developed a friendship, and Matt would in time share his interest in developing a course in the sociology of love, partly as an antidote to the depressing effects of studying crime for a living. Margaret was confident that Matt was just the person needed to complete the team. A cordial introduction was followed by hours of discussion during which the autumn afternoon sun set with hardly a notice. Something new had begun as daylight faded into dusk; a theologian and two sociologists became partners in launching a new field of study around the core concept of godly love.

Exploring how ordinary mortals interact with God necessarily involves peering into a spiritual world that is shrouded in ambiguity and clothed with metaphor. Albeit from differing perspectives, Stephen, Margaret, and Matt shared awareness that such inquiry was seemingly mysterious and impenetrable with questions centering on issues of life and death, illusion and reality, time and eternity. Transcending the material world readily amenable to the five senses into a nonmaterial or spiritual world seemingly requires familiarity with another way of knowing as it seeks to deal with questions about the nature of God, the essence of love, and the meaning and purpose of life. The dominant materialistic worldview of modern humanity has put a particular spin on these cosmic concerns, but scientific skepticism and time-bound technologies have not silenced the sixth sense of spirituality that remains widespread in American society. Deep streams of spiritual energy still can be found beneath the materialistic surface of American culture to provide meaning and spiritual empowerment for at least two-thirds of Americans.

We have tried to capture some of this energy through interviews with 120 Christian exemplars of benevolence and their collaborators, like the one that produced the narrative by Klaus Kugler that opened this chapter. We interviewed well-known public figures—ranging from Anne Beiler, founder of Auntie Anne's Pretzels and one of the most successful female entrepreneurs in American history, to Jim Wallis, best-selling author and spiritual adviser to President Barack Obama—as well as those who serve others in significant ways without ever receiving awards or public notice of any kind. Our interviewees represent the diversity of the US population, from conservatives like Beiler (who delivered a kickoff speech for the Republican National Convention in 2008) to liberals like Wallis or Leah Daughtry (the latter served as CEO of the 2008 Democratic National Convention Committee [DNC] and chief of staff to the DNC chair). We conducted interviews with people from different, age, racial/ethnic, and socioeconomic groups, holding a variety of theological, political, and social viewpoints.

Results from our wide-ranging qualitative data were used to develop a survey instrument to collect data from 1,208 randomly selected Americans from across the United States, supplemented by hundreds of more targeted survey responses, to explore the relationship between spirituality and benevolence.[13] The Godly Love National Survey (GLNS), illuminated by the thick description of in-depth interviews, provides a unique account that reflects the experiences of millions of spiritual and religious people who claim to have encountered the deep love of God and seek to share this love with others. The purpose of our book is not to prove the existence of God or to advance the position that religion-based benevolence is more effective or desirable than secular counterparts. Instead, we hope to initiate a conversation that is too often lacking about the role that religious and nonreligious experiences play in convincing people to try to help others and make the world a better place. We focus on Christianity because the vast majority of Americans self-identify as Christians—and because our research shows that their religious experiences do make a difference in their willingness to serve others.[14] We need more in-depth studies of other traditions and the nonreligious in order to have a comprehensive dialogue, but this book is a starting point.

While there is little doubt that Americans live in a public culture that has been increasingly secularized, private spirituality continues to have a direct impact on individuals and communities. Scores of books have been written on "toxic churches," with their rigid beliefs and sometimes harmful practices; but there is another side to the religious coin, namely, religious and spiritual experiences commonly promoted by churches that have positive influences on families, friendships, and communities. We believe that one (if not "the") heartbeat found in this dynamic process of divine-human interaction is love—love that finds expression in the dialectical dance between God and humans. Indeed, as we were writing these words, the national magazine *USA Weekend* (which reaches 48 million Americans each weekend) arrived in our local newspapers. The cover story was "How Americans Imagine God." The article notes that Americans have many different images of God and includes this quote:

> No two are the same, and each is intensely personal and deeply passionate. Still, one gleaming, common thread weaves throughout: For Americans today, God, quite simply, is love. Christians, Hindus, Jews and Buddhists alike describe a loving presence who offers a pathway to goodness, peace, and brotherhood. Some imagine him, or her, as limitless energy; others, a force of nature as great as the ocean and as dear as a baby's smile.[15]

In an earlier work intended for theologians, social scientists, and others who may be concerned with the theoretical and methodological details that are foundational to our study, we used select qualitative interviews from our research to describe a process of divine-human interaction captured by our concept of godly love.[16] In this new book, which aims for a broader audience, we build on our previous work by using nationally representative statistics from the GLNS and by making more thorough use of our interview data. We have had several years to reflect on our findings as part of a sustained dialogue with our larger research team, composed of nineteen prominent social scientists and theologians from a variety of traditions. We expect our findings will be of interest not only to professional scholars of religion and altruism but also to lay readers who may be less concerned with theories and methodologies than they are about how real people claim to have experienced God's love and attempt to pass that love on to others. Our empirical research supports the thesis that a decided majority of Americans are engaged with divine love and this engagement positively affects not only their personal well-being, but also that of friends, families, and communities.

Although only our three names appear on the cover of this book, we would not have been able to collect our data and make sense of our results without the support of the aforementioned nineteen additional scholars from a variety of social science and theological disciplines who joined us as members of our extended research team.[17] Their diverse perspectives have helped us develop an interdisciplinary perspective, and we will reference some of their important work that our grant funded throughout this book.[18] The conversations we had about godly love with our research team helped us think through some of the initially puzzling findings we uncovered.

The concept of godly love may resonate with some readers, while others may have some reservations about it. To the skeptics, we respond that mythic tales, metaphysical treatises, and theological statements can influence human behavior and, when appropriate, should be factored into social scientific research. From a social psychological perspective, if spiritual realities are believed to be true, they can and do often have real consequences. Although the limitations of social science prevent researchers from judging the metaphysical *truths* claimed in different spiritualities, its methods do enable the investigation of the *consequences* of deeply held convictions and experiences. It is beyond the scope of science, for example, to prove the existence of God or the reality of a spiritual world; but the tools of social science do permit us to collect facts about religious beliefs and reports of spiritual experience, using them to explore possible consequences of the nonempirical. These findings should not be summarily dismissed (as often done in social science) by relabeling positive effects as "placebo" and negative ones as "pathology." As we will demonstrate throughout this book, experiences, even spiritual experiences that cannot be proven, do appear to produce lasting consequences that can be identified and assessed.

Is Godly Love Alive and Well in America?

Experiencing the love of God is the heart of religion. Unlike the love described in a well-known Shakespearean sonnet, however, most human perceptions of love—even divine love—do not involve "an ever-fixed mark that looks on tempests and is never shaken."[19] According to Wayne Jacobsen, one of our interviewees as well as an author and public speaker who played a major role in the editing and publishing of *The Shack*, human understanding of divine love is often more like a child engaged in tearing the petals off a daisy—"God loves me, he loves me not." Wayne describes his thirty-four years of "daisy-petal Christianity" as being like "the schizophrenic child of an abusive father, never certain what God I'd met on a given day."[20] Statistics, collected as they are at one point in time, are always more fixed than the dynamic stories told by interviewees. Yet statistics play an important role in supporting our thesis that experiencing God's love has important implications for benevolence by providing a skeletal framework of numbers for our broader story about godly love.

Select figures from the GLNS will give the reader a sense of the importance of spiritual phenomena within the context of American culture. The United States is more religious (regardless of whether the dimension is private devotion, public ritual, or religious experiences) than other Western countries, including Canada. Increasingly, however, the term "religion" itself has come under question. From the pens of militant atheists to daily news reports, religion often has been presented in a negative light. Even some conservative evangelical Christians have come to denounce "religion" as a dark spirit that corrupts "true faith," as they warn believers to beware of harboring a "religious spirit" of self-righteous laws and legalisms. Suddenly a question asked in surveys for decades—"How religious are you?"—has become suspect, forcing scholars through the painful process of sorting out spirituality (spiritual practices and experiences) from religion (rituals, doctrine, and organizations). Judging from our survey responses, however, for most Americans being "spiritual" and being "religious" appear to be nearly analogous terms.[21]

As found in our national survey, religion is reported to be important for 83 percent of the American adult population; the corresponding figure for the importance of spirituality is 88 percent.[22] There is, as these figures suggest, a high correlation between the two concepts. For example, 82 percent of those who say that religion is extremely important in their lives also claim that spirituality is extremely important. Whatever else they may be, the clear majority of contemporary Americans tend to consider themselves to be highly religious and spiritual. For some analytical purposes it is useful to separate religion and spirituality, but the statistical differences, as we will see, are negligible. In order to provide an introduction to the survey findings, we compare those who are both very religious *and* very spiritual (58 percent) with Americans who are *neither* religious nor spiritual (9 percent).

Spirituality and religiosity in America are commonly linked to a personal relationship with a *loving* God. Almost half (45 percent) of all Americans feel God's love at least once a day, and 83 percent have this experience at least "once in a while."[23] This finding will play an important role in our analyses, as many previous works have not assessed religious experiences in terms of love. Those reporting to be more highly spiritual and religious are also more likely to have regular experiences of a loving God.[24] It is fair to conclude that not only do Americans claim to be highly religious and highly spiritual but also that the clear majority experience God's love. According to our survey findings, being religious and spiritual provides an important context for considering the big questions of life. Those who reported that they are highly religious and spiritual also contend that they have a clear sense of the purpose of their lives. For example, nearly all (98 percent) of those who report that religion and spirituality are very important to them agreed or strongly agreed with the statement, "I have a strong sense of purpose that directs my life." The figures for those who claimed to be neither religious nor spiritual dropped to 68 percent.[25]

The effects of spirituality/religion do not stop with feel-good personal experiences. We also noted that the experience of God's love was believed to increase compassion for others. A clear majority of all survey respondents (83 percent) acknowledged that they "felt God's love increasing their compassion for others," and 53 percent claimed this is an experience they have "on most days" or more often.[26] Perhaps not surprisingly, self-identifying as religious and spiritual, regularly sensing God's love, and a strong sense of existential well-being are all statistically related to reports that feeling God's love increases compassion for others. In other words, the awareness of God's love not only fuels a sense of personal meaning and purpose but it also seems to stoke the fires of compassion.

But can these subjective perceptions lead to acts of benevolence? To put the question another way: do experiences of the divine actually have a helpful effect on the lives of others—can they make our world a better place in which to live? This is a central question and is a theme that will be developed through interview narratives and the presentation of survey findings in the chapters that follow. However, we would like to provide a sneak preview of some statistics that bear on our guiding question—an appetizer for the full-course analysis that follows. Our results suggest that these self-described personal attributes and experiences may indeed bear the fruit of good works.

Survey respondents were asked whether they went out of their way "to assist people in my community who are struggling," whether they "often come to the aid of a stranger who seemed to be having difficulty," and whether they "regularly provide financial support to local charities." A *Community Benevolence scale*, composed of the answers to those three questions, is the measure of good works employed in this preliminary examination. Based on what statisticians call bivariate analysis (studying the relationship between two variables), we found a significant statistical relationship between experiences of divine love and community benevolence. Those who score higher on the *Divine Love scale* are also likely to score higher on community outreach; those who score lower on community outreach are also likely to score lower on divine love.[27] For example, 42 percent of those who scored low on the Community Benevolence scale also scored low on the Divine Love scale, compared with 12 percent who scored low on divine love and high on community benevolence.

We tested these preliminary findings further by using multivariate analysis. Multiple regression analysis permits the simultaneous use of more than one indicator ("independent variables") that may have an effect on our outcome measure or "dependent variable." Our big research question, as we have noted, centers on the relationship between spirituality and benevolence. Bivariate analysis shows that there is indeed a positive relationship between experiencing God's love and community benevolence. Multivariable analysis allows us to test for other possible "causes" of benevolence. Perhaps it is "really" age or gender that is "causing" this finding. Perhaps older people and women were more likely to be included in the sample, were more likely to be benevolent and also "happened" to be spiritually inclined. Multivariate analysis, a technique we will use throughout our statistical assessment, is a procedure that allows us to determine whether perceptions of divine love are really contributing to benevolent actions—or whether benevolence is "caused" by something else (perhaps commonly used demographic measures). To test for such a possibility, we added the independent variables of age, gender, race, education, and income to the Divine Love scale to determine what effects demographic variables have on community benevolence. The results of multiple regression analysis showed that of these six indicators—divine love, gender, age, income, education, and race—experiences of divine love are the most important factor in accounting for differences in community benevolence.[28]

We believe we have a solid foundation with this and related findings to continue to develop our narrative about godly love. Experiencing God's direct and personal love contributes to existential well-being and a greater compassion for others, which may further enhance benevolence. Although experiencing the love of God is not a necessary cause of benevolence, our survey finding suggests that a personal and experiential knowledge of God's love is indeed an important factor that has been too long overlooked. Godly love does appear to be alive and well in America. In chapters to follow, we systematically analyze the results of our interview and survey data to further explore this idea.

An Overview of the Chapters

A personal and loving relationship with God has a ripple effect that affects both personal well-being and interpersonal relationships. This is the key to unlocking the analysis and presentation found in the chapters that follow. Chapter 2 considers adaptations shaped in part by demographic differences (like race, ethnicity, religious denomination, gender, education, and age), differences in worldview (naturalistic and spiritual), and different degrees of extensity in caring and compassion (from family/friends, to community, to all of humanity). The next four chapters focus on specific types of spiritual experiences and the roles they play in the unfolding of godly love.

Chapter 3 employs the survey findings to create a typology into which we classify the five primary exemplars whose narratives appear throughout our book. The typology consists of four distinct yet permeable categories that represent important patterns in the experience and expression of godly love: (1) Global Mystics, interviewees with high scores on both extensive benevolence and a spiritual/mystical worldview; (2) Global Planners, those with high scores on extensive benevolence but low on the spiritual worldview; (3) Local Mystics, those with low scores on extensive benevolence (although still highly benevolent at the local level) but high scores on the spiritual worldview; and (4) Local Planners, those with low scores on both extensive benevolence and spiritual worldview but high scores on benevolence at the local level. Chapter 4 focuses on spiritual transformation and personal experiences of a loving God. Spiritual transformation commonly begins in a quest for the sacred, often leading to the experience that Protestant evangelicals have called "being born again." Being born again is one example of the broader social psychological concept known as "primary spiritual transformation." Spiritual transformations, often accompanied by a persistent lifelong calling, are fortified with secondary changes in pathways that people take to the sacred. This chapter explores the statistical relationship between some select variables that reflect spiritual transformations, including being born again, a sense of divine call and destiny, and an accompanying sense of existential well-being.

Chapter 5 describes how godly love is energized through prayer that seemingly releases what sociologist Pitirim Sorokin has called "love energy." As demonstrated through survey statistics and illustrated through the stories from the lives of exemplars, prayer is far more than a monolithic practice that can be measured (as it commonly is) by asking how often someone prays. Although active or devotional prayer is nearly universally practiced among American pray-ers, forms of receptive prayer are also quite common. Active prayer and two approaches to receptive prayer (prophetic and mystical) work together in deeper experiences of divine love. Chapter 6 explores how our respondents often were able to "see beyond circumstances" when faced with pain and suffering in ways that were self-sacrificial and self-affirming. Some forms of populist theology have tended to minimize suffering, but most of our interviewees confronted their pain directly, sometimes as expressed anger at God. Continuing to weave together survey data with narratives, chapter 6 describes three faces of holistic healing in relating to the divine—anger with God, inner or psychic wounds, and physical healing. Findings from the surveys and the enriching stories from the interviewees showed how joy and suffering could work together in strengthening an ongoing love relationship with God.

Clearly the loving relationship that the majority of Americans profess to enjoy with God is rich in detail and filled with dynamic interaction. The concluding three chapters develop the link between experiences of divine love and benevolence that we identified as the major theme of our book. Chapter 7 focuses on the benevolent activities associated with godly love, especially as these are carried out with human partners. It shifts the spotlight away from personal experiences of divine love toward works of benevolence that are the fruit of both human and divine collaboration. Using the typology we created to select and classify the interviewees in chapter 3 as Servers (engaging in community service), Renewers (working to revive the church), and Changers (advocating peace and justice)—we examine further some basic

differences found when comparing the three groups. Chapter 8 responds to
the widespread concern, perhaps best articulated by Oliver Wendell Holmes,
that "some people are so heavenly minded that they are no earthly good." Our
national survey suggests that this concern is misplaced: regardless of how
benevolence is measured, religious experiences (particularly those associated
with divine love) are a catalyst for benevolence. Previous research has found
religious helping networks to be important for benevolence, but this work
has been unable to help us understand why. Our interviews help us understand the subjective nature of benevolence and how what actually "counts" as
benevolent service varies across social and political groups. Our concluding
chapter returns to the "big questions" that we raised at the beginning of the
book and summarizes what we have learned from our research as we attempt
to answer them. We find that cultural contexts are central to any assessment
of spiritually empowered benevolence. In the next chapter, we begin to
explore some of these contexts, particularly the spiritual worldview that is at
the center of godly love.

2

Diversities in the Experience and Expression of Godly Love

IN THE FIRST chapter we discussed how loving God and experiencing God's love leads to expressing benevolent love in collaboration with other people, and we referred to these dynamic interactions as "godly love." These love relationships involve personal adaptations, and no two accounts are exactly the same. As we present the stories of exemplars of godly love, we will see that each is fascinating, informative, and perhaps at times a bit of a stretch for the modern reader's mind. Woven into these seemingly unique stories, however, are larger patterns that we have gleaned from the interviews and used to shape our broader discussion of love as the heart of religion. The highly personal and unique accounts mirror differences that are filtered through what we have called *cultural grids*—perspectives that reflect racial, ethnic, and gender differences as well as religious ones. These cultural grids are foundational for the identification of four ways that godly love is expressed. We introduce these conceptual types in this chapter and then use this framework to categorize our prime exemplars in the next chapter.

One cultural grid for describing variations in godly love (perhaps not surprisingly) is grounded in religion—religion in the sense not of denominational affiliation, religious beliefs, or religious practices, but of a particular religious perspective or worldview. Its modern base is found in historical Pentecostal churches like the Church of God in Christ (the nation's fifth-largest denomination) and the Assemblies of God (the nation's ninth-largest denomination), which are often characterized by an alternate religious reality. This alternate reality includes speaking in tongues, reports of divine healing and miracles, and "hearing" directly from God, with followers who say they walk and talk with God.[1] The historical wing of this religious movement is commonly traced to the first decade of the twentieth century, but since the middle of that century it has been adopted and adapted by many others— often called *neo-pentecostals* or *charismatics*—found in mainline churches and in the growing number of nondenominational congregations.[2] The pentecostal worldview is widespread, as reflected in the Godly Love National Survey (GLNS) finding that approximately one out of four (27 percent) Americans self-identify as pentecostal or charismatic Christians, a ballpark figure that may be low, with many more Americans reporting pentecostal-like experiences.[3] There appears to be a pentecostalization of Christianity in America that reflects an increased globalization of pentecostal Christianity, particularly in Africa, Asia, and Latin America. With an estimate of over one-half billion followers, pentecostalism has been called the "fastest growing religious movement in the world."[4]

It is important to emphasize that there is no single "pentecostal" or "charismatic" denomination or doctrine either in the United States or globally.[5] (American followers cannot even agree to a common identifying label.)[6] There are many "pentecostalisms" (we prefer to use lowercase p for the broader sense and to designate pentecostalism as a global movement, while we reserve uppercase P for historic Pentecostal denominations). These can be found under the single umbrella of an alternate worldview of Christianity that stands in contrast to well-organized and doctrinal denominations whose practice, if not theology, recognize that freedom of religious experience can be institutionally dangerous and seek to limit it. The pentecostal perspective offers a set of lenses, as it were, to see beyond a "normal" sensate world commonly limited to the five senses in order to access a parallel world of the spirit where conversations with God, experiencing miracles, and seeing angels are normative.[7] Of course many who attend classic Pentecostal churches do not adhere to this pentecostal worldview, reflecting an evangelicalization of pentecostalism.[8] Just as pentecostals populate most denominations to some degree, so do non-pentecostals appear in older denominational Pentecostal churches. It is the pentecostal worldview, and the experiences it encourages, that matters—not the name of the church.[9]

Unlike the Pentecostals of the early twentieth century, who were at war with modernity, contemporary American pentecostals pragmatically embrace science and technology while holding fast to the miracles and mysteries of an era seemingly gone by. Nomenclature for those sheltered by this wide pentecostal umbrella is diverse and shifting with each new wave of pentecostal revivals, making it difficult to create good survey questions to measure pentecostal self-identity. Those involved in the revivals of the 1990s, for example, were likely to self-describe as being "in the river," while "Full Gospel" was the common renewal term for the 1950s, "charismatic" was the descriptive term for the "new" pentecostals of the 1960s and 1970s, and "Third Wave" became yet another designation during the 1980s. Throughout this book we will use the inclusive term "pentecostal" (with a small p) to refer to a combined group that includes those from historical Pentecostal denominations as well as to charismatics and neopentecostals in non-Pentecostal denominations. These are the two most common designations for those who share in this alternate reality where the Spirit of God is not simply *believed* to be a religious doctrine but is *experienced* as an active collaborator in daily life. We use "Pentecostal" (uppercase) to refer to those from historic Pentecostal denominations only.

In sum, contemporary pentecostalism is an identity that encompasses a worldview which (unlike that of the founders of Pentecostal denominations in the early twentieth century) now embraces the culture of the modern world while also proclaiming access to the nonmodern world of spirits and the work of the Holy Spirit. Pentecostal Christians commonly report encounters with the divine as well as at times with angels and demons, insisting that seemingly supernatural events are in fact normal Christian living. They are known to see the world (in varying degrees) through different cultural lenses than those who do not embrace this form of Christianity.[10] The pentecostal cultural grid is unevenly distributed among different religious denominations, some of which are better hosts than are others. As we will demonstrate, significant differences in experiencing divine love were found among the common denominational groups identified as Catholic, Hispanic Catholic, mainline Protestant, evangelical Protestant, Hispanic Protestant, and black Protestant and those who claimed no affiliation with a religious faith.

Race (white or black) and ethnicity (Hispanic or non-Hispanic) have also proven to be important in marking vibrant Christian subcultures: blacks and Hispanics are generally more religious and pentecostal than most Euro-Americans. Age, education, income, marital status, and gender (other commonly used demographic measures) also hypothetically have different effects on religiosity and on benevolence. We examined our hypothesis about the effect of these background variables on experiencing divine love by simultaneously testing for the relationship that these seven demographic markers—race, age, education, income, marital status, gender, and pentecostal identity—have with a four-item scale we constructed to measure experiences of God's love (which we have labeled the Divine Love scale).[11] We found that four of the seven descriptive measures were not related to the experience of divine love, but three were—self-identifying as pentecostal; being female; and being black or Hispanic. Of these, *pentecostal identity was the strongest predictor.*[12]

Cultural Grids as Filters of Divine Love

While doing preliminary analysis on our survey findings, Margaret recalled how she first became aware of the importance of cultural grids for processing personal religious experiences. Her classroom was a luncheon conversation she had three decades ago with a prominent sociologist who had come to hear her paper on the charismatic (neo-pentecostal) movement. Paranormal religious experiences (e.g., speaking in tongues, prophecy, and miraculous healings) once limited to sectlike Christians in Pentecostal denominations (sometimes disparagingly called "holy rollers" because of their exuberant worship) were then sweeping through mainline Protestant denominations, as well as the Catholic Church.[13] With services commonly held in rented auditoriums, hotel ballrooms, or conference halls across the country to accommodate large interdenominational crowds, the charismatic movement had become national news and the subject of some social science research. Margaret was surprised to see Theodore (Ted) Abel enter the professional meeting where she was delivering a paper on the movement. This distinguished professor emeritus was best known for his work in sociological theory and his role in establishing the prestigious department of sociology at Columbia University instead of scholarship on the sociology of religion. She was delighted when Ted approached her after the session, introduced himself, and asked her to join him for lunch. During a leisurely lunch Ted shared his spiritual journey that brought him from agnosticism to faith.

Ted was raised Roman Catholic in Poland during the early decades of the twentieth century, rumor has it in a wealthy Polish family that was able to provide him with an elite education. He lost all interest in religion, however, as he studied sociology as a graduate student. By the time he began his teaching career in the United States in the late 1920s, Ted considered himself an agnostic. An epiphany occurred many years later when he made a trip to his native Poland in search of reconnecting with his homeland. When he entered a familiar Catholic cathedral, he experienced what he would come to call "a visit from God." At first he did not know what to make of the cloud of awe that seemed to envelop him in love—was it God or was it a surge of nostalgia? Then something happened for which he had no words or explanation—he began to speak softly in a mysterious language. The more he spoke (prayed?) in this language, the more he felt wrapped in the cloud of awe and the more deeply loved he felt. The experience went on for some time, and soon Ted no longer questioned that what he was experiencing was somehow the presence of God.

Ted would return to the practice of his Catholic faith, but he never talked about the mysterious "strange language." He had no cultural grid for presenting it, no language for describing it. Had this happened in a Pentecostal church, he would have been told he had been given the "gift of tongues" (known as glossolalia to anthropologists and linguists who study the phenomenon), a prayer language that signaled his being baptized in the Holy Spirit. Twenty years would pass before he found the label and a grid for his unusual experience. He was staying at a hotel where charismatic Christians were gathered for a Saturday night worship service. Hearing the vibrant and lively music as he was passing through the lobby, Ted wandered into the ballroom to observe the joyful celebration. In the midst of the prayer and worship he heard the sounds of "strange languages" similar to what had come out of his mouth in that Polish church two decades earlier. In talking with some of the worshippers after the service he learned that the experience is known as "speaking in tongues," a "prayer language" given by God for worship and personal encouragement. Equipped with an explanation that included biblical references for the practice, Ted was now able to make sense out of his seeming anomalous experience. In other words, he was given a cultural grid—something he did not find in either his Polish or American Catholic culture—for a religious epiphany that had occurred decades earlier.

Like Ted, we all interpret the happenings of our lives, including religious ones, within the parameters of the social worlds in which we find ourselves. The numerous research findings demonstrating gender differences, for example, suggest that men and women see their worlds differently (as reflected in the adage "Men are from Mars—women are from Venus"). Complementing general observations of gender differences are specific findings, such as those that repeatedly show that women are more likely to regularly attend church, to engage in private spiritual devotions, and to report spiritual experiences than men are. And there may be cultural reasons aside from prejudice and discrimination as to why most churches remain largely segregated on Sunday mornings. The GLNS shows that African Americans and Hispanics are much more likely than Euro-Americans to report experiences of God's love. Perhaps this is one reason nonwhites seem to prefer the lively and exuberant worship that stirs familiar emotions of a heartfelt "knowing" of God's love to the more sedate services commonly found in Euro-American congregations that focus on finely crafted sermons that engage the mind but not the body. Furthermore, both women and nonwhites are more likely to report that they are either Pentecostal or charismatic Christians, an approach to Christianity that provides a nonmodern spiritual grid in which supernatural experiences are deemed to be normal. We will take a closer look at some of these differences, including denominational affiliation, gender, racial/ethnic differences, and pentecostal self-identification for a better understanding why some are more likely than others to report extensive and enduring experiences of God's love.

Denominational Grids and Experiencing God's Love

There are scores of recognized Christian denominations in the United States that are commonly reduced to several religious families. Traditional groupings include Catholic (comprising 17 percent of the GLNS sample), evangelical or conservative Protestant (24 percent of the sample), mainline Protestant (15 percent), and historically black Protestant (10 percent).[14] In our analysis we have also included the following as distinct groups: Hispanic Catholics (8 percent of the sample), Hispanic Protestants (4 percent), and, for comparative purposes, those who claim no religious affiliation (14 percent). Although all of the Christian denominations would teach about the love of God, the degree to which it is *experienced* differs greatly. As shown in figure 2.1, the

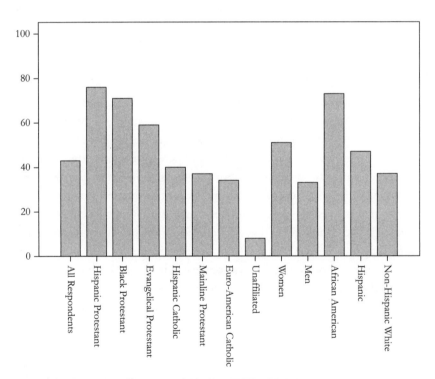

FIGURE 2.1 Percentage of American Adults Scoring in the Highest Third of the Divine Love Scale, by Denominational Affiliation, Gender, and Race/Ethnicity

(*Source*: 2009 GLNS; *N* = 1,208)

percent of those who score high on the Divine Love scale ranges from 76 percent of those who self-identify as Hispanic Protestants and 71 percent of black Protestants to 34 percent of Euro-American Catholics. Evangelical Protestants (59 percent) were more likely to experience high scores on divine love than were mainline Christians (37 percent) and both Hispanic (40 percent) and Euro-American Roman Catholics (34 percent), as well as those unaffiliated with any religious denomination (8 percent). Experiencing God's love with frequency is related to religious denomination: some denominational groupings provide significantly better grids for experiencing the divine than others do.[15] Why the differences? Why is it that affiliation with some groups is related to a greater likelihood of experiencing God's love with frequency and through a wider range of experiences? One key to addressing such questions can be found in exploring demographic traits of those respondents who reported the highest scores on the Divine Love scale, namely women, nonwhites, and Hispanics.

Women as Lovers

"Women are from Venus": so goes the cliché identifying them with the Greek goddess of love, while men are metaphorically linked with Mars, the Greek god of war. The GLNS survey indicates that there may be some truth to this adage. Men (28 percent) were twice as likely as women (14 percent) to have scored low on the Divine Love scale; and, as shown in figure 2.1, while slightly more than one-half of the women (51 percent) placed in the high category, only one-third of men (33 percent) did. Our findings on male/female differences for experiencing divine love mirror gender differences commonly reported for religiosity and spirituality. There is considerable evidence that women are more likely to be interested in and involved in religion than are men. Whether these differences are due primarily to nature (biological factors) or nurture (social influences) is still open for discussion. Most likely both nature and nurture are woven together in complex patterns as social influences built on biological foundations.[16]

Sheri, one of our interviewees, is now an ordained minister in a Pentecostal denomination that was once known for its preaching about the fearful effects of God's judgment.[17] Her story illustrates how family influences (in this case her mother) can override the effects of a particular denominational perspective, which included a maternal nurturing of Sheri's early childhood experience of God's love and call to ministry. Sheri narrated how her mother provided her with an outlook that tempered the denominational grid with its many rules and regulations and its image of a God who was more of a stern judge than a lover. Despite the many hellfire-and-brimstone sermons of her youth and young adult life, Sheri claimed that she always found the arms of God to be "soft and safe"—adding with a hearty laugh, "Interesting, isn't it—growing up in a Pentecostal church?" With a broad smile she spoke of an experience she had as a child of five or six years old when she felt the warmth of God's loving embrace as she lay curled up in the back of the family car during a long road trip: "I felt in my little heart at that age just this profound experience with God—his incredible closeness, his presence." When asked why she never internalized the "hellfire and brimstone," as reported by other interviewees from her denomination, she attributed her spirituality to memories of this childhood experience and to her mother. With a chuckle and a twinkle in her eyes Sheri described her mother as "a petite, quiet, lovely, loving woman who may have sinned once in her life." It was her mother who helped Sheri to safeguard the memory of her intense personal experience; it was also she who encouraged Sheri as she began a path of ministry that was increasingly riddled with roadblocks even though her denomination had a history of ordaining women. "My mom defined for me what I had kind of known about my life—the love of God and his call on my life to ministry."

Throughout history, religious traditions and their cultural grids have been shaped and dominated by men, who (at least in contemporary culture) have been less religious than women.[18] Yet there may also be an important and largely unrecognized undercurrent in organized religion (as Sheri's story illustrates) where feminine influence prevails as loving mothers model godly love for their children. They may be teaching their daughters—and their sons (and perhaps even their husbands)—how to safeguard mystical experiences in a materialistic world that often lacks a suitable grid for interpreting things of the spirit.

Race, Ethnicity, and Communal Spirituality

According to 2010 US census figures, whites make up 72.4 percent of the population—63.7 percent if Hispanic whites are excluded from this figure. Hispanics comprise 16.3 percent of the population, while African Americans are reported to comprise 12.6 percent.[19] It is thus important to examine the results from the GLNS for information that can be gleaned about the spiritualities of these two large yet underresearched faith groups, both of which score higher in experiencing God's love than Euro-Americans.

Figure 2.1 demonstrates that respondents who self-reported as African American were twice as likely to have frequent and intense experiences of divine love compared with those who said they were "white" and "non-Hispanic" (73 percent of blacks, compared to 37 percent of whites). Looking at this finding from another angle, only 5 percent of the African American respondents (compared with 24 percent of the whites) were found in the lowest category of divine love scores. African Americans appear to have a strong cultural grid for experiencing divine love; its roots arguably go back to slavery. Historically the black church has played a central unifying role in African American culture in ways that are different from Christianity's effect on Euro-American or American Hispanic society. As slavery gave way to emancipation and segregation of the races and black Americans found themselves in bondage to both legal and de facto restrictions that prohibited them from freely participating in white society, the church became an important safe haven. The renowned black sociologist E. Franklin Frazier pointed out nearly five decades ago that the African American church was an agency of social control, economic cooperation, educational development, and an arena of politics. It was the principal "refuge in a hostile white world."[20]

African American religion has undergone changes over the past half century since Frazier wrote about the black church. Educational, employment, and economic opportunities have opened up for more blacks, and the church is no longer the only refuge in a hostile white world. Some contemporary scholars question the extent to which there ever was a "'single' black church," but all would recognize that African Americans "have built a mosaic of religious practices that for many form a core element of their identity."[21] With increased affluence over the decades, the worship of some black churches emulated the more sedate mainline white Protestant congregations. More recently black megachurches have sprung up alongside white and multicultural ones to replace many old storefront churches and small family-based congregations. Although religious structures and practices may have become more diversified, what does not seem to have changed, as reflected in our survey data, is the African American belief that "religion was best when it led to a direct, personal encounter with God."[22] Renita Weems, a Bible scholar, famed preacher, and ordained elder in the African Methodist Church, has noted how when Christianity was introduced to slaves centuries ago, it was in the form of Protestant Christianity that "emphasized a piety that can be felt and experienced with the senses." Although there are exceptions, in general black worship has been traditionally more experiential and embodied than the typical Euro-American Protestant or Catholic service. As an increasing number of black Americans moved into the middle classes, they did not swell the membership of the mainline denominations. Instead, contends Weems, "a new class of Black social elites has emerged in recent years, who seem to welcome the updated twist on that 'old time religion'" with neo-pentecostal "jubilant praise." In sum, our survey findings on black religious experiences support those who argue there is something unique and unifying about black styles of religion that constitutes a "socially alternative cultural core," which includes "full engagement of the senses in worship, intimate prayer, cathartic shouting, triumphant singing, politically relevant religious education and prophetic preaching."[23]

Similar but more complex patterns for religious and spiritual experience exist for the more diversified Hispanic communities. Unlike most African Americans whose ancestors shared a common history of slavery and segregation in which black Protestant religion (commonly Baptist or Methodist) provided a unifying force, Hispanic peoples are bound together with a common language but are divided by differing cultures. These subcultures are represented in their respective countries of origin—countries in South America and Central America, Mexico, and the Caribbean nations—in which indigenous spiritual practices were often mixed with Catholicism. Further adding to potential cleavages is the conversion of increasing numbers of Hispanics from an often nominal cultural Catholicism to a highly committed evangelical Protestantism, more specifically to historical Pentecostalism and its neo-pentecostal offshoots. It is here that we observe vast differences in religious experience among Hispanics. As we have seen, Hispanic Protestants (76 percent) exhibit high scores on the Divine Love scale, a figure similar to those of black Protestants (71 percent). Hispanic Catholics (40 percent) score somewhat higher than Euro-American Catholics (34 percent) on the frequency and intensity of experiencing divine love, but both groups of Catholics demonstrate significantly lower rates of religious experience than their Protestant counterparts. To put this important finding another way, Catholic Hispanics are nearly half as likely to report frequent and intense experiences of God's love than Hispanic Protestants are.

There are undoubtedly many reasons for this difference in the frequency and intensity of religious experience between Catholics and Protestants in Hispanic communities, but perhaps the most important reason is rooted in the respective theologies of the two major streams of Christendom. Joseph Varacalli sums up this reason as follows: "The Catholic position on religious authority can be compared to the quintessential Protestant perspective in which the Holy Spirit is viewed as being in direct and unmediated relationship with the individual believer.... Catholicism is a religion that is not only inherently communal and social but is one that argues that the official institutional Church is a non-negotiable and indispensable mediator between God and the individual believer."[24] Catholic priest-sociologist Andrew Greeley first noted the vast differences between Catholic and Protestant religious experiences in research he did in the 1970s. When interviewed by the now-defunct popular social scientific magazine *Transaction* about these findings, Greeley acknowledged the effects of Catholic theology on religious experience as he quipped, "If you have papal infallibility, who needs religious experience?" In short, the difference between Protestant theology that is grounded in individual spirituality and Catholic theology that focuses on divine authority within a hierarchical community has created the different cultural grids that are reflected in our survey findings. Catholics, whether black, Hispanic, or Euro-American, are less likely than their racial/ethnic counterparts to report frequent and intense experiences of divine love.[25]

Experiences of divine love thus are clearly not equally distributed among various groups of people—men differ from women, Catholics differ from Protestants, conservative Protestants differ from mainlines, black and Hispanic Christian cultures differ from Euro-American ones. But differences among these demographic and denominational categories tell only part of the story. There is yet another factor, which we introduced earlier, that we found to be an even more powerful predictor of feeling loved by the divine. The pentecostalization of Christianity that can be found in all denominations is more important than any of the demographic factors in accounting for experiences of divine love.[26]

Dancing with the Divine in Pentecostal Christianity

Historically religion has played a major role in providing a worldview or a comprehensive framework for interpreting human existence over the centuries. In more recent times so-called modern thought would arise to challenge the faith and colorful metaphors of the ancient religious fathers and mothers through the often stark empiricism and rigid rationalism assumed to be necessary for the scientific method. The stage was soon set for an ongoing cultural battle between religion and modern science. While great thinkers continue to wrestle with questions about whether science and traditional religion are mutually exclusive or are capable of coexisting as part of a larger "truth" system, our research suggests that millions of Americans have comfortably combined the natural world of science and the supraempirical world of faith in their personal lives.[27] This is particularly true for the group of respondents who self-identified as Pentecostal or charismatic Christians, referred to in this text as "pentecostals." What can be said about the larger pentecostal movement, whether reflected in classic Pentecostal denominations or its neo-pentecostal charismatic streams, as we have argued at the beginning of this chapter, is that pentecostal Christianity is more about a distinct worldview than about organized religion. Its worldview is holistic in its ability to integrate natural and supernatural, material and spiritual, premodern and modern phenomena into an alternate way of perceiving reality. If some groups experience religion through the adherence to divine commands and in fidelity to creeds—through the metaphor of law—pentecostals might be better understood through the metaphor of dance: dancing with the divine in an experiential mode of being that emphasizes the felt presence of God.[28]

The pentecostal worldview is found in all Christian denominations, and its adherents are likely to be involved in a dynamic and personal relationship with a God who is up close and personal. We saw this divine-human relationship reflected in the story of Sheri, whose intense experience of God as a small child marked the beginning of a lifelong relationship with the divine—a God she describes as "soft and safe." Throughout our interviews and confirmed with survey statistics we observed the important role that divine intimacy plays in personal lives as men and women reach out to others in lives committed to human benevolence. More than gender or denominational affiliation, self-identifying as a pentecostal Christian is the best single predictor of "knowing" (in a heartfelt way) the love of the divine. We raise a two-pronged question: Which religions are supportive of the pentecostal worldview and what is it about this worldview that serves as a cultural grid for intense, frequent, and ongoing experiences of divine love?

As figure 2.2 shows, slightly more than one in four GLNS respondents self-identified as pentecostal or charismatic (27 percent). Pentecostal Christians are found unevenly distributed in all denominations, reflecting the pattern reported for experiencing divine love. Half of all Protestant and Catholic Hispanic (50 percent), nearly half of all African American (44 percent), and slightly more than a third of evangelical (37 percent) respondents acknowledged that they were pentecostal. Mainline Protestants (19 percent), Catholics (23 percent), and "other Christians" (21 percent) were significantly less likely to claim religious identity as either a pentecostal or a charismatic Christian. Although represented in all streams of Christianity, the pentecostal worldview is found to be stronger in some cultural groups

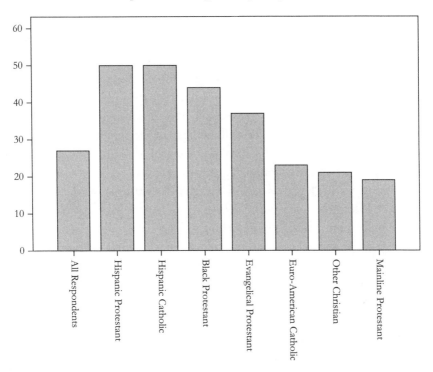

FIGURE 2.2 Percentage of American Adults Self-Identifying as Pentecostal or Charismatic by Denomination

(*Source*: 2009 GLNS; N = 1,208)

than in others. By no means, however, is it limited to Pentecostal congregations and to nondenominational churches that self-label as "charismatic."

The pentecostal worldview is nurtured by a wide array of communities—Pentecostal and charismatic congregations, parachurch organizations, networks and conferences, radio/television, and virtual networking—where followers can learn to move with the flow of personal religious experience and find grids for interpreting these experiences. What is shared in these live and virtual communities is a common transcendent worldview that speaks of a world of possibilities rather than particular doctrines, defined ritual practices, or denominational involvement. Pentecostal reality is a curious blend of premodern miracles, modern technology, and postmodern mysticism in which the natural world is mixed with the supernatural. Signs and wonders analogous to those described in premodern biblical accounts of dreams and visions; prophetic proclamations; miraculous, divine provisions; and other ways of knowing beyond the five senses are expected as normal events in the lives of believers. It is an approach to knowing that challenges an overly rational modern empiricist way of thinking with a world of spiritual possibilities.[29] As pentecostal theologian Jackie David Johns notes, "[A] Pentecostal paradigm for knowledge and truth springs from an experiential knowledge of God which alters the believer's approach to reading and interpreting reality."[30] Pentecostals thus see the world through different lenses—lenses that according to our research findings are powerful and world-transforming.

We return to Sheri's story for an illustration of the pentecostal worldview that blends the material and spiritual—or, if you will, the natural and the supernatural—that can be found in pentecostal narratives. Sheri received her new metaphysical glasses through which she views the world when she was only a child, but they are lenses that have served her well throughout her life, through good times and bad. In retelling the story as an adult, she used sensate facts to set the stage for recounting her intense childhood experience of God's love: "I must've been about five or six, because we were on our way home from my grandmother's house in Glendale and I still fit in the back of the car—you know those great big old cars we had back in the late '50s? I fit in the shelf between the back seat and the back window." Sheri was enjoying the ride as she began to talk to God: "So that was where I was laying, and I was stretching out and I was looking up through the back window, looking at the stars and everything. And I said, at five years old: 'God, I love you and I want you to use my life.'" She felt that heaven then broke through and words started to fail. Sheri tries to describe what happened: "I had this profound experience with God—his incredible closeness, his presence. That was the altar." Sheri, as we saw earlier, shared this "treasure" with her mother, who undoubtedly helped her daughter to keep the experience from being relegated to the realm of fleeting and childish illusion. The treasured memory is an ongoing gift of grace for Sheri: "I have thought in the very difficult times in my life since that experience: 'Sheri [she says to herself], God heard you when you were a little girl, and it's hard for the prophets. It's hard for the preachers. It's not an easy life. So you remember—God heard you when you committed yourself and put yourself on the altar.' And of course, at the time, at five or six years old, who understands the ramifications? I'm not sure I still do."

In short, at the center of the pentecostal cultural grid is an alternative worldview—often seen as primal or primitive relative to modern rationality—that validates transforming spiritual experiences. Narratives like Sheri's often begin with a memorable experience that opens them up to further divine-human encounters. The heartbeat of the pentecostal worldview is relational encounters with God through which pentecostals often feel they are being empowered through the Holy Spirit. These experiences are regarded as normative, and they shift the way in which individuals (with support from their pentecostal communities) interpret their transrational world. Pentecostals tend to be suspicious of creeds, believing that "knowing" comes from a right relationship with God rather than through reason or even through the five senses. Theirs is a God who can and often does defy the laws of nature with the miraculous and unexplainable. Without doubt the Bible holds an important place in their worldview, but for many it is a kind of catalyst and litmus test for the authenticity of personal and corporate experience rather than a manual of rigid doctrine and practices.

Love and Power Encounters

There is an often-undetected tension to be found in pentecostal thought between viewing paranormal experiences attributed to the Holy Spirit as being centered in power or being centered in love. This tension can be gleaned in the theologies (denominational and populist) that have emphasized the initiation into the realm of the spirit, commonly known as *baptism in the Spirit* (or *Spirit baptism*). Some have focused on Spirit baptism as a power encounter with God; others have preferred describing it as a "baptism of love," as "liquid love," being "bathed in love," and as the "flame/fire of love."[31] Although love and power, as suggested by our data, do work in tandem to empower one to love God and neighbor, arguably the focus has been more on power than on love.

Leif Hetland, a missionary from Norway now living in Alabama, is a well-known pentecostal speaker. He has been called "an apostle of love" in some countries where he has ministered, and he proved to be one of our most articulate interviewees when talking about the subject. He notes that, unfortunately, love and power do not always come as a package deal. After describing a particularly intense experience of divine love, Leif confessed to us: "I'd been baptized by water before, and I had a Spirit baptism where I experienced power. And I love power, but I was not comfortable with love—and if you're not comfortable with love, you're not comfortable with God." This epiphany came during a small meeting to which he had been invited, where a couple of well-known pentecostal leaders prayed over him while a musician played a song about the Father's love. He described his experience in this simple way: "I lay on the floor, and there was just waves and waves of love that just flowed throughout my body." He went on to say:

> I was no longer living *for* God, I was living *from* God. I had an A-plus on my report card. I didn't have to do anything any longer for him

and I became totally free. I came home and all I wanted to do was to receive love and give love, and that became my identity. Before the identity was "What am I doing for God?"—the Great Commission [evangelize the world as a missionary]. Now it was the Great Commandment—loving the Lord thy God with all my heart, with all my soul. You cannot love him if you don't know how much he loves you. There was a healing of my image of God, then there was a healing in the image of myself and then there was a healing of my image of other people and then healing my image of the world. It was kind of a process that took place on that floor that day. I had new glasses, 20/20 vision.

Although he still "loves the power" and claims to see miracles at the meetings he leads around the globe, Leif now believes that the benevolence dictated in the teachings of Jesus must be "rooted and grounded in love."

I think that love is the fruit that comes of being in the Spirit.... Christ-like qualities in you that are flowing out of your life because you are in him and he is in you. You are a son (or daughter) and all that you do is love the Father and in his perfect love you receive love and you give love. That is what the Great Commandment is all about.

Heidi Baker, another missionary whose stories will be recounted throughout the book, also refers to the Great Commandment as she connects love and power. In reflecting on her thirty years as a missionary to some of the economically poorest parts of the world, she argues that God "is love, and so we cannot separate the first commandment from the second." She goes on to state, "There are many callings, but none higher than to give water to the thirsty and food to the hungry." Why undertake such missions? Because she has been privileged to experience the grace of God's love, which empowers and sustains her, as well as other blessings:

Missions is our joy, the simple, logical outcome of knowing Jesus. We have life and hope; others don't. We have reason to rejoice; others don't. We have love in our hearts; others don't. We have food and clothes; others don't. We have health; others don't. We have family; others don't. We have no reason to be anxious; others are weighed down with cares. It is obvious that the calling of every believer in Jesus is to have a part in correcting these imbalances.

Sowing love and hope where they are missing, feeding the hungry, promoting health and well-being—for Heidi Baker, anyone who has deeply experienced the love of God must correct any "imbalances" in the distribution of these goods. This is "obvious" to her, as it is for many others who have experienced the heart of religion.

Pentecostal Worldview and Benevolence: A Typology

Self-identifying as a pentecostal Christian is the leading single sociodemographic characteristic for describing persons who frequently experience divine love. It is a better descriptor than age, degree of education or income, white or black, or male or female. While some of these demographics, as we have seen, are related to experiencing divine love and to having a pentecostal worldview, they are less important for providing a cultural grid for the supernatural experience of love than is the pentecostal worldview itself, a perspective that can be found in most streams of Christianity. Ninety-five percent of those who self-identified as pentecostal Christians scored as either moderate or high on the scale of questions measuring the frequency and intensity of experiencing God's love, compared with 73 percent of those who do not self-identify as pentecostal or charismatic. Thus, while only 5 percent of pentecostal respondents scored low on experiences of divine love, 27 percent of non-pentecostal Christians reported that they rarely if ever have this experience. It is safe to say that experiences of God's love by "Main Street mystics" are common and mirror the transcendent worldview of millions of Americans.[32] These experiences are not limited to personal enjoyment, but they appear to be related to benevolence.

Our analysis of the survey data provides numerical support for this contention that knowing the direct and personal love of God plays an important role in the expression of human benevolence. Of course, not every highly benevolent person is highly spiritual (although the odds are that spirituality is an important part of their lives), and we are careful not to overstate our findings by suggesting that only those who know the deep love of God can be benevolent. But what we can say with confidence is that experiencing God's love intensely and frequently is a better predictor of doing good for others than are commonly used descriptors of age, income, education, gender, and race. In that sense it supports a better understanding of the Great Commandment of godly love, a command that calls women and men to love God above all and to love their neighbor as they love themselves. It is not simply a matter of men and women loving God but *the knowing that they are loved by God* in the very depths of their being that empowers them to live lives of benevolence. This is especially true for benevolence that extends beyond near-universal claims of caring for family and friends by working for the betterment of local and global communities. Although it is fashionable in some circles to minimize the spiritual dimensions of highly benevolent leaders, such as Martin Luther King Jr. in the Christian tradition, Gandhi in the Hindu context, or Badshah Khan in the Muslim one, it is clear that religious experiences were central to their missions.[33]

Ideal Typologies in Perspective

What we have done in this chapter is to present a hypothetical social construct or *ideal type*, a concept that we have described but which does not exist in "pure form" in real life. Ideal types are useful for discussing in simple and predefined terms more complex human processes that involve many parts. These components can shift with the sands of time and place—sometimes even while researchers are gathering their data. Ideal types are thus more like sand castles than figures carved in stone, but establishing such concepts allows us to see important patterns even though specific cases would probably not fit all the details used in describing a particular ideal type. For example, we have talked about the spiritual worldview of Pentecostal-charismatic Christians, but undoubtedly not all 27 percent of survey respondents who self-identified as pentecostal Christians would agree with all of the points we presented as ones they share. Scholars of pentecostalism—whether theologians, historians, or social scientists—do agree that pentecostalism has provided believers with a distinct religious worldview. This pentecostal worldview, however, is an ideal type that serves as a proxy for the supernaturally oriented faith of real people who might embrace some, most, or all of its common tenets and experiences. So while we use ideal types for discussion purposes and demonstrate what seems to be true about them through statistical findings, we will also employ interview narratives for illustration. This will prevent us from losing sight of the stories of real people from whom these statistics are derived.

Another strategy was pursued by Distinguished Professor of Political Science John Green. An important member of our research team, and codirector of the GLNS, John has moved beyond the binary opposition of "pentecostal" or "non-pentecostal" and instead looks at the presence of certain "markers" of pentecostalism. These may include self-identifying as a Pentecostal or charismatic (pentecostal), but also experiences such as praying in tongues (glossolalia), receiving divine emotional or physical healing, being baptized in the Holy Spirit (an experiential second baptism, contrasted with water baptism), and other pentecostal experiences. With this method, it is possible for people who do not self-identify as pentecostal to be analyzed as experientially pentecostal, or as having a worldview that is more or less pentecostal. This strategy is important for assessing divine love experiences as well as benevolence.[34] Later in the book we will explore the relationship between benevolence, pentecostal markers, and experiencing divine love. We will see that different pentecostal experiences (especially healing and prophecy) affect the experience of divine love, which in turn affects benevolence.

This argument for the use of fluid ideal types to describe pentecostal identity also can be made for the construct of the *extensity* of human love. Acts of benevolence not only take countless forms (e.g., giving emotional support, money, or time) but can also be assessed in terms of the extensity reflected in the most likely recipients (family, close friends, or "strangers"). Our focus here is not on the nearly universally expressed relational love for family and friends but rather on the less often reported extensive benevolence that reaches out to "strangers" in the community and beyond. It may not be surprising that people love their families and friends, but there is interest and often admiration when intense love is shown to strangers near and far away. The GLNS asked twelve questions to measure the extent and depth of the respondent's love for others—was this love generally limited to family and friends, or did it extend to the larger community and beyond national boundaries?[35] As we will discuss later in the book, the findings of our survey suggest that divine love helps to explain differences not only in the degree of benevolence toward family and friends, but also in the more extensive benevolence demonstrated in caring for the larger community and being a citizen of the world.

In sum, just as there are many shades of love found in caring and benevolence, so too are there differing degrees to which people embrace pentecostal identity.[36] In the next chapter, we use the two ideal-type constructs that we have discussed here—pentecostal worldview and extensive benevolence—as the two axes of a fourfold typology we created to classify our rich and diverse interviews. In selecting five individuals from scores of godly love "exemplars" as primary representatives of these categories we intend no prejudice or preference for one type over another. The diversity we have found in how people experience and express godly love is itself an important finding, and one that we continue to explore in the next chapter.

3

Introducing the Exemplars of Godly Love

BEFORE THEY CONSTRUCTED the initial draft of the survey question-naire for the GLNS, Matt and Margaret interviewed over one hundred exem-plars of godly love—men and women from varying walks of life who were notably regarded as benevolent within their own communities, and many of whom had received awards and honors in both secular and religious contexts for their self-giving service to others. There was much diversity: young and old, black and white, Hispanic and Euro-American, liberal and conservative, urban and rural, famous and unknown. All had significant ties to the United States, and virtually all were American by birth. They resided in a dozen dif-ferent states representing all regions of the country, although a few were born in Germany, Norway, Bulgaria, Sweden, Canada, and Puerto Rico. Even if they did not use the label, the vast majority felt comfortable identifying as "pentecostal," as we have defined it. Except for the relatively few "collaborators" we interviewed who partnered with exemplars in benevolent work, their life stories reflected a loving intimacy with God calling them to partner with a divine plan. Together they provided invaluable insight into the relationship between divine love and benevolence as we constructed the survey question-naire and then interpreted the findings.

The benevolent outreach for most of these interviewees could be catego-rized according to three definable areas of service. They include *community service* (outreach to people in need, such as a homeless shelter); *renewal/ revival* (the supernatural revitalization of the larger church through the bib-lical practices recorded in the book of Acts, such as prophecy, healing, mira-cles, deliverance, and speaking in tongues, believed to be signs of the coming kingdom of God); and *social justice* (actions taken to effect changes in social and political structures). More often than not, however, exemplars provided examples of hybrid ministries in which one service was paramount but other services were also part of the ministry. For example, the practice of healing

Table 3.1 Types of Benevolent Service

Type	Focus
1. Servers	Engaging in community service (e.g., serving meals at a soup kitchen, providing medical help at a free clinic, giving shelter to the homeless)
2. Renewers	The supernatural revitalization of the larger church through the biblical practices recorded in the book of Acts (such as prophecy, healing, miracles, deliverance, and speaking in tongues), believed to be signs of the coming kingdom of God
3. Changers	Advocacy or direct action intended to alter inequitable social arrangements, foster peace and justice, and bring institutions into conformity with the kingdom of God (e.g., protesting military operations, working to pass legislation that provides greater access to health care, standing in solidarity with oppressed groups during rallies, influencing public opinion through words and deeds)

(spiritual, physical, and/or emotional) is quite prominent in the lives of many exemplars, but it can be viewed as a subtype of renewal/revival because of the strong focus in early Christianity on healing. In other words, healing ministries provide a kind of outreach that seeks to revitalize the larger church and draw attention to practices that were once normative. Healing comes close to being a subtype of community service, but the emphasis on the supernatural distinguishes it from homeless shelters and soup kitchens, which are primarily focused on meeting material needs rather than spiritual ones. This distinction is somewhat arbitrary in practice, as some ministries were more holistic, offering food, shelter, and spiritual healing as well as various kinds of physical and psychological healing. In most cases there is an easily identified dominant theme.[1] We refer to people engaged in these three different ideal types of ministry as *Servers*, *Renewers*, or *Changers*, respectively (see table 3.1).

As we have done in the previous chapters, we will continue to draw from the range of these interviews for our illustrations, but a special spotlight rests on five interviewees whom we will introduce in this chapter and whose stories will unfold throughout subsequent chapters. Each one has been placed within a typology (see table 3.2) that has been constructed from the GLNS survey questions on extensive benevolence and on pentecostal identity. The typology consists of four distinct yet permeable categories: (1) Global Mystics, interviewees with high scores on both extensive benevolence and the pentecostal

Table 3.2 Godly Love Exemplar Typology

		Extensive Benevolence	
		High	Low
Pentecostal Worldview	High	**Global Mystics** (H. Baker)	**Local Mystics** (S. Witt)
	Low	**Global Planners** (P. Alexander)	**Local Planners** (A. Beiler, H. Daughtry)

worldview; (2) Global Planners, those with high scores on extensive benevolence but low on the pentecostal worldview; (3) Local Mystics, those with low scores on extensive benevolence but high scores on the pentecostal worldview; and (4) Local Planners, those with low scores on both extensive benevolence and pentecostal worldview (but high on benevolence at the local level).

Global Mystic: Heidi Baker (Iris Ministries)

Although Heidi Baker holds a PhD in systematic theology from King's College London, what immediately struck Margaret, even prior to the formal interview, was Heidi's simple childlike faith. With a warm voice that seemed to bring spring to a cold autumn Pennsylvania day, Heidi began our time together by saying, "Most things in our life are not compartmentalized. It's all about him, loving him and making his love felt to other people. It's just so simple!" We referred to some of life's "big questions" in chapter 1, including the issue of delineating one's responsibilities to other people. For Heidi it is all about love and changing the world through the simple power of love in action. She is "compelled by love."[2] When she senses that God has put a person in her path, she has no choice but to stop and literally be God's love in that moment. This obedience to love might require her to adopt an orphan, respond with kindness to an attacker, expose herself to a deadly disease, or feed the multitudes.

Despite the Herculean work performed since 1980 by Iris Ministries,[3] the international ministerial organization founded by Heidi and her husband Rolland, Heidi insisted, "It's never about me. We all just do our little thing, but that's exciting! We can't take on the responsibility where we think, 'If we are not there it all falls apart.' That's a very sad thing. It's about the body [referring to the body of Christ, i.e., the Church] and the family [the family of God] and all of us doing our part. It's very freeing—and it lets us rest, giving us a place where we can rest in the Spirit." Heidi's voice was beginning to lift from a serious to a playful tone, as she spoke of the revival-style meditative prayer common in revival circles: "We can lie down; we can soak; we can get wrecked and get up again. Isn't that good? I like that." Loving God and knowing God's love for her empowers Heidi to love in amazing ways, to be seen as her story unfolds.

The website describing the mission of Iris Ministries offers a clear picture of an organization that is affecting lives across the globe. Its succinct opening statement reflects the godly love we heard about in our interview with Heidi:[4]

> Iris Ministries is a Christian organization committed to expressing a living and tangible response to those commandments that Jesus called greatest: "Love the Lord your God with all your heart and with all your soul and with all your mind and with all your strength, and, Love your neighbor as yourself." It is our conviction that the Spirit of God has asked us to make this love concrete in the world, incarnate in all our thoughts, our bodies, our lives, and our every action. Iris Ministries exists to participate in bringing the Kingdom of God to earth in all its aspects, but most especially through our particular calling to serve the very poor: the destitute, the lost, the broken, and the forgotten.

Heidi and Rolland both believe that God was the Divine Choreographer who had planned the steps leading to their meeting and their marriage. (Heidi reported that God had told her in prayer that she would "marry Rolland Baker" before she ever met him—even providing his last name so she would not be confused.) But we chose Heidi for our metanarrative not only because she cofounded Iris Ministries[5] but because, like Mother Teresa[6] before her, she spends time traveling the globe, drawing others into the divine dance whose basic steps are found in the Great Commandment. Born in an affluent American family in Laguna Beach, California, in 1960, Heidi encountered God at age sixteen in response to an altar call by an evangelist while serving on an Indian reservation, and she has followed Jesus by serving the "poorest of the poor" for over three decades. Thousands have followed Heidi as she has modeled and taught others about the power of divine love.

Heidi's husband Rolland confessed to needing "a real-life example of Jesus living in someone to such an extent that I would be inspired and motivated to consider living the Sermon [on the Mount] as not only realistic but also the only viable way to approach life and ministry in the Lord." He shared how this "need" has been met by Heidi. Rolland's description of his wife is perhaps the best introduction we can provide to demonstrate why we have chosen Heidi Baker as an exemplar of Global Mysticism. In the foreword to Heidi's book *Compelled by Love,* Rolland writes of Heidi:[7]

> I know that our Lord has many such monuments of His grace among His people who are often hidden in the far corners of the world, but for me that encouragement came during the late 1970s when I met Heidi in a small charismatic church in Dana Point, California. She had a privileged upbringing, living on a private beach, and lacked for nothing in education, comforts, and opportunity. But even as a small girl growing up, she pulsed and radiated with a consuming hunger for God. Radically influenced by her sixth-grade teacher who had been a missionary, Heidi's heart turned toward the poor and suffering of other cultures. That teacher turned out to be my mother, and so our families became interlinked. When I met her, she was a pure, idealistic flower child in the Spirit, a teenager who at sixteen had already been mystically taken to heaven and commissioned by Jesus to be a missionary and a minister to Asia, England, and Africa....Here was someone who could take no thought for tomorrow, seek first His Kingdom and His righteousness under any circumstance anywhere in the world, and in the most childlike simplicity pursue heaven on earth—in spite of all opposition and discouragement.

We will continue to follow Heidi in the chapters that follow as she and Rolland move from southern California to living out lives of love in Asia, England, and Africa, observing her ongoing connection with and increasing influence on pentecostals in North America.

Global Planner: Paul Alexander (Sider Center on Ministry and Public Policy at Eastern University; Pentecostals and Charismatics for Peace and Justice)

Like Heidi and Rolland Baker, Paul Alexander, a theologian and peace activist, has a ministry that transcends local and national communities. Whereas Heidi and Rolland focus on reaching individuals around the world with the message and personal experience of divine love, Paul's emphasis is on the structural changes needed to rid the world of injustice and war. To return to our question list in chapter 1, Paul's "big question" might be "How am I to live in a conflict-ridden world?" In response, Paul turns to Jesus, whose very life serves as the answer. For Paul, love requires peace and social justice that goes beyond the typical evangelical understanding of the teachings of Jesus that has in recent decades been aligned with an emphasis on personal salvation and conservative politics.

Such was not always the case for Paul, as reflected in his self-description as a "Christian/Pentecostal boy in Kansas": "I was a good kid; I wasn't a rebel; I was helpful in the church.... I was a leader. I was student congress president in high school. I was the Christian leader who did things pretty well. I was supposed to do things well and try to help the people who were backsliding." When the interviewer interjected that his "consciousness of social justice was pretty limited," Paul laughed and replied, "Well, I would not have been *anti–social justice*. I was simply *pro–social injustice*." Paul then stopped short, hesitated, and added, "I don't want to be condemning of folks who are still like I was at that time." Paul's answer to the question, "Who is my neighbor?" was much more narrow in his youth than it is today. His vision of social justice now includes everyone, oppressed and oppressor alike, without respect to national or other humanly constructed boundaries.

Paul grew up in a loving and devout Pentecostal family; his love for God was intimately intertwined with familial affection. He commented, "I think I probably experienced God's love through the love of my parents, my grandparents." The Pentecostal church in which he was raised, however, was "puritanical" and "pietistic," and it left him with a stern and punitive image of God—"a god of wrath, judgment, and you've got to get everything right." While growing up, Paul kept the rules—he didn't go to movies, engage in public swimming, drink alcohol, do drugs, or go to dances. There was somewhat of a discontinuity, however, between the legalisms then emphasized in his denomination and Paul's experience of love. As Paul explains:

> So God was related to those things [religious taboos]. But maybe my loving experiences with people overwrote, meshed with, and really worked with that definition of God to where God is watching everything you are doing. If you're in a movie theater and Jesus comes back, you're probably not going to get to go [with him]. That's the kind of sermons that I heard [he laughed]. That is what was preached. So I definitely had a view of righteousness and holiness. Then I became extremely judgmental myself. I was super self-righteous. What I didn't see was the greed and the racism and the sexism. Those things were not

pointed out to me. I had everything else right, but I did not—capitalism was not critiqued.

Paul graduated from a Pentecostal university and seminary in the mid-1990s still enmeshed in a strict and outmoded culture of a Pentecostalism in flux, and in time his religious faith "really started crumbling and falling apart." He would soon become an agnostic "follower of Jesus." Paul opens his book *Peace to War* with the following brief account from his spiritual journey:[8]

> I was a freshman in a Pentecostal college in 1991 when the United States ousted Saddam Hussein from Kuwait. I cheered as Operation Desert Storm began and the missiles rained down. My friends and I enjoyed watching the war on television, and I thought the song, "Bomb, bomb, bomb…bomb, bomb Iraq" (to the tune of "Ba Ba Ba…Ba Barbara Ann" by the Beach Boys) was hilarious. I was a tongues-talking, pro-war, hardcore patriotic, Assemblies of God follower of Jesus. If somebody had told me that the Assemblies of God, the denomination of my four-generation heritage, had been officially antiwar for its first fifty years, I would have thought they were crazy.
>
> Six years later, when I found out most early Pentecostal denominations has been "pacifist," I did indeed think it was about the dumbest thing I had ever heard. But it so intrigued me that I was drawn to the topics of Pentecostals, war, violence, Americanism, and patriotism as a moth to the proverbial flame.…My understanding of Christianity died, my understanding of God died, my faith died, I died.

Although the parochial and nationalistic Pentecostal religion of Paul's youth proved inadequate for the maturing scholar, he was ordained and remains a minister with the Assemblies of God. At the same time, he recognizes the significance of a pentecostal worldview with "signs and wonders" and its "world of miracles" that he credits as a major reason for Pentecostalism's growth.[9] Paul felt "compelled" ("I think led by the Holy Spirit") to found an organization known as Pentecostals and Charismatics for Peace and Justice "that would be a catalyst to help fulfill what God wants to do in the world."[10] Through his research, writing, and university teaching, Paul works to bring about a more just world by challenging pentecostals and evangelicals to return to what he believes are basic teachings of Jesus on peace and justice. Yet his approach to global ministry differs from Heidi's in that it places less emphasis on supernatural gifts. He is more of a Changer than a Renewer, in our typology.

In fact, the Changers in our sample were generally less "pentecostal" than the Renewers.

The coming kingdom of God preached by Jesus and proclaimed by Christians—a kingdom that gives a taste of heaven to a hungry and broken world—is a theological theme we found coloring the interviews of many exemplars. Although Heidi spends approximately one-third of her time traveling the globe speaking about a coming kingdom where love is the primary language, living out the kingdom for Heidi has always involved serving the "poorest of the poor" in countries far removed from Western affluence, where the reality of the supernatural is more apparent. Paul's approach to ushering in the coming kingdom, on the other hand, has its focus on a need for structural changes to bring about a more peaceful and just world. With a primary goal of changing existing structures to conform to biblical mandates, Paul tends to place less emphasis on affective changes in individuals, the unusual manifestations of the Spirit, and supernatural forces. Both Heidi and Paul are examples of extensive benevolence with a high sensitivity to global needs that transcend national boundaries, but there are differences in the way they live out their shared faith in Jesus. In short, Heidi better reflects the alternate primitive worldview of pentecostalism, with its supernatural "signs and wonders," while Paul's approach to pentecostalism mutes the primitive with a strong call to pragmatic action. Both reflect what pentecostal historian Grant Wacker described as a hallmark of pentecostalism—a blend of premodern primitivism and modern pragmatism—but their paths differ in the use of these two basic elements.[11] Despite having earned a PhD in systematic theology, Heidi displays a simple and childlike faith, and her mystical stories of supernatural encounters with God are beyond most common spiritual experiences of those of us in the modern Western world. (These stories include resurrections from the dead, supernatural healings, and the multiplication of food, much like accounts found in the ministry of Jesus.) Paul, on the other hand, is a Pentecostal theologian who sounds a biblical call for justice as he describes the need for planned social action. Although the primitive and the pragmatic can be found in both Paul and Heidi, Paul is decidedly less likely to frame his narrative with experiences of pentecostal power and possibilities than Heidi is.

Local Mystic: Steve Witt (Bethel Church Cleveland)

Steve Witt, founding pastor of Bethel Cleveland (known from its founding in 1996 until recently as Metro Church South),[12] illustrates yet another expression of godly love in which the primitive and the pragmatic are inter-twined. Like Paul, Steve earned his undergraduate degree at an Assemblies of God (A.G.) college, but he would soon drift away from historic Pentecostalism toward newly emerging neo-pentecostal groups where primitive supernatural experiences and revivals were more likely to be found. At the same time, Steve is a spiritual entrepreneur who deftly intertwines the pragmatic into his life and ministry that reflects what he learned as a child from his union-leader father.

Although his family moved away "from being a basic blue-collar family" as his father became a union leader, Steve grew up during a time when manufac-turing was king in the now aging and decaying city of Cleveland, Ohio. When he was eight years old and his mother was in the hospital as a result of a ner-vous breakdown, a Pentecostal woman came in and prayed for her. His mother was instantly healed, and after she was released from the hospital they began attending a Pentecostal church. It was there, Steve reported, that "I had a very strong experience where I laid on the floor at the age of ten. I was speaking in tongues and it was very powerful. That kind of was a benchmark defining moment for me." Steve would in time attend a Pentecostal Bible college and found two churches in Cleveland (while earning his master's degree in the-ology), but experiences of the supernatural were never far away. For example, during his interview with us, Steve succinctly described an unanticipated move from Cleveland to New Brunswick, Canada, as follows: "God visited me in a very supernatural way and called me to go to Canada—that I was to go there in preparation for a revival that would touch the nations and the world." Steve and his wife, Cindy, together with their four children, would move one thou-sand miles to New Brunswick, where he founded a third church. And as fore-shadowed in his divine call to Canada, he was among the first wave of pilgrims to visit the Toronto Airport Vineyard when a major revival broke out in 1994.[13] (Two years later Steve would heed another prophetic call, this one to return to Cleveland where he presently serves as lead pastor for four congregations in northeastern Ohio that are known as Bethel Cleveland [Middleburg Heights, Brunswick, Madison, and Akron] Church.)

The revivals that swept across the globe in the 1990s have had lasting effects that are reflected in the ministries of both Heidi and Steve. Personal proph-ecies, a sense of divine empowerment, and the "signs and wonders" of super-natural experiences are heightened by revival fires. But while Heidi remains an apostle to the nations and a citizen of Mozambique, Steve Witt's enthu-siasm for being a global itinerant minister during the height of the revival eventually would wane. He would come to recognize that Cleveland was to be his focus. Cleveland—pejoratively dubbed the "mistake on the lake" where the "river caught on fire"—has been the subject of repeated prophecies over the past couple of decades. These prophecies point to Cleveland's "unique calling and role in the Kingdom"—prophecies that Steve Witt has embraced in a way that blends the entrepreneurial spirit of his union-leader father and the mystical spirit of his pentecostal mother.[14] As we were preparing this account, the local Akron, Ohio, newspaper reported that Bethel Cleveland had purchased property that until recently housed a Catholic parish. Located at the exit of the expressway leading to downtown Cleveland, with the University of Akron to the north and a blighted inner-city neighborhood to the south, the old church provided a perfect location for another Bethel Cleveland church. In the article Steve shared: "Our dream is to plant multiple church locations to provide outreach in neighborhoods throughout the Greater Cleveland area, which includes the Akron area, by releasing, deploying and empowering lay people to go out and meet the needs of people who need the love of God. We've got an outrageous goal to plant one hundred groups of at least one hundred people. The Akron location is our fourth. We still have ninety-six to go."[15]

Relative to other categories in our typology of pentecostal exemplars, Steve scores high on pentecostal identity and experience but (because of his focus on a particular locality) is lower on extensive benevolence than either Paul or Heidi. As we will see as his story unfolds, Steve is convinced that needed change can best be brought about through praying with people, which he believes holds the key to changes that will impact social structures. During his interview, Steve described the power and effects brought about by individuals changed by prayer as being like "Trojan horses all through the culture—doctors, lawyers, teachers, factory workers." He adds, "If I can teach those people that they're called of God into that place, then they can rise up. Now it becomes (particularly in time of economic or otherwise downturn or disaster like we are facing right now) the moment for which the church was made." Thus his vision for Bethel churches is to equip members of his congregations to "bring the kingdom of God" into their communities—to transform their workplaces and neighborhoods as they are led and empowered by the Spirit. Twenty young people from suburban Bethel churches who have moved into Slavic Village, an old ethnic neighborhood in Cleveland currently suffering from high rates of crime and home foreclosures, serve on the front line. Through their commitment to living in this area and with the help of other Bethel congregations, they are working to transform Slavic Village into a viable community with improved economic, social, and spiritual health.

Steve described some efforts to prepare his members to make a difference in the community as follows:

> That's why we prepared this summer two hundred people for deliverance and healing ministries. That's a lot of people! Right now we've got forty to fifty people coming tomorrow night for fresh prophetic training. So if persecution comes upon America—maybe not overt persecution but where we are in a state of crisis where leadership is needed—we will be ready.... People will say, "I want to be ready for a time that kingdom believers can emerge and advance the kingdom unlike any time before." We may be on the outer edges of that right now. So we get people ready to move broadly into the streets and into their neighborhoods.

We close this short introduction to Steve and Bethel Cleveland with a succinct description of this pastor's dream:

> My dream for this church is a community of people that on the surface at any given time may look like one thing or another, but if you scratch deep enough, you're gonna see these three things underneath: solid theological understanding, a value of the experiential, and a practical exercise of what we call "engaging." We talk about equipping and engaging, which are really two different things. Equipping is all about education. Engaging is about experience. Equipping is about being a student. Engaging is about being a servant.

Local Planner 1: Anne Beiler (The Family Center of Gap)

The exemplars we have introduced thus far, despite their many differences, do share white middle-class backgrounds that have provided them with a common grid for many of their life experiences. Heidi, Steve, and Paul were all raised in solidly middle-class Euro-American Protestant homes. The two exemplars we have selected to represent the Local Planner corner of our typology of pentecostal identity and extensive benevolence—where scores for mystical experiences are lower and the benevolence displayed is more local than global—are from significantly different backgrounds. Our first is Anne Beiler, whose Auntie Anne's Soft Pretzels can be found across the malls of America, a successful entrepreneur and cofounder with her husband Jonas of the Family Center of Gap. Anne was born into an Old Order Amish family, but her parents joined the somewhat less strict Amish-Mennonite church when Anne was three years old. The Family Center in Gap, Pennsylvania, which opened in the fall of 2008 (with the money derived from the sale of Auntie Anne's Inc.), "brings together the resources, services, and community connections people need to be well—mentally, spiritually and physically." The succinct mission statement found on its website reflects the Amish value of being a helping community: "The Family Center exists to help families thrive by providing a hub of interactive services which offer a healing presence, foster healthy relationships and model community cooperation."[16]

Anne and her husband Jonas were both raised Amish—Anne in an Amish-Mennonite community that allowed for cars and electricity, and Jonas in an Old Order Amish community, with its horses and buggies, in Lancaster County, Pennsylvania. Important lessons about family and community were woven into the fabric of their lives. When asked in our interview about events that shaped her, Anne responded without hesitation, "My family, growing up in the Amish culture with eight children and parents that care for me and love me (but never told me they loved me)." Anne went on to develop this thought by sharing how she had "a mom and a dad there any time of the day or night" and not remembering "a time coming home when I was alone." Two important and recurrent facts about Anne's life are found in her response to our opening interview question: first, the value she placed on Amish community; and second, the lack of open communication and expression of affect (although she was not aware of the latter until much later in life). Anne then added, "So my family history is very not perfect, but there is a foundation there that I believe really set me for life." Although her family was poor, she learned at an early age the joy of giving.

Anne also differed from Heidi, Paul, and Steve in another important way. While the benevolence of our first three exemplars is rooted largely in religious service organizations, Anne Beiler, with an eighth-grade Amish education, was thrust into a secular marketplace when she and Jonas left the Amish community, a shift that opened the door to the seemingly serendipitous founding and growth of Auntie Anne's.[17] The organization "grew from a single outlet to more than 950 locations worldwide, with a workforce of more than 10,000."[18] The success of Auntie Anne's Soft Pretzels was welcomed, but it reportedly was not the Beilers' passion. It has always been their desire to reach out into the larger community with the resources they have been given, a passion that has come to fruition with the Family Center. When Anne spoke of the financial problems her family had as she was growing up, she also noted how the seeds for benevolence were planted in the midst of the difficulties:

I think it was during that time that it was put in my heart that I wanted to make a difference. I wanted to help my parents—I knew that—and I wanted to help people. Maybe it's because I saw people help my parents; I don't know. I think it's safe for me to say that was the beginning of my awareness of being poor and struggling because of family.... It was my purpose. My purpose was to give back and that's where it started. I learned at a very young age, it's never about going to work to get a paycheck for me. And I work just as hard, probably harder because I had a purpose.

When Matt interviewed Anne on August 28, 2008, on the sprawling campus of the Family Center of Gap—then still under construction—she was putting the finishing touches on an inspirational address that would be delivered to a television audience of millions on September 3 at the Republican National Convention for the McCain/Palin presidential ticket. Whereas Margaret's interview with Jonas that day was full of laughter, Anne's interview with Matt was very different in tone. The powerful, optimistic speaker who appeared at the RNC a few days later was instead thoughtful, and even touchingly vulnerable, as she wept over the tragic events of her life. These events include the accidental death of her daughter involving a tractor driven by Anne's sister, as well as infidelities involving a pastor who also abused another of Anne's sisters as well as another of Anne's daughters. Anne now feels empowered by her relationship with a loving God to share these details, as she has done in her autobiography, so that her story may empower others who have experienced tragedies and abuse to tell their own stories and be healed.[19] Whereas Heidi describes being "wrecked" by a direct encounter with the love of Jesus, Anne was undone by the love of her husband, who instantly forgave her indiscretions and stood by her unconditionally. Godly love unfolds in myriad ways, as we will see throughout this book.

Local Planner 2: Herbert Daughtry ("People's Pastor," National Presider of the House of the Lord Fellowship, and a founder of the National Black United Front)

Herbert Daughtry has been called the "People's Pastor" (a title he cherishes) for his long tenure as pastor of the House of the Lord Fellowship in Brooklyn, national presiding minister of the House of the Lord churches, and his activist career.[20] Despite a ministry that crosses many localities and includes international work, we classified Daughtry as a Local Planner, given that his social activism has been directed toward a specific people group and has largely focused on the United States. Although not confined to a single community, as is the case with the Beilers in Gap, Pennsylvania, and Steve Witt in northeastern Ohio, Daughtry's ministry is local in the sense that it is limited to a call for social justice for people of African descent. Perhaps more than any other exemplar in our study, Herb Daughtry represents the voice of an Old Testament prophet for whom love dances to the timbre of justice. Cornel West (professor at Princeton University, author, civil rights activist, and prominent member of the Democratic Socialists of America) describes Daughtry as follows:[21]

> Herb Daughtry is one of the towering prophetic leaders of his generation. Pastor of the world-known House of the Lord Pentecostal Church for nearly forty years, founder and first chairperson of the National Black United Front, and leader of the African Peoples Christian Organization, Rev. Daughtry has touched the lives and inspired the hopes of thousands of people. He certainly has enriched my life—as friend, mentor, comrade, colleague and fellow Christian.

Matt, accompanied by the Flame of Love Project team member A. G. Miller, Daughtry's longtime protégé and a religious studies professor at Oberlin College, interviewed this towering figure in a multipurpose room at his church in Brooklyn, New York, on a cold day in January 2009. The room was filled with artifacts from the church's history, including civil rights and social justice signs, banners, buttons, and photographs. Herb was initially accompanied by one of his daughters, who refused on his behalf the survey form Matt had placed before him. With a skeptical demeanor, he inquired about why our research project was "necessary at this particular time." His posture seemed to be asking, "In a world of suffering and injustice, what good will result from this interview that will benefit the oppressed?" If we failed to provide an adequate answer, who could blame him for canceling the interview and getting on with more important matters? In fact, he did cancel our first attempt to interview him the day before due to illness, and the only reason we were able to meet with him on that day is that his illness required him to cancel a flight to Atlanta. To say this was a last-minute arrangement was an understatement: we almost missed our return flight to Cleveland in an effort to get his complete narrative.

Yet it was a compelling narrative, and fortunately A. G. was able to make a persuasive case that there was value in sharing his story with us. It goes without saying that we would not have even gotten an invitation to meet with him if not for A. G. Thanks to this interview, we were also able to interview Daughtry's wife as well as one of his daughters (who was serving as the CEO of the Democratic National Committee). Each interview we conducted had a unique feel. Some interviewees expressed a kind of nervous energy, others (like Heidi) a warm glow of abiding love. Paul and Anne both shed tears, for very different reasons. Jonas's soft-spoken responses reflected a striking inner contentment of a humble Amish man. Steve's more intellectual responses reflected his advanced degree in theology while paradoxically including accounts of prophetic voices. Herb was more serious than the others, as fitting a man whose whole life has been spent, as he notes, "at the point of pain." And that, in his view, is where the servant of God ought to be. This is not to say that he lacked humor or warmth, but he seemed burdened by the afflictions he sees in his community. The grievances are significant, and in his role as a prophet Herb seeks to bring awareness to these issues in a way that will lead to healing. Many of his stories do not have a happy ending, as his well-known involvement as spiritual mentor to the murdered rapper Tupac Shakur illustrates.

Daughtry's awareness of the injustice leveled against African Americans is rooted in his childhood in Savannah, where he lived on "the dividing line" between the black and white neighborhoods. He set the stage for his interview with Matt and A. G. by sharing how his earliest awareness of racial inequities was formed: "I would stand on the street (this was before I was eight years old) and look southward and there were gleaming white houses. The lawn was manicured; the streets, clean. But looking then northward was the black part of the neighborhood, and there were shanties and gullies in the streets. The street was not paved. I would wrestle with this conspicuous contrast." After his parents separated, he would go back and forth between Savannah and Augusta, where his sense of the "imbalance" between white and black communities would increase. Herb began to play Robin Hood while working for a Chinese merchant, stealing from the "rich" and giving to the "poor." He would be caught—and fired from his job: "You go to the movies and everybody applauded Robin Hood. That's all I was doing. I didn't need those potatoes and greens and stuff that I was stealing. But, in any event, you know what happened!" In 1953 he would be convicted of armed robbery and assault charges, and it was while in prison that he had a religious conversion that would change the rest of his life.

Herb Daughtry's ministry has had its share of controversy. His younger protégé, Cornel West, describes it as follows: "Like the prophets of old, Rev.

Daughtry often has been misunderstood. His sincere outrage against injustice and social misery has challenged the status quo and unsettled the powers that be—of the White House, State House, City Hall, Wall Street, *The New York Times* or *Daily News.*"[22] For Daughtry and his followers, the prophetic call requires applying the Gospel to the conditions of the community, a call that involves the acquisition of power, as reflected in the following statement that Daughtry refers to as "my theme":[23]

> We were being beaten and killed because we are powerless. We must develop power. Every group acts on behalf of its own interests. I added that when political and economic power have been equitably distributed, I would gladly stand on the steps of City Hall or elsewhere and declare that creed, color, and ethnicity do not matter. Until then, we must organize ourselves and act with self-interest.

For Daughtry this struggle for power is a God-given American right, as seen on one of his YouTube videos: "It has always been a belief in our family that we had a covenant with the Almighty—a covenant that said if we did our part—that is to say if we worked with and struggled for the people—that God in turn would make our lives meaningful and worthwhile."[24] Daughtry certainly has his share of critics—his book *No Monopoly on Suffering* was written largely in response to criticism—and benevolence is always in the eye of the beholder.[25] But few can doubt that his participation in godly love has made his life meaningful.

Different Choreography, Same Dance with the Divine

In response to a question about the relationship between love and power that Margaret asked Heidi during her interview, Heidi responded that she saw the two as wings of the same bird. While Herb might concur with Heidi's observation, it strikes us that their conceptions of power are strikingly different. While Heidi is certainly a woman of action as well as prayer, she uses the language of love and relies on a supernatural power (including miracles) to right wrongs, whereas Herb emphasizes a human struggle against injustice—a struggle that he believes has been ordained by God and endorsed by a divine covenant. Like Paul Alexander's call, Daughtry's ministry centers on a biblical cry for social justice that embodies more pragmatic action than primal divine empowerment. Paul, a Pentecostal from the Midwest, on the other hand, has a focus on peace that is arguably more global in application.

And while the Beilers recognize the leading of God in establishing the Family Center at Gap and the divine provisions that came through Auntie Anne's, there is little talk of paranormal experiences, prophetic calls, and miraculous events that are common to the more pentecostal-driven ministries of Steve Witt and Heidi Baker.

What all do share in common, however, is a sense of a divine call—of a partnership with God. Their lives present diverse answers to our "big question" about how different people come to recognize and work out their purpose in life. Whether they represent the new face of global pentecostalism that is transforming Christianity throughout the world (as Heidi does); a dream to revitalize a dying city within a larger stagnant urban area (as we see with Steve); a compelling prophetlike drive to resolve racial injustice in a local community (as with Herb), or economic injustice across the globe (as with Paul); or the reinvention of values found in the Old Order traditions of the Amish for the modern world (as reflected in the lives of Anne and especially her husband Jonas), all of our primary exemplars have had deeply personal and life-transforming encounters with the love of God. They would argue that their lives are richer and more meaningful, and their benevolence more far-reaching, as a result.

In short, their experiences are deeply rooted in godly love interactions. If we imagine godly love to be a dance, God is the primary partner. But human partners are important too. None of the accomplishments of our exemplars would have been possible without the help of other people and human organizations. The choreography is different depending in part on the social networks in which the exemplars are embedded, as the life histories of our five primary exemplars demonstrate. Although the next three chapters focus on the interactive relationship between God and the exemplar, their human collaborators are never far away. Our final chapters will attend to the human interactive network as we wrestle with the perennial problems inherent in evaluating benevolence. But first, chapter 4 explores how our exemplars of godly love learned to partner with God by focusing on their respective stories of spiritual transformation. We also discuss how these stories illuminate our survey statistics that reflect the thoughts and behaviors of millions of Americans.

4

Partnering with the Divine

SPIRITUAL TRANSFORMATION
AND GODLY LOVE

IN 1980, UNIVERSITY student Bob Ekblad traveled for a year through
Central America, where he had a powerful life-changing experience as he
found himself in the midst of a civil war. After surrendering his life to God a
few years earlier at the age of seventeen, Bob knew that his primary calling
was to serve the poor. He described how he and his wife had worked alongside
the Mennonites ministering to the needs of the poor and refugees in
Guatemala—even using their status as American citizens to, as he described it
in his interview with us, "provide protection for the refugees by serving as
human shields." He listened to the people he met and learned firsthand the
horrors of war. Bob found himself in a lived history lesson that would change
his understanding of American politics and his identity as an American.

> I mean my country has put in these dictatorships that have been killing
> hundreds of thousands of people. And I've never learned about it until
> now. What else has the United States done?... When I learned that in
> fact it was true and what we did was just like... I mean really diabolical,
> that caused such a crisis for me, in terms of my American identity. And
> I've never learned about it until now. I was a history major in college,
> and I had been misled. But anyway that experience being in Central
> America and in both seeing that our country had been consistently on
> the side of injustice and that what we have been taught was just kind of
> the opposite of what we are.

When Bob returned home with his wife and lectured about what they saw in
Central America they found little acceptance in the conservative evangelical
churches in which he was raised. "The evangelicals and charismatics all said

that we were liberal communists. And they didn't listen to anything that we had to say. In fact, they were consistently on the side of the US policy. It was very disheartening. It caused me to distrust anything that they were saying." Bob would describe much of his life until 2004 as a Christian social activist "estranged from the body of Christ charismatic [pentecostal]. Years of ministry among the poor in war-torn Central America and among undocumented immigrants and inmates in labor camps and a jail in the United States put me at odds with my government and with many evangelicals and charismatic Christians who supported its wars and laws."[1] Yet over these years Bob still felt he was "making progress" in his work to "combat the roots of poverty and oppression through contextual Bible study, sustainable development and human rights advocacy."

Just as it did for most other Americans, 9/11 marked an epiphany for Bob, albeit in a direction somewhat antithetical to the patriotism that seemed to blanket the country after the attacks on the World Trade Center and Pentagon. During his interview Bob elaborated on his increasing discontentment with his ministerial work, service that seemed to lack power:

> When 9/11 happened the patriotism was so strong that I just felt like everything I'd been doing on the education front was for nothing. It was like nationalism couldn't be combated through education. It had to be something spiritual. That was beyond what I was. You know, my paradigm for how change happened, wasn't deep enough. And that coincided with methamphetamines hitting the streets. When meth hit … that was such a potent drug and was so destructive that 9/11 and meth kind of caused me to really hit a crisis, where I just felt like the gospel that I'm bearing is not, doesn't have the power to save.
>
> You know, it doesn't have the power to save these people who are caught up in severe nationalism and pride, national pride—you know, the mainstream. It doesn't have the power to save them from its realism and from all the trappings of the American culture. It's not powerful for the mainstream and it's not powerful enough for the margins, because the people that have been coming to my Bible studies weren't getting free from meth. They were just getting destroyed.

As his discontent increased, Bob became more desperate and "longed to see more of God's power to bring transformation." It was only after his wife attended a revival conference at the Toronto Airport Christian Fellowship— where Heidi Baker was one of the main speakers—that Bob would become open to pentecostal Christianity. Bob and his wife were both moved "just seeing there was someone, kind of like us in a way, working with the poor who was talking about being touched [by God] and then seeing fruitfulness in their lives." Two months later, in 2004, Bob would venture to a conference at the Toronto church: "My desperation for breakthrough in ministry became so great that I ventured across the line into an ecumenism broader than I'd ever considered—attending a pastors' and leaders' conference at the infamous Toronto Airport Christian Fellowship" (now Catch the Fire Toronto).[2] He described himself as "truly open," as he sought to look beyond the point of disagreement to what he might glean from the conference that would empower his ministry.

Bob was not disappointed. He elaborates on his spiritual transformation in an article on his website:[3]

> I was struck from the start how much the Holy Spirit was moving during a session on the importance of forgiveness. As the speaker taught and prayed vivid memories came to mind of offenses and judgments held against people in my distant past who I felt compelled to forgive. After another stirring session on Jesus's ministry announcing the Kingdom of God I lined up to receive prayer with hundreds of others for greater fruitfulness in ministry, and soon had my turn before a young man from the UK on the ministry team. His words opened me up as he spoke what only God could have shown him.
>
> "I see you in a circle of men in red uniforms, I think they are prisoners," he started out, getting my rapt attention. "The Father is saying 'I am delighted how you love my prisoners and I'm going to give you deeper revelation from the Bible that will make their hearts burn,'" he continued, moving me with this reference to my favorite picture from the Emmaus road story in Luke 24:13 before a final unexpected clincher. "He is releasing an anointing for healing on you so your words will be confirmed with the signs that follow." I fell to the ground overcome by the Spirit, my hands burning. I continued to be touched more and more by the Holy Spirit at that conference in ways that transformed my life and ministry.

Godly love begins with a spiritual experience and an invitation that commonly includes a call requiring a response. The call to benevolent service is part of an ongoing process we call *spiritual transformation*, which brings about a qualitative change in a person's relationship with the sacred. As Bob's narrative indicates, spiritual transformations unfold throughout the life course and are bound up with personal experiences as these are shaped by broader social events; in his case, 9/11 and the proliferation of methamphetamine were particularly important. Our interviews with godly love exemplars like Bob provided a wealth of powerful stories of spiritual transformation as these extraordinary Americans shared some of the most significant events in their lives that brought them to where they are today. We have provided some examples of spiritual transformation in previous introductory chapters. The life accounts of nearly all of our interviewees abounded with fascinating stories in which bits of heaven seemed to touch the earth—long and short narrations, sometimes sprinkled with laughter or tears, which described the call and response.[4] Some of these experiences proved to be life-changing. Sheri's coming into an awareness of God's personal love as a five-year-old child when she realized God was "soft and safe," described in chapter 2, provides one simple yet life-altering account of a spiritual transformation. It is an experience that remains vivid and pivotal in her life nearly five decades later and reportedly continues to have a profound effect on her spiritual journey as she ministers to people in need.

Psychologist of religion Kenneth Pargament says that a spiritual transformation—"a fundamental change in the place of the sacred or the character of the sacred in the life of the individual"—may be *primary* or *secondary*.[5] Sheri's primary experience of God in the back seat of the old family car as she gazed at the stars through the back window is her personal and unique story. Primary spiritual transformation takes on an indeterminate number of forms and takes place in countless different settings—experiences like the birth of a child, a moving religious ritual, a quiet time of morning prayer, a late summer sunset on a beautiful beach, a hike through a multicolored autumn forest, or attending the passing of a loved one. Primary spiritual transformations are of seemingly infinite variations, but each provides a unique and often dramatic preview into the world of the sacred for the one reporting the experience. In Sheri's case, her experience as a five-year-old was but the first step in a lifelong commitment to a loving God and his call to follow him in the service of others.[6]

Secondary transformations provide new directions in living out a divine calling. They do not mark a change in goals or destinations but rather they represent changes "in pathways people take to the sacred."[7] Sheri's original pathway, for example, was that of a full-time evangelist before she went on to earn her PhD and began teaching at a university. At the time of the interview she had just quit her university position and due to health problems was again about to change pathways. Yet her primary commitment to following God wherever he called her to serve him seemed as strong and unwavering as ever. Bob's story also provides a good illustration of the importance of both primary (e.g., his initial surrender to God) and secondary (e.g., his involvement in social justice) transformations. In sum, although narratives commonly begin with a very particular and memorable personal experience, spiritual transformation is more of a lifelong journey dotted with secondary transformations than a single transitory event.

Survey Statistics and Spiritual Transformation

Throughout this book, we weave together foundational statistical findings from the GLNS with the interview narratives of exemplars of godly love. Survey statistics apart from lived experiences can provide only a pale reflection of the rich and varied experiences of spiritual transformation. Numbers are useful and interesting, but statistics by themselves are unable to capture the movement and flow of spiritual transformations as an ongoing process. At the heart of the problem is finding words that hold the same meaning for the diverse populations represented in a good national sample. Even the best of survey instruments used in national and global studies have difficulty capturing the many cultural grids and their particularistic linguistic expressions for religious and spiritual phenomena.

Yet the GLNS is no less important for our understanding of godly love than the qualitative accounts of religious experience are. Perhaps the greatest importance of the survey is that it provides solid empirical evidence demonstrating that spiritual experiences are alive and well, transforming individual lives and communities, in American society.[8] The survey results permit us to create a statistical skeletal form and then clothe it with rich and colorful narratives from exemplars that breathe life into its dry bones.

We have already reported on some statistically significant relationships between experiencing the love of God and higher scores on benevolent activities, experiences grounded in both *spirituality* (the individual experience of the sacred) and *religion* (institutional beliefs, denominational affiliation, and religious practices). Those respondents who claimed to be both spiritual and religious were much more likely to score higher on experiencing divine love than those with lower scores.[9] Through the use of the GLNS data we also showed that a surprisingly common pentecostal worldview in which the Spirit of God is experienced in everyday lives can be found throughout contemporary American Christianity. Self-identifying as a Pentecostal or charismatic

Christian is a factor more important than demographics that are commonly used in social science research for understanding the relationship between divine and human love. The 27 percent of the sample who said they considered themselves to be Pentecostal and/or charismatic (pentecostal) were significantly more likely to score high on the Divine Love scale.

Furthermore, our findings affirm the normality of seemingly paranormal spiritual experiences and how these experiences transcend, albeit unevenly, a wide array of denominational affiliations. One common marker of religiosity in surveys that we have not yet considered—one that promises to be significant for understanding spiritual transformation—is the experience of being "born again." This is commonly understood to mean accepting Jesus as one's personal savior and receiving the assurance of salvation, although the precise meaning varies across cultural groups. As figure 4.1 shows, 42 percent of the GLNS reported having this spiritual experience. It was found to be much more common among evangelical (82 percent), Hispanic (80 percent), and African American (71 percent) Protestants than among mainline (33 percent) Protestants. Clearly it is a label and nomenclature more likely to be used by Protestants than by Catholics: only 11 percent of Euro-American and 41 percent of Hispanic Catholics claim to be born again.[10] These survey findings suggest, however, that being born again may be an important catalyst in primary spiritual transformation for many Christians.[11]

As we continued our statistical analysis with our ears attuned to the voices of our interviewees, an even more important factor than being born again would emerge as one that is statistically related both to experiences of divine love and to increased benevolence. Those who reported that they believed their lives mattered to others, that they had a sense of destiny working in their lives and a strong sense of purpose that directed their lives, were also more likely to experience divine love and to demonstrate benevolence toward others.[12] We called the general phenomenon tapped by these three survey items—lives that mattered to others, a strong sense of destiny, and a strong sense of purpose—*existential well-being*.[13] In sum, existential well-being demonstrated moderately strong statistical relationships with higher scores for experiencing God's love and with benevolence (toward family, friends and neighbors, local community, and beyond).[14]

It does appear, however, that members of some religious groups are more likely to report higher scores on existential well-being than others are. Evangelical (33 percent) and black Protestants (36 percent) are significantly more likely to claim that their lives are high in meaning and purpose than mainline Protestants (22 percent), Jews (20 percent), Catholics (18 percent),

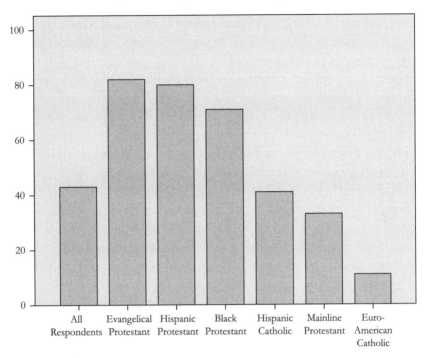

FIGURE 4.1 Percentage of American Adults Self-Identifying as "Born Again" by Denomination

(*Source*: 2009 GLNS; *N* = 1,208)

and those who are unaffiliated with any particular denomination (16 percent). Those who self-identify with the pentecostal worldview are more likely to report their lives to be filled with meaning and purpose (31 percent) than those who do not claim pentecostal identity (22 percent). Of particular interest for our discussion of spiritual transformation in this chapter is the relationship between existential well-being and benevolence, including the role that self-identifying as a born-again Christian may play. Over three-fourths (77 percent) of those who *did not* regard themselves as born-again Christians scored low (i.e., in the bottom quartile) on existential well-being, compared with less than one-quarter (23 percent) of self-described born-again Christians.[15]

We present this assortment of relevant statistics to demonstrate that, while the narratives of our select group of interviewees may seem extraordinary, they reflect the spiritual transformations of millions of Americans represented in our national sample. A clearer description of the role that particular cultural grids play in such findings emerges only as we allow our interviewees to speak into this numerical analysis. What we observe is that some primary spiritual transformation (e.g., being born again)[16] is what commonly ignites the spark of divine love. With this experience of God's intense love often comes a calling to follow God in developing a life of benevolence. A strong sense of existential well-being enters into a dialectical relationship with acts of benevolence. The sense of a divine call and destiny empowered by experiences of divine love in turn serves as a catalyst for benevolent attitudes and actions, which then further enhances a sense of existential well-being in a process that is consistent with what psychologists, economists, and management scholars describe as a "virtuous circle" (see figure 4.2 for one possible pathway).[17] In this model, equilibrium is not necessarily the end state. Ongoing experiences of God's love, if they occur with increasing intensity or take on deeper significance, may set in motion a feedback loop that leads to more intense or effective acts of benevolent service.

We are not implying that the nonreligious are incapable of participating in a virtuous cycle that fosters benevolence. Instead, we are simply identifying a pathway for a particular group of people that is central to their commitment to and enactment of benevolent work over the course of their lives. More research is needed on how an analogous or different process might work for the nonreligious. In addition, this model is just one example of a number of permutations. For some, the primary spiritual transformation would not be described as a born-again experience. For many, well-being might precede taking benevolent action or receiving a divine calling. We have simply illustrated one path in a diverse process. The point is that regardless of the specifics, primary and secondary spiritual transformations are involved in a virtuous circle that fosters benevolence.

In addition to data from our interviews, our national survey also provides support for the importance of experiences of divine love and a sense of divine calling, in concert with increased existential well-being, to a life of benevolence.[18] We are unable to test the time-ordering of the model displayed in figure 4.2 due to the cross-sectional nature of our survey data. But when taken together, the survey and interview findings suggest an interplay between divine love, divine calling, and existential well-being that predicts higher levels of benevolence. The flow of the circular model of virtue in figure 4.2 is well illustrated through the narrative of missionary and evangelist Heidi Baker, a journey that she asserts has been compelled by the love of God.

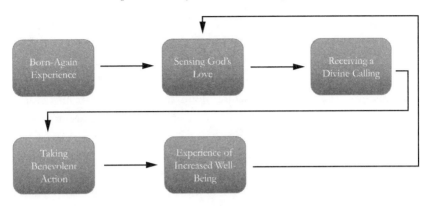

FIGURE 4.2 The Process of Benevolent Spiritual Transformation

Heidi Baker: A Case Study of Spiritual Transformations
Threefold Primary Spiritual Transformation

As a child Heidi was often taken to an Episcopal church by her nonpracticing Catholic father and her Episcopalian mother. She described her parents as being "not particularly religious"—"my father was Ivy League Catholic, left God at Stanford...and my mother was not very strong in her Episcopal faith." When Heidi was four years old, shortly after her brother had died, she was in the hospital battling encephalitis. Fearing for the loss of another child, her parents prayed, "If you will spare our daughter, you can take her and you can use her and you can have her for your glory." Heidi defined this act of parental dedication and promise as their surrendering her to God's plan and purpose: "My parents, who barely knew him, literally lifted me to God....And God took me—he took me and so my life's not my own." So began our interview with this remarkable missionary and evangelist whose life and message are having a global impact.

When asked by Margaret to identify a few of the factors or events that have shaped who she is today, Heidi responded without hesitation:

> Okay, I can absolutely identify that—March 13, 1976. I was living on an Indian reservation as an American field service student and someone called to me, "Come to a revival." I did not know what that meant. I was killing roaches in the dormitory, and I said, "I don't care what a revival is." I just wanted to get away from the roaches, so I went. Seriously, that's the only reason I went. I wanted to get away from the bugs.

Little did she know that the revival service—where she was but one of perhaps three white faces among five hundred American Indians in attendance—would change her young life forever. The Navajo preacher in full Indian dress "was screaming how he always hated white people, just hated them," bringing great discomfort to the petite white blond sixteen-year-old from affluent Laguna Beach, California. But then the preacher began to share how Jesus came into his life and showed him love for all people—and that he had stopped hating white people! Heidi laughed as she jovially added, "I was very relieved because I was there really sticking out. No blending for me."

Even as a young child, Heidi loved God: "I loved Him and I prayed and I had a hunger in my heart." She asserts, however, that she "did not understand fully the born-again experience of salvation" as a personal experience of primary spiritual transformation that she would mark as the beginning of her spiritual journey. She was drawn by the preacher's account of "how he met a man who taught him to see people from the inside, and how to love…He talked about our sin and our need for forgiveness and faith in Jesus." When he gave an altar call, not one person responded—except Heidi.[19] She described this to us as follows:

> I felt like God himself just took hold of my shirt and pulled me; I was
> the only one that night. I went forward just sobbing and crying. I was
> saying, "God, save me; get rid of my sin." I was powerfully transformed
> that day. I was sixteen years old, and I have never looked back. That is
> the most important, defining moment of my life.

The next night Heidi was taken to a Holiness Pentecostal church by the pianist from the previous evening's revival service, who said to her: "I am so glad you are saved, but now you need the Holy Ghost."[20] Heidi told us through a simple statement what happened next in an experience commonly known as "being baptized in the Holy Spirit [Ghost]": "I fell to the floor, prayed in tongues, rolled down—I was a holy roller! I was fully initiated in this church that was just wild Pentecostal fire. I gave myself to him [God]. I just said, 'Just take my life.' I was transformed."

The third most important event happened just two months after Heidi was born again and baptized in the Spirit (May 1976), an event that seemingly sealed the first two experiences with an intense mystical experience and a call: "I was fasting and praying because these people told me that you must fast and pray and love Jesus and read the Word [the Bible]. I was so hungry for God." She continued:

And on that day in May, I felt God—really all I can tell you is that he just stepped into the room. I was in this little loud church—a little tiny loud church—and suddenly I could not hear the preacher. I could not hear the piano playing on two sides. I was taken up, either I was taken up or he came down. And I heard, the only time in my entire life, the external, audible voice of God.

I was surrounded in white light. He said, "You are called to be a minister and a missionary, to go to Africa, Asia, and England." I have never looked back and I have never doubted that day. He transformed me. He said, "You are to be married to me." Oil ran down my arm. I came out three hours later and they told me I was frozen there for three hours. I had my hands lifted, and I did not twitch, and I did not move, and I did not hear a single sound in church.

When I came out of this vision, I started laughing hysterically. I didn't know what was going on. I was just so full of joy that God could choose little me—that he would call me to himself and that I could be chosen to preach. I had never seen a woman preacher. I'd never heard of one—never knew they were allowed to preach. In my background there were no women in ministry. But I heard God. I would never deny it. The next day—as a sixteen-year-old—I stepped out and started preaching on the streets. I have been preaching now for thirty-three years. I am in love; I'm really, really in love.

These three events—a salvation experience, being baptized into a baptism of love, and receiving a call to minister and preach—remain intimately intertwined in Heidi's mind as she proceeded to share the unfolding of her adult life and ministry. And her benevolent service to others has been remarkable, involving repeated brushes with death as well as miracles, as we will share throughout this book. Heidi's story provides an exemplary illustration of a primary spiritual transformation in which intimacy with God brought empowerment for service and a strong sense of divine destiny at a very young age. The stage had been set for a lifelong dance with God and a living example of our metaphor.

The Metaphor of Dance

Most of our respondents did not speak the language of metaphor. But Heidi's description of spiritual transformation included her story of how, as an aspiring young ballerina, she would lay aside her toe shoes after a dramatic encounter with her Divine Lover. After twice putting her love of dance on the altar of sacrifice, she realized her life itself was a divine dance. This metaphor captures the mood of the pentecostal worldview evident in our interviews. Religion in this mode is not a cognitive assent to a creed or the ritualistic participation in group activities. It is instead an exuberant, Spirit-filled waltz through the highs and lows of a life of meaning. At times God is perceived as leading the dance, at other times the individual must step out in faith, trusting that the divine dance partner will follow and lead the next step. Dance implies joyful, bodily participation in spiritual transformations, at least on occasion, as the Spirit of God moves through the body.[21]

The legalistic, conservative little Pentecostal church that would become Heidi's first spiritual home considered dancing of any kind sinful. In response to the urging of her new mentors and fueled by an intense love of God, sixteen-year-old Heidi would surrender her passion for dance—not only that of becoming a professional ballet dancer but being able to dance at all. The sacrifice was painful, both psychologically and physically, as we see reflected in her words:

> That hurt. When I was sixteen, that hurt a lot. In fact, that was like ripping my right arm off. . . . I remember the day of laying my toe shoes on the altar and saying, "Here, Jesus. Here are all my dreams. Six days a week, hours and hours of training since I was eight years old, for this that I think is my destiny. Here it is on the altar." I remember the pain of that and in my body too. Because when you stop training, it hurts.

With her call to ministry and missions in focus, Heidi would complete high school and select a college to prepare for the ministry to which she believed God had called her. Although her parents would have preferred an Ivy League university, her mother said that she could select any college she wished, as long as it was academically accredited. Heidi chose Southern California College (now Vanguard University of Southern California) in Costa Mesa, a Christian college that had moved away from the extreme Pentecostal legalisms that once permeated this former Bible college. When Heidi went to register for classes, the first person she saw was Babe Evans, "a Christian woman wearing pants, makeup and big hoop earrings. I was sure that I was in the wrong place!" Babe asked her about her "spiritual birthday"—which happened to be on that very day. Babe responded, "Happy birthday, honey! Jesus told me it was your birthday." Through Babe the process of freeing Heidi from religious legalism would begin: "I learned that it was what was in the heart, the inner person, not outward appearances that mattered. God told me that He had led me to lay down all the externals so that I would long for Him alone. It was my heart that mattered to Him."[22] Don Baldwin, an Assembly of God minister and a professor of theology at the college, would become a special mentor as Heidi sought to discern the details of her call. Baldwin spoke prophetically into the pain that Heidi still felt about giving up her dream of dancing: "Heidi, God wants you to dance again. He's going to give it back to you."

While still a college student, Heidi met Rolland Baker, the grandson of a Pentecostal missionary to China whose story of a powerful revival of supernatural gifts among children helped to shape Rolland's own ministerial call. As both believed God had directed, Heidi and Rolland would soon marry. Together they would go to Indonesia, and it was there that Baldwin's prophetic promise was fulfilled. Heidi found freedom to weave dance into liturgical worship in the ministry she and her husband Rolland had begun. Heidi did dance again. Together with Rolland she led dance-drama crusades in the Philippines, Taiwan, Indonesia, and Hong Kong for some six years. Somewhat unexpectedly, Heidi would hear her Divine Lover instruct her "to lay them down again [the toe shoes]—lay them down again and sit with the poor." She would obey, as she surrendered the dance ministry for working with addicts and the poor, first in Hong Kong and then for a time in London where she and Rolland worked with the homeless while pursuing their PhDs in theology. In 1995 the Bakers and their two biological children would leave London to follow a divinely perceived call to serve "the poorest of the poor" in Mozambique, a country they now call home. They founded Iris Ministries (at the time of this writing the name was changing to Iris Global) in 1980. It started in Asia, where it was focused for twelve years, eventually shifting to a small street ministry and later a modest orphanage in Mozambique. Now it cares for some ten thousand Mozambican children in villages and in church-based orphan care centers while serving as an umbrella organization for over ten thousand churches in Mozambique.[23] The toe shoes remained on the altar of sacrifice.

Toward the end of her interview, Heidi would return to the topic of her love of dance with yet another narrative replete with divine serendipity. She is now a frequent international speaker at revival meetings often held in impoverished areas of the world, and her next account was set in Brazil:

> I was doing a big meeting and the glory of God fell. It was a powerful meeting. They had these amazing ballerinas dancing, with a prima ballerina leading the troop. They knew nothing of my background. I did not say a word. As I was preaching, I couldn't stand up. The power

of God was so strong, and I was on my face. At the end, the prima ballerina came to me, and she gave me her toe shoes. She said, "Jesus said to give you my toe shoes. You're dancing with him around the face of the earth, leading the multitudes into his kingdom." Then another dancer gave me her flat shoes and said the same thing—at a different time and not knowing what the other had said. I was ruined! I was ruined because the Lord was saying, "You are dancing. You are fulfilling your destiny, and I know everything and here are the toe shoes." It was an amazing moment for me.

This notion of being "ruined," mentioned by Heidi, is quite common in many religions, although the language employed to describe the experience may differ. Indeed, the heart of spiritual experience is a dramatic shift in life goals and core values that accompany the experience of "rebirth" in which the old self dies and a new, better self emerges. In Christianity, this is the classic spiritual transformation of being born again, often accompanied by dramatic emotional healing, the overcoming of addictions, or the restoration of broken relationships with God and often with people as well. Jesus captures this idea in John 12:24: "Truly, truly, I say to you, unless a grain of wheat falls into the earth and dies, it remains alone; but if it dies, it bears much fruit."

Our interviews suggest that the core experience that drives the godly love model is the death of the old "me." We suggest that if one is armed only with a cognitive transformation (e.g., assent to a belief system or creed), but without the deeper, emotional experience of rebirth, the likelihood of developing into an exemplar of godly love is limited. The pentecostal worldview that we have described, and that Heidi's experience embodies, reflects this deep, transformative process of rebirth born of a radical encounter with the grace and purity of God's freely given love. This finding is consistent with much other scholarship on spiritual experience. For example, one summary argues that "brokenness is the best predictor of spiritual experience," which leads to an encounter with a divine energy that is "profoundly loving and accepting beyond words," followed by a radical shift in which core values are "turned upside down," resulting in "insights" that "appear to rewire the person" and their "approach to life."[24] In other words, being "ruined" or "broken" does not lead to helplessness and apathy, but instead paradoxically empowers a life of benevolence because of the birth of a new self. The loving presence of God, experienced in a pentecostal (i.e., deeply experiential and affective) way, is the key to this rebirth. Heidi's ongoing spiritual transformations with a loving God constitute, for her and for many others, the heart of religion that empowers her to spread the message of love in word and deed to people around the world.

Diverse Experiences of Spiritual Transformation

Heidi's narrative of spiritual transformation is multifaceted but seemingly danced out on the stage of the word she believed God himself gave to her: "You are called to be a minister and a missionary, to go to Africa, Asia, and England." There is little in her privileged background to suggest why she would choose to give herself to a life of self-giving service, but it appeared that her sensitivity to the poor was reinforced in part through her parents, who often took her to Mexico on camping trips and who "had an unusual sensitivity to the poor."[25] In between the lines of Heidi's fascinating stories of spiritual transformation we see empathic (even if not particularly religious) parents who did care about the poor and spiritual mentors who introduced her to the world of pentecostal possibilities. In introducing Heidi Baker in the last chapter we labeled her a Global Mystic, demonstrating love that is highly extensive and replete with a mystical walk with God that empowers her life and ministry. Renewal or revival centered in neo-pentecostal experiences is central to her identity, empowering her compulsion to love without bounds and her commitment to the service of the poor, especially in Mozambique. Steve Witt, a neo-pentecostal church founder and pastor in the Cleveland, Ohio, area, also has been transformed by ongoing religious experiences, including those of the revival of the 1990s in Toronto that transformed Heidi and Rolland's ministries.[26] Heidi has been a frequent revival speaker at Steve's church over the years, and they both are involved with a network of revival ministers. Steve's account of his spiritual transformation has been ongoing and has taken several pathways leading him to Bethel Church and with the ministry we have described as one of a Local Mystic.

Spiritual Transformation and Coming Home

Although he lived in Canada for part of his life, Steve Witt now lives out his call as a church founder, pastor, and community visionary in Cleveland, Ohio, the city in which he was born and raised. The founding pastor of Bethel Church Cleveland began his story of spiritual transformation by saying, "I really went to church since I was about two weeks old—went to a Methodist church here in Cleveland and then for whatever reason my parents shifted over to a large Baptist church." His childhood, he says, was that of "a knowledge-based Christian" who "accepted Christ into my life because my parents accepted Christ—it was my culture." At the age of ten, while accompanying his mother as he would do to the front of a Pentecostal church she had begun to attend (where people "would just hang out, wait for God, and then God would touch them"), he had an experience of his own. Steve describes this experience as "a benchmark—a defining moment for me." Reflecting his desire for a supernatural Christianity that is relevant to the modern world, Steve prefers to use contemporary vernacular that is shy of spiritual jargon. He went on to talk about this "benchmark" experience as "becoming connected," adding: "I lay on the floor at age ten, and I was speaking in tongues. It was very powerful." The original "head knowledge" that prompted him to "accept Christ" seemingly prepared him for this new experience that Pentecostals would call "being baptized in the Spirit." (Most evangelicals would agree that together these two events qualified Steve for born-again status, but he refrained from using the term in his interview.) Two years later, while on a youth retreat, Steve felt "a kind of warming, if I can say that, that came over me and an understanding that I was supposed to prepare for ministry." Looking back on that recurrent feeling and his understanding of it, Steve added: "We had a theology back then that kind of focused and elevated on a specific call, that people that went into ministry had 'calls.' It wasn't a career choice; it was a God choice." Although the memory of that experience would never leave him, Steve explained, "As you enter your teen years, you start to drift a little bit away. You get your own ideas of what you want to do." He noted that his father wanted him to become a lawyer. The devout Pentecostalism of his mother was slowly being eclipsed by the lure of secular culture.

Steve described himself as "drifting farther away from the Lord" during a time when his father became leader of all the labor unions in northeastern Ohio, a development that moved the blue-collar family into white-collar status. It would take another spiritual experience that he called "a visitation from God" to bring him back to a renewed response to his call to church ministry:

> The only way I can describe what it (the visitation) was like was it was like a bird coming. I was in a parking lot of a college; it was like a bird flying by my head—you know, it kind of makes you dart a little bit. A bird flew by my head, but there was no bird there! Immediately the impression was put into my mind, kind of like "Are you going to do what I asked you to do?" So it was at that point that I radically prepared

myself to go away to Bible school (that's all I knew to do) and get ready for ministry. That would have been in 1975–76; I did what I knew to do back then, which in that culture—at that time—was you get your hair cut, you change your clothing, you know. You get ready to become spiritual!

But Steve did not find his experience at a Pentecostal Bible school to be a direct path to spirituality. He described it as "a season of training but also a season of real strong disillusionment." He was disillusioned by "the stuff going on that was obviously outside the spirit of what we believed in, and I found myself kind of in the group of those on the radical fringe of the school—the type that got kicked out." So instead of pursuing "spiritual things," Steve bucked the religious culture of the college. Steve "ran for student government (and got elected), wrote a gossip column for the school newspaper, and enjoyed disagreeing with authority." He would graduate and take a position at a Pentecostal church as a youth pastor, only to suffer another debilitating and disillusioning blow. The wife of the pastor of the church where Steve was employed came to Steve complaining about her marriage to his boss! After only four months in congregational ministry Steve resigned, feeling unprepared for ministry and even more disillusioned. He thought getting more education would help to better prepare himself to respond to the call and began to pursue a master's degree in pastoral psychology ("which now seems absurd, knowing my personality," Steve added parenthetically). And he would plant his first church. "I was really an entrepreneur at heart, and that [church planting] was the closest thing to starting a business in the church. I quit seminary [although he would later finish his master's degree] and quit my job and we went full force into starting a church in April 1980." But all did not go well; Steve was "basically kicked out of the church I had planted." He founded another church, and with it came another divine visitation: "God visited me in a very supernatural way and called me to go to Canada—that I was to go there in preparation for a revival that would touch the nations and the world. We planted our third church; I was now twenty-nine years old."

The seeming "bunny trails" would go on for several more years as his new church in Canada grew in numbers but Steve continued his spiritual quest. The Canadian revival promised to Steve by God through prophecy years earlier would come to pass in January 1994 in Toronto. Through the so-called Toronto Blessing at a church near Canada's international airport (now known as Catch the Fire) Steve had an experience that he describes as "being baptized in the spirit of 'I don't care.'" Through this transformative experience Steve was finally able to put aside church politics and congregational discontent that haunted him throughout his pastoral career and begin really "running after God." Steve described the aftermath of a sabbatical from his congregational ministry and the fruits of the Toronto experience as follows:

> I had gotten a sabbatical before Toronto, and I returned physically restored but not spiritually restored. I go to Toronto—the capstone of the sabbatical really took place in Toronto. I just go—and got absolutely freed. I regurgitated laughter so much that it opened up an ancient well inside of me. It was exciting. You know what? It was an absolutely, totally new ball game! I was back to the future. I went back to a 1975–78-ish excitement and revitalization....I'm about thirty-seven now, feeling really matured in this thing. I've been burned a few times—majorly. I still love God. I'm ready to go at it again. I was ready to tackle it.

Steve's church in New Brunswick, Canada, would be revitalized and show new growth, like many other congregations impacted by the revival. But as 1995 drew to a close, Steve received a prophetic word about "geographic relocation and new headquartering," to which he added, "I was in this long enough to realize I'd seen enough of the fingerprints that God was about to do a transition in my life." Shortly after this general prophecy another prophetic friend of Steve's said to him, "You are about to go back to Cleveland." After six months of "huge prophetic confirmation over and over again, from magazines, from television, from friends, from people I didn't even know," Steve left the thriving congregation he had started in New Brunswick to return to the unknown in Cleveland. Steve laughed as he said, "The newspaper in Canada where I was couldn't figure out why I was leaving, and that I was going back to nothing. There was nothing here! So the headline actually said something like I was leaving to wait. That's what it was."

Although the new spiritual pathways that have been forged throughout his life sometimes seemed to be going nowhere, our description of Bethel Church that began in chapter 2 suggests that Steve Witt has always been on the edge of religious cultural change as he sought to fulfill the call on his life. Since the revival he has aligned with other spiritual entrepreneurs who seek changes in the churches that will affect the larger community—community change brought about through a Spirit-powered Christianity that is relevant for the twenty-first century.

Spiritual Transformation Reshaped by Tragedy

Narratives, as do the lives they represent, necessarily unfold within particular cultural contexts. The stories of personal spiritual transformation as told by Heidi and Steve—especially the ease with which they both talked about experiencing God in their lives—mirrors a contemporary American pentecostal culture where God is up close and personal. Although our survey findings suggest that many Americans share the same loving image of God, our interviews demonstrate that some find him easier to talk about than do others. The impact of cultural and familial factors in narrations of personal encounters with God is particularly evident in a close review of Anne Beiler's interview with Matt. While many if not most of the interviewees would immediately launch into an experiential account of a spiritual birth or awakening when asked about the events that made them who they are today, Anne's account began with her family: "There's something about the family of origin that we are born into, and that's where all of us get our start. No matter how, what the family looks like, it's how we start out in life." Anne's narrative would stream without interruption as she told Matt how her family struggled financially, described the generosity and willingness of other family members to help, and shared how her desire to help others stemmed out of this familial experience. Acknowledging that she has been able to talk about these things only within the past few years ("Amish never talk about issues in your family or things that are going wrong"), Anne was aware of how her family's problems affected her and her desire to help resolve them: "I think it was during that time that I put this in my heart that I wanted to make a difference. I wanted to help my parents. I knew that, and I wanted to help people. Maybe it's because I saw people help my family." Anne couldn't wait to get out of school, and by the age of fifteen she was working as a waitress and giving her small income and tips to her parents. She went on to say: "It is okay; it is what I wanted to do. It was my purpose. My purpose was to give back, and that's where it all started."

When Anne paused, Matt raised a question about the nature of her relationship with God during that time, to which she responded:

> I don't think that it came as much from the fact that Jesus died for me on the cross as it did from the fact that my parents had a need. You know what I'm saying. At that age I'd accepted Christ (when I was twelve); I accepted Christ so I could go to heaven, so I could miss hell. You know, a very basic doctrine there.

It was only after a few more probing questions by Matt that a narrative of Anne's spiritual transformation began to emerge. Her Amish-Mennonite culture was not one to encourage self-disclosure. When Anne was twelve years old, her family went to a controversial Amish-Mennonite revival meeting—controversial because Amish (even the less conservative "Beachy Amish" in which she was raised) do not hold revivals. That experience left a lasting memory. When a call was made by the revivalist to come forward "to accept the invitation for Christ," Anne, despite strong reservations, found herself responding:

> That's a bold thing in a church setting. I mean, I'm in the front row, and you have to walk out. It was just—the pressure was on because, believe me, this was something we never did before. I remember it just got so intense for me that I had to. I couldn't stop myself. That's when I responded to Christ and gave him my life.

Matt then asked Anne how she felt: "I just felt like this whole burden—like I was a terrible sinner—and it's just been lifted from me. I knew I wasn't going to hell now." Anne added that much was said about going to hell in the Amish-Mennonite services. "I always felt that God was kind of stern; he was commanding and he was very demanding."

It wasn't until Matt asked her if she had experienced "Spirit baptism and speaking in tongues" that Anne reported encountering a softer face of God. She believes she was actually born again at the age of twenty when she and her new husband began attending a less strict Mennonite church, an event she prefers to call her "spiritual awakening": "That's when I became tuned into the fact that God is more than a religion. God is more than outward externals. God is more than, 'Oh, he's going to keep me from hell.' I began to understand there's more to life, my spiritual life. I just couldn't get enough of reading the word of God, study Bibles, books about prayer and God."

During this time Anne said she began to feel connected with God—"and I felt a peace that was calming to me. I would never talk to anyone about the fact that I read the Bible and prayed. Again, that's very cultural." Her image of God began to shift from that of a father who is "up there just looking at me; I better behave" to a focus on Jesus and talking to him as a friend. "I became so hungry; there's no other word for it. I just wanted more of Jesus. Suddenly I wanted to become more like him. Maybe I can't be like him, but I can follow him. And so when I received the baptism in the Holy Spirit, I can only say there was a—I almost want to say it was like an out-of-body experience. I don't even know if I've ever talked about this. But it was so powerful; it was so powerful."

When Matt asked her to set the stage for this experience, Anne spoke of attending a woman's prayer group that "talked a lot about baptism in the Spirit and speaking in tongues." Anne then began to seek the baptism in the Spirit only after consulting with her husband Jonas; he agreed with her that it was biblical to seek the Holy Spirit. She commented, "This was kind of like an act of obedience. By now I wanted to be filled with the Spirit. It was an act of obedience on my part and my husband's part at the same time. So we both received the speaking in tongues, and I came away from there feeling really shook up. I mean, I went, 'Wow!' For a year I'd been pursuing this, thinking about it, praying about it, questioning, seeking. So, 'Okay, wow, this is it!'" She seemed at a loss for words to describe what had happened and how much it meant to her. For five or so years after that Anne spent more time in prayer than she had ever spent before, time that was typically filled with a sense of intimacy with the divine. Anne described this transformation as follows:

> From that point on, I got so it was more about my time with the Lord than anything else. I became—my communion with Jesus and my times with Christ, were just experiences that I can't—I would have to really, you know—go back there and think about how wonderful that was.... It was so good. I was feeling emotional, but also very real. I could spend hours in prayer, just in this presence. It was definitely a period in my life that I have never been to since.

Anne referred to this period as a "time in my life of great joy—spiritually, physically, in every way I felt like a whole person. I was somebody in Christ. I had found my identity." What may be seen as an extended journey of primary transformation would come to a tragic end when her nineteen-month-old daughter was killed in a farm accident. The narrative of this tragic event that would drastically change Anne's life and this pathway of her spiritual journey is best told in another chapter.

Spiritual Transformation Birthed in Crisis

Although Herb Daughtry says he "grew up in church," his spiritual transformation could be labeled a life-changing "jailhouse conversion." As noted in our introduction to this social activist pastor, even as a child Herb was aware of the racial injustice in the segregated South. His interview was filled with memorably sad accounts of what today we call "school bullying," with much of it instigated by teachers. Having come from the South to Brooklyn, Herb said, "I became a buffoon—at least I was treated as a buffoon," as teachers and students alike would make fun of his accent. He described one childhood account—"just to show you the insensitivity and the racism"—during which he was instructed to pick a card from a deck and he picked the card that said, "Imitate a little colored boy eating watermelon." He was torn, wondering what he should do, as everyone's eyes were on him:

> Should I get up and throw this card in the teacher's face and storm out? Should I go through with the act? What should I do? What I decided to do—I still have deep emotional feeling. I decided, "All right; you want me to be a fool, I'll act like a fool." I took my hand and tried to do a watermelon piece. Of course, obviously, I hated everything. I hated the principal, the school, me and everybody else.

Herb's young life was a series of negative experiences—"just went from one negative experience to another." Through his own pain, however, he developed "a sensitivity to other people's pain, the hurts." Herb continued, "I could never engage in the kinds of things that would bring pain because I had so much of it from other people. In fact, the biggest fight I had was over somebody else, over a bully trying to take somebody else's money." And it was the pain of his mother that softened his spirit to receive a religious transformation. By the age of fifteen, with "no kind of supportive peers," Herb "just got into some negative stuff" and was arrested. The police were by no means friends and mentors to black youth; for Herb, verbal abuse was the norm, and physical brutality was tolerated. After his first arrest, Herb said he became a hero to his peers. They had adopted an adage: "Live fast, die young, have a good-looking corpse.' So you don't be thinking about other people and all that stuff. You just live the way you want to live." But when he was facing some long jail time for two counts of armed robbery and assault, he came face-to-face with himself and with the pain he had caused his mother:

> So it was there, February 1953, that my mama came to see me, and I finally got to look in her face. It looked like she had aged. Her hair had turned gray, it seemed furrows were deeper in the brow, just haggard. It sort of hit me as never before that I had contributed to this because nobody gave her the problem that I did. Because, you know, up to that point you sort of live [thinking], "Oh, I'm only doing this to myself."

So at the age of twenty-two Herb Daughtry took a good look at himself and gave his life over to God:

> I said, "Lord, here is my life. I put my life in your hands. I don't know if I am not trying to manipulate now. I don't know. I've been trying to get over for so long. I've been negative and manipulative and deceitful and deceptive for so long. I'm not sure what I am doing. But as well as I know myself, I want to put myself in your hand." That was February of '53. And I can't say that I got hit by fireballs or that angels tapped me upside the head. But deep down, within my very being, I knew that a change had happened, and I would never be the same.

Although Herb recalls being active in church in early childhood—"singing and down on my knees calling 'Jesus, Jesus, Jesus'"—he had no frame of reference for the "mysterious experience" that proved to change his life in 1953. Despite the filthy and dirty conditions and the bad food at the precinct where he was being temporarily held, Herb was at peace:

> So the surroundings I'm seeing were deplorable. They were deplorable, they were oppressive. Even in that state, as well as I knew myself and as well as I can remember, all of the external pressures and discomforts was minimized. Something had happened that was more significant than anything that was happening around, and it didn't make any difference. Where I was, I wanted to play with it—think about it— meditate on it.... In this precinct there may be not more than five or six cells, so there's nobody for me to communicate with. There's no distractions, in other words. Even the deplorable physical surroundings were not a distraction for me. Nothing was.

Herb had a lot of time to consider how he would plea—"because obviously I'm pleading 'not guilty,' that's what you usually do." Then Herb added, "But that is not consistent now with my newfound faith. Interesting: [he paused, then laughed] immediate moral conflict!" Herb would refuse to use questionable tactics to get less jail time: "I pleaded guilty to the charges." His arrest and incarceration would come to be seen as a gift from God:

> If God had not allowed me to be put away—like, put on ice, so to speak—I would not be here. There's no way I should have been around as long as I was. I mean, the kind of chances I was taking with people's

money and lives.... The penitentiary saved me in the sense that it extri-
cated, or got me out of a situation which was where I was destined to
die early like most of my friends.

Herb said this "salvation experience" brought with it so much more; it would
be soon followed by a call to become a preacher:

> So when I went to jail (I had been in the county jail), I then felt led that
> [his experience of God] was more than just salvation—it was more
> than being saved. I knew that something good was happening, but
> then I began to feel that it was more—that I was being called to more.
> I remember sitting down with a paper and pencil, saying, "Okay, if I'm
> going to be a preacher, then I got to do some studying."

Theological Spiritual Transformation

The accounts of spiritual transformation told by the exemplars of godly love
were stories seeking to describe new birth, indwelling of Spirit, awakening,
epiphany, as told within various religious cultural grids provided by
Christianity. The accounts differed as to the degree that heavenly music
replete with visions and visitations, as compared with natural human forces,
played in the transformation. Some, like Heidi's and Steve's accounts, reflected
the timbre of supernatural activity that flowed seemingly without effort;
others, like Anne and Herb, seemed more grounded in the sounds and language of secular life and required some gentle probing for the details of memorable spiritual experiences. Although born and raised a fourth-generation
Pentecostal during a time and place when walking in the supernatural and
eschewing involvement in "heathen" society were normative, Paul Alexander
represents what we have called a Global Planner (lower on supernatural experiences but high on extensive benevolence). Paul now serves as a professor of
Christian ethics and public policy at Palmer School of Theology (Eastern
University). Like few others in our study, within Paul's interview are references to stories of paranormal pentecostal events, tempered through the
reflections of a theologian, centered on the calling of a global peace activist.[27]
Paul's unusual path took him through the Pentecostal commitments of being
born again and Spirit baptism as a child—to a time during young adulthood
when he realized he was an agnostic "follower of Jesus" who was not able to
believe in a "god who seemingly cared little about human suffering." Paul

gradually would come back full-circle to his Pentecostal faith, as an ordained Pentecostal minister, peace activist, and professor seeking to influence both his religious tradition and the students he teaches.

Paul tells his story with ease, often with humor and sometimes through welling tears. In response to Paul's simple statement "I was filled with the Holy Spirit when I was twelve years old," Matt asked him to describe "how that unfolded." Paul said, "That's hard for someone that's raised in the church. The story of, you know, I was saved when I was five. That's kind of my story." Matt said, "Okay," looking at Paul to continue. As it turned out, Paul's "story" evolved as one rich in details, struggles, emotions, and theology. Paul immediately continued:

> I got saved again and again and again. I was saved repeatedly at many ages all the way through [he laughed]. So that's my story. I went to a Christian school that was Baptist one year, and they would sing this song [he began singing]: "It was on a Monday somebody saved me." And I am like, "How do you know? I didn't know if it was on a Tuesday, Wednesday, Thursday, Friday, Saturday, or Sunday. I got to stand up when they sang "It was on a *someday* that Jesus saved me" [he laughed].

Paul's Spirit baptism was more memorable, more as a process than the single event when he first spoke in tongues. He says he remembers more about the intense desire to speak in tongues than the actual event: "I can't remember. I wish I could remember. I just remember the desire." Paul continued:

> I just remember many times of praying at Wheat State Camp [in Kansas] in the evenings, sometimes for several hours and often for other friends. I remember my close friends, Nathan Brewster and my brother Mark or my other friends would just be with their hands in the air, weeping and sometimes jumping. My experience of prayer at those times were usually lying on the floor—not slain in the Spirit, not out, but laying on the floor and weeping with my face in the carpet. That's what I remember. Those were the kind of emotional experiences in the times of prayer that I had.

This was something that Paul acknowledged he had "not actually talked about much in my whole life," as Matt and Margaret raised questions about his emotional responses. In retrospect those times seemed to Paul to represent communal cathartic experiences with good friends: "As it wanes, you kind of start to realize that everyone is kind of coming to a collective end. My tears kind of dry up, and I can just lay there peacefully. I'll get up and go back to my pew or chair. Sometimes it feels really good, as if you have really worked through something." During one of these times of prayer and fasting as a first-year college student, Paul was praying for the salvation of Muslims when "I felt called to Muslims as a missionary." Paul described this period of his youth as being "so happy": "I guess thinking afterwards like in my life since then, there was this period—the precritical time—where it's just the received practice and I participated in it, uncritically in college and kind of through grad school."

Then came what Paul termed "the time of silence, the dark night of the soul," during which he and his wife "were just completely losing our faith. These late nights of, there was weeping involved then, but it wasn't glossolalia. I mean it wasn't prayer; it was just frustration with the pain and suffering of the world. Where is God in this darkness?" Paul describes his journey at this point: "I'd gone through losing my complete faith, trying to go with, 'Okay, I'll be an atheist but I'll follow Jesus.' So Christian atheism was part of this. Because Jesus was pretty cool and I am starting to realize he was a revolutionary. He was radical. He took on the system. He got murdered by an empire of religious elites. All this stuff going on; I can get into this."

Paul's struggle seemed to require a theological response rather than simply lying on the carpet in tears as he did as a child. A primary question was rooted in the common theological position on Jesus's suffering and death in much of conservative Christianity. Paul noted, "There are different theories of atonement. I would learn there's a nonviolent atonement. The fact is that this kind of killing of a son by his Father doesn't work very well [he laughed]." His was a two-faced theological struggle as "I started realizing just how absolutely ridiculous my faith was; it really started crumbling and falling apart," coupled with his wife's "deep compassion and her empathy and identity with the suffering of the world." His wife's timeless question became his question as he began to wrestle with what kind of God would allow human suffering. Paul's old concept of God was dead, but the new one had yet to be born.

This rebirth was to come gradually, in part through his discovery that his Pentecostal denomination had once been pacifist (a fact that became the topic for his doctoral dissertation). Paul's reconversion came as a "gradual awareness" rather than through some mystical revelation or response to an altar call. At first he was able to accept Jesus only as a good and smart teacher, but he explained, laughing, that Jesus "got murdered, so he's not that smart!"

He noted that Jesus did "some amazing stuff," but Paul "wasn't ready to buy the God thing again; that kind of grew on me little by little. Then I eventually admitted to myself—I guess I had to admit—that it doesn't work [theologically] that Jesus is just a good teacher." He recognized the grace of God "drawing and inviting" him, but his recommitment to God was experienced primarily "by working through it with my students and my friends." Paul explained why his answers had to be more than experiential:

> I was resisting certain theological constructs that I didn't want to hang together any more. If accepting God means the all-powerful, all-loving God (with a suffering world and he could fix it and doesn't), that I was not going back to. So other theological explanations of the nature of the world were important to me. Because the issues were theological, I mean existential related but connected, the answers had to be that as well. I just couldn't be experiential. I mean, I don't think it could have been. I don't think I could have just felt love for a God or felt good about this anymore. [Others] can feel good about that God— absolutely. But I couldn't.

Toward the end of our interview, Margaret asked Paul about the paranormal experiences that are so often found in pentecostal accounts, asking him if they were familiar to him as a child. He referred us to his new book, *Signs and Wonders: Why Pentecostalism Is the World's Fastest Growing Faith,* to read some of these familiar stories.[28] While Paul seems to accept the accounts of miracles and divine serendipity he shares in his book, his second transformation has set him on a somewhat different path with its emphasis on nonviolence, justice, and peace.

The Journey toward Spiritual Transformation

As we have seen, the journey toward spiritual transformation follows many different paths and involves fundamentally different kinds of experiences. For example, Herb's jailhouse conversion (a *primary* transformation), which occurred in the wake of a deeper understanding of his mother's suffering, differed dramatically from the less experiential and more existential *secondary* transformation that set Paul on a new path toward social justice. It is little surprise that distinct kinds of spiritual transformations also lead to different types of benevolent outreach, ranging from community service, to revival/renewal, to social justice. But we should not lose sight of the big picture in attending to details. There is a common theme in all of the stories: powerful experiences of spiritual transformation (often taking the form of feeling born again) lead to a deeper sense of God's love and a calling to benevolent action, which in turn promotes existential well-being. Causality is notoriously difficult to establish, especially given that the GLNS collected data for only a single point in time and our interviews were retrospective accounts. We do not claim to have proven a time-ordering. Moreover, our interviews revealed notable departures from our "virtuous circle" model in figure 4.2, particularly as well-being ebbed and flowed over time.

Perhaps it is better to think in terms of a dialectical dance among these experiences, rather than a unidirectional causal flow. We can say conclusively that spiritual transformation, experiencing God's love, receiving a call (even if this changes over time), engaging in benevolent service, and attaining a higher level of well-being are the key ingredients in the contemporary American experience of godly love. This holds true in the narratives of benevolent exemplars and is confirmed in the GLNS statistical analyses of ordinary Americans.

We are just beginning to scratch the surface of these complicated interrelations. We will devote subsequent chapters to more fully consider issues such as prayer, suffering, collaboration with other people, and different understandings of the meaning of "benevolence." These and other issues figure prominently in the lives of Americans who have encountered a loving God and attempt to live out the Great Commandment as a result. The point we would like to stress here is that spiritual experience and transformation provide the foundation for subsequent steps in living out a calling. As National Public Radio correspondent Barbara Bradley Hagerty explains, "Half of Americans claim to have experienced a life-altering spiritual event that they could circle on the calendar in red ink," and this explains why "even the twentieth century, with its Freuds and B. F. Skinners, its technological advances and scientific reductionism, could not quash Americans' yearning for the divine."[29]

Hagerty is in good company in drawing attention to the importance of spiritual transformation in the lives of most ordinary people, even as both scientific and public discourse have marginalized this phenomenon. From William James's 1902 classic *Varieties of Religious Experience* to William Miller's update *Quantum Change*, published a century later, the lived reality of life-altering spiritual experiences simply will not go away—even as secularization continues in the public sphere.[30] Our findings, along with the larger body of work, demonstrate that godly love profoundly reshapes how a person experiences reality and interacts with other people. At the center of this dramatic change is a "loving presence" that can turn personal values "upside down."[31] The striving for power, pleasure, and wealth becomes replaced by spiritual growth and generosity.

Heidi's personal experience with what pentecostals call the "baptism of the Holy Spirit" demonstrates this process of being turned upside down:

> I just felt overcome. I felt overcome by the Holy Spirit and I just fell more in love with Jesus and I wanted to just be fully possessed. That might frighten people, but I pray that every day of my life: "Possess me fully, Holy Spirit." (So I wouldn't call myself "classical Pentecostal," in the sense that I look for a filling every day [rather than in a single encounter].) Every day I'm looking for another filling, another filling, another filling because I want to pour out to every single person that Jesus puts in front of me. And so I'm continuously seeking to be more baptized. I'm looking for that. I'm looking for the participation in the divine nature completely: "Take me, God. Empty me out." So it's a continuous pursuit of love and being filled and poured out.

For Heidi and many others, the ultimate aim of this process is not self-aggrandizement, but becoming empty so that she is humble enough to serve others in the most mundane ways, yet empowered by the Spirit to accomplish the miraculous. She aspires to be last, not first, in the upside-down kingdom of God. Paradoxically humble but powerful, this is the effect of spiritual transformations on her. As anyone who has spent significant time with her will tell you, it is not uncommon for her to rise early in the morning to make breakfast for her children, colleagues, and friends, who help her meet the needs of orphans in Mozambique, or to spend significant time affirming and praying with the person cleaning her hotel room when she is on a speaking trip to the West.

What is the meaning of well-being for such a person? It is not material success, prestige, or the adoration of other people. Well-being is redefined in terms of doing God's will and being the face of God for others. Heidi is not typical, even among our sample of exemplars—some of whom are quite comfortable with the materialistic lifestyle of the "untransformed" American. But reading through the transcripts of our interviews, it is difficult not to be struck by the incredible personal sacrifices our interviewees have made and the way in which they "count it all as joy," channeling the well-known words of James 1:2.[32] Yet spiritual transformations are only part of the story. Once transformed, a person must be sustained in the context of difficult life circumstances. This sustenance is the fruit of prayer, the subject of our next chapter.

5

The Breath of Prayer

ENERGIZING GODLY LOVE

IT CAN BE said that breathing is to physical life what praying is to spiritual life. To say that breathing is necessary for human life is to state the obvious. Professional dancers, yogis, runners, weightlifters, singers, skaters, and many others can testify to the importance of learning to use and control the common act of breathing to advance their skills. Just as there are recognized physiological connections between breathing and heart rhythms that affect bodily strength and endurance, cultural wisdom throughout the ages has posited a spiritual connection between breath and prayer. Although some traditions are more explicit than others in asserting the relationship between breathing and praying, we are less concerned with techniques than with their metaphoric potential. Some forms of prayer explicitly make use of breathing techniques; many do not. Just as different breathing techniques can be used to enhance physical goals, so too can varying prayer activities promote ongoing spiritual transformation.

For many pray-ers the phenomenon we call prayer is three-part, not unlike the three-part breath practiced by yogis. The first part, sometimes assumed to be all there is to prayer, involves devotional prayer activities that focus on the pray-er. These prayers commonly are said in private or in public gatherings, as prayers made in intercession for others, petition for personal needs, thanking God for blessings, seeking forgiveness, or uttering words of adoration. They may be ritualistic in form, including recitations from memory or reading from a book of prayers. More often they are colloquial or extemporaneous prayers directed toward the divine. For some, prayer is limited to such nearly universal practices in which the person is the primary actor. Many active pray-ers go beyond what a non-pentecostal philosopher of religion (whom Margaret encountered at a conference of evangelical leaders) described to her as "leaving messages on God's answering machine."[1] Most pray-ers report that God does return the calls—at least on occasion. These pray-ers find themselves entering into two-part breath where active prayer is complemented by prophetic dialogue with the divine. Still others commonly experience three-part prayer, active prayer that flows into prophetic dialogue and sometimes into mystical union. Like Brother Lawrence, the seventeenth-century French Catholic mystic whose little book continues to be widely read, they are learning to "practice the presence of God."[2]

The GLNS and our rich interview data support our analogy between praying and breathing. Just as breathing provides energy for the body, prayer can be seen as a multifaceted medium through which pray-ers come to know divine love. Using a concept of the Russian-American sociologist Pitirim Sorokin, we see prayer as a type of "love energy." Sorokin, the founder of Harvard University's sociology department and a master theorist and pioneer in the sociology of love, wrote a classic treatise in the 1950s with the descriptive title *The Ways and Power of Love: Types, Factors, and Techniques of Moral Transformation*.[3] We drew heavily from Sorokin's work as a theoretical foundation in designing the Flame of Love Project, and its influence remains important as we seek to present and interpret our research findings on prayer and their relationship to love energy. Especially relevant for our discussion of prayer and godly love is Sorokin's proposal about the production and generation of love energy and its role in empowering altruism. According to Sorokin, love energy is commonly generated through the interaction of human beings, but he hypothesizes that it is possible that "an inflow of love comes from an intangible, little-studied, possibly supraempirical source called 'God.'"[4] Although the methodology of social science does not provide the tools for proving whether or not God exists and interacts with humans, we have already demonstrated that most Americans *believe* that they have (at least on occasion) interacted with the divine—and that this interaction *does have an effect* on benevolent attitudes and behavior.[5]

In the last chapter we caught glimpses into life-changing prayer experiences in the stories of spiritual transformation shared by our exemplars of godly love. Heidi's mystical accounts included divine visions and voices that set her on a lifelong path of love, with a focus on the poorest of the poor. Steve's account was much like those of the "Main Street mystics" whom Margaret described in her book of the same title dealing with a modern pentecostal revival, replete with an increasing ease in hearing the voice of God through his spiritual senses and confirmed by others on similar journeys. Anne's humble Amish-Mennonite background differed in part due to a cultural reluctance to talk about religious experiences, yet she too recalled the heavens breaking open in what she called her "awakening" as a young newlywed.

Herb's life-changing experience in his jail cell exemplified a personal spiritual breakthrough without the affect of black religious services that he knew as a child. Paul, reared in the revivalist milieu of small-town traditional Pentecostalism, seemed wary of the mystical experiences of his childhood as he heard his invitation to benevolent service through involvement with a Mennonite community to work for peace and justice. The transformation accounts are not only descriptive, but they raise questions for us to review using the lenses of our national survey data. Are there common features of prayer to be found in these seemingly diverse experiences of spiritual transformation? How do the stories of the exemplars fit with the highly representative statistics we have collected on prayer? And, most important, what role does prayer play in godly love?

What Do Social Scientists Know about Prayer?

A consistent and repeated finding about prayer in America over the past six decades is that the overwhelming majority of Americans say that they pray. Ninety percent of those surveyed for a Gallup Report in 1948 acknowledged that they prayed; thirty years later in 1978, a nearly identical proportion (89 percent) reported that they prayed to God. In 1988, the year of the Gallup Survey for a groundbreaking book on prayer by Margaret and George H. Gallup Jr., 88 percent of all respondents acknowledged that they prayed to God.[6] The decline over the next twenty years has been negligible. The 2008 Baylor Survey reports that 87 percent of Americans pray at least once in a while, and an identical figure is found in the 2009 GLNS. Furthermore, a clear majority—68 percent—of all GLNS respondents say they pray at least once a day, a figure that is identical to the figure reported by the 2007 US Religious Landscape Survey conducted by the Pew Research Center's Forum on Religion and Public Life.[7] As in these other surveys, women were found to pray more frequently than men; nonwhites and Hispanics more frequently than Euro-Americans; and older people more than younger people.[8]

Despite such well-documented facts about the frequency of prayer, social scientists have been slow to wrestle with the complexities of this Gordian knot. While researchers continue to gather information on the frequency of prayer—certainly an interesting and important fact—it has not proven to be a particularly good measure for exploring whether prayer makes a difference in people's lives.[9] Although the near universality of the practice of prayer by Americans has been clearly established by survey researchers, pray-ers are probably not all doing the same thing or having the same experiences while praying. So while we are able to secure statistics on the frequency of prayer, less is known about what these numbers represent. When questions about the nature of prayer activities are included, as they have been in some more recent surveys, they have focused on one form of prayer—devotional prayers of petition or intercession (praying for family or friends, for healing, for a job, etc.) that fail to tap into the heart of prayer. Despite the findings amassed by Margaret and her colleagues suggesting that prayer experiences may be more important to assess than simple figures on the frequency of prayer, some researchers have been content to stop with demonstrating that the vast majority of Americans do pray rather than exploring whether and how praying makes a difference in the lives of pray-ers or in their communities.

In sum, prayer is an activity that can be counted much like other personal, religious, social, or political activities—like being a vegan, going to church, attending a movie, or voting on election day—and researchers have been faithfully counting the practice for decades. Yet social scientists still know little about three-part prayer as devotional human activity, dialogue with the divine, and mystical union. A short narrative of an experience Margaret had as a hospital chaplain at the time she was analyzing her early survey findings may help to demonstrate one major—but largely unresearched—difference lying just beneath the surface of the near-universal American activity we call prayer.

Going beyond Frequency: Soliloquy, Conversation, and Communing with the Divine

By the time Margaret began working at a local hospital as a volunteer chaplain in 1992, she had completed two survey research projects on prayer, noting that it was not how often people prayed that made a difference in self-reports of well-being but whether they experienced God through their praying. Although significant, this basic finding was long on statistics but short on narratives that might illuminate the stories behind the numbers. One day as Margaret was making her daily hospital rounds she visited a retired colleague who had been recently admitted as a patient. Sam was a delightful but loquacious older gentleman with whom she had never had an opportunity to discuss her faith, even after years of knowing him. (Unknown to Margaret, Sam must have been following the newsletter she then edited for the Christian Sociological Society, where she wrote openly about prayer and prayer experiences.) Toward the end of the visit Margaret asked Sam if he would like her to pray with him. After he responded affirmatively, she then asked if there was anything in particular for which he would like prayer. Sam said, "Yes, there is. You seem to hear from God. I want to hear from him." Margaret nodded and then prayed a simple prayer, including the petition that Sam would indeed learn to hear God's voice. A couple of months passed before Margaret had the opportunity to talk with Sam again. One of the first things he asked was, "Do you remember the prayer you said for me?" Margaret replied, "Yes, I do; and what is it that God has said to you?" Sam continued:

> Well, the first thing I heard was "Sam, get off the line." I stopped talking and I sensed (in my mind) that God was clearly saying again, "Get off the line." I was confused, when God said for a third time, "Sam, get off the line; the two of us cannot talk at the same time."

Sam had moved from prayer as a soliloquy to prayer as conversation—beyond talking to God in his own words (as 95 percent of pray-ers do) without waiting for a reply to waiting for God to speak (as most pray-ers eventually do at least on occasion).[10] By the time we talked by phone Sam was comfortable with just being in the divine presence where there was no need for words. He had moved from talking to God, to conversing with him, to silently communing with the divine presence.

Like spiritual transformation, prayer is more than an act—it can be described a journey toward union with the divine. Through the statistics collected in the GLNS and the stories of the exemplars, we are able to move beyond knowing that the vast majority of Americans pray toward a better understanding of this multifaceted concept and exploring the role prayer plays in godly love. We constructed three prayer scales—devotional prayer activity, prophetic conversation, and mystical communion (see table 5.1)—to explore further the prayer journey reflected in Sam's short narrative. We were interested in the possible relationship between these prayer measures and the survey scale we have been using in this book to measure respondent experiences of divine love. Our statistical (multiple regression) analysis found a strong relationship between these three prayer measures and knowing God's love. *Frequently engaging in an array of devotional prayer activities, experiencing prayer as a conversation with God in which the pray-er listens as well as talks to God, and enjoying mystical communion with the divine all contribute to an increased sense of knowing God's love.*[11] Prayer is a process that begins with a purposive encounter and that (at least for some) progresses to loving union with God. These prayer indicators provide the empirical data to support our

Table 5.1 Types of Prayer

Type	Focus
1. Devotional Activity	Purposive human activity that reaches toward the divine (e.g., thanking or worshipping God; praying for needs of self and others)
2. Prophetic Conversation	Hearing God in a direct and supernatural way and responding (e.g., receiving revelations from God or sensing a divine call to perform a specific act and then moving in faith to manifest God's will)
3. Mystical Communion	Feeling the presence of God or experiencing union with God (e.g., sensing God in a way that words cannot express)

assertion that prayer indeed is an important medium through which humans are empowered with what Sorokin has called "love energy."

Our statistical findings support and identify three distinct yet interrelated movements of prayer: purposive, devotional, human activity that reaches toward the divine; prophetic dialogue with God that emerges out of silent waiting for a response; and experiential transcendent union with the divine. We considered the effects that demographic differences—age, gender, income, education, and race/ethnicity—had on these three prayer forms. The impact of the demographics proved, for the most part, to be negligible.[12] What did help to explain differences in devotional prayer activities, conversations with the divine, and mysticism was whether the respondent self-identified as a Pentecostal and/or charismatic Christian. (This finding reflects the typology that we developed in chapter 3 to introduce four major types of exemplars.) Those respondents who professed to be pentecostal were significantly more likely to experience all three of the prayer forms. They were more likely to actively engage in prayer activities with great frequency than those who did not self-identify as pentecostal, to enter a more receptive prayer mode that facilitated divine-human communication, and to report mystical experiences that reflect altered states of consciousness.[13] Taking these survey findings and illuminating them with accounts from narratives from our interviews suggests that prayer journeys commonly include human activity that opens the pray-er toward a greater human receptivity of the divine presence and toward the transcendent experiences of mystical union with God.

Prayer as Human Activity

The vast majority of Americans pray. Only 12.5 percent of our respondents said they never pray; 62 percent claim to pray with great regularly. Thirty-two percent said they prayed once a day, and another 30 percent indicated that they prayed more than once a day. Three-fourths of the respondents (75 percent) *regularly* directed their prayers toward thanking God for blessings received, praying for the needs of others (68 percent), worshipping God (66 percent), and asking God for guidance in making decisions (64 percent), with a significantly smaller percentage (40 percent) indicating they pray regularly for their own personal needs. These five items were used to construct the *devotional prayer activity* scale that tapped into ways men and women reach out to the divine. Some of these prayers were surely soliloquies where the pray-er did all the talking; others included a conversational component where the pray-er seemed to hear from God; and still others were accompanied by some degree of mystical union. These three prayer forms are not mutually exclusive; rather, they resemble a river with tributaries flowing in and out of the main stream of human effort found in the process of prayer.

The devotional activity scale is a more complex measure than simply asking a respondent whether he or she prays. It provides a window for a range of prayer foci including the worship of God, petition for personal physical and spiritual needs, and intercession for the needs of others. Moreover, this act of praying appears to support the other two primary measures of prayer found in the GLNS. For example, over one-half (52 percent) of those who scored high on prayer activities also scored high on hearing from God (prophecy), in comparison with only 7 percent who scored high on prophecy but indicated they were infrequent active pray-ers. Frequent prayer seems to be an even more significant precedent for experiences of mystical union. Sixty-two percent of those who scored high on prayer activity also scored high on the mysticism scale, compared with the 4 percent who scored low on prayer activity and who were high on mysticism. The occasional pray-er is not likely to be engaged in either divine-human dialogue or in mystical union.

The active prayer journey commonly begins with a ritual practice—a child kneeling by the bed saying "Now I lay me down to sleep...," a teenager's monologue asking for divine help in getting out of a difficult situation, a Catholic reciting the rosary, or a Protestant's devotional reading of the Bible. Some rituals are more formal than others; some are solitary, while others take place in groups. The journey of active prayer commonly brings a deep sense of peace, a deeper awareness of God's love, and a sense of meaning and purpose in life, as reported by our survey respondents. For most pray-ers, however, the ritual of active prayer is complemented, at least on occasion and over time, by a divine-human conversation as the pray-er begins to discern the voice of God.

Prayer as Prophetic Dialogue

In the pentecostal world where heaven seems to break through with its mystery and miracles, the prophetic is less about foretelling the future than about hearing from God.[14] Not everyone who prays would claim dependence on God for instruction and guidance. The popular adage "God helps those who help themselves" (erroneously thought even by many Christians to be a quotation from the Bible) is deeply engrained in American culture. Rather than focus on self-reliance, Christian norms stress the need to surrender to and to rely on God, with the expectation that he will lead and empower the pray-er to do the seemingly impossible. Despite the popularity of self-help books that promote self-reliance, the majority of Americans still acknowledge at least occasional experiences of divine direction, either directly from God, through the prophetic words of others, or through circumstances that are interpreted as the voice of the divine. Undoubtedly one of the most common experiences— for those who sense the voice of God and who see visions of the heavens as well as for those who do not—is a sense of calm and peace that prayer can bring to the pray-er. This awareness of tranquility that commonly accompanies prayer appears to be a first step in moving away from a sole reliance on prayer activities toward more receptive prayer stances that transform prayer monologues into dialogues. As we saw in Sam's story, transformation commonly involves being still and listening with one's own spirit for the Spirit of God.[15]

Like many of our interviewees, especially those raised in conservative Christian homes as she was, Anne Beiler reported that her childhood prayers were formal and disciplined, addressed to a God who was stern and strict— "commanding and demanding," says Anne. Although she said she knew that she could pray anytime, Anne described her prayers as a young Amish-Mennonite girl more in terms of ritual than affect:

> Well, when I prayed I always knelt. I knew I could pray anytime, you know, but I was very disciplined at night praying by my bedside. As I got older, I felt like longer periods were better. I think that had to do with my longing to know God in a deeper way—that started when I was twelve, thirteen, fourteen. So my relationship with God was

going to church every Sunday, reading my Bible every day, praying every night, no matter what. I never went to bed without reading my Bible and praying, never.

When Matt asked for more detail, Anne acknowledged that her disciplined prayer did bring spiritual tranquility. As we saw in the last chapter, Anne "accepted Christ" at the age of twelve in order to avoid going to hell. It was a memorable experience of being born-again: "I remember feeling like this whole burden—like I was a terrible sinner—had just been lifted from me. I guess it's true; we are sinners. And when we invite Christ in there is just this light that went on for me." The light continued to flicker for Anne offering a sense of peace and of connection with God during prayer: "I did feel a connection with God. And I felt a peace that was calming to me. There was something very calming about my discipline of Bible reading and prayer."

When she was twenty, Anne reported a spiritual transformation that she alternately described as "like being born again" and as her "spiritual awakening." Jesus became her friend as she experienced what pentecostal Christians call the "baptism of the Holy Spirit" or the "baptism of love." Although she was unable to find adequate words to describe it, she alluded to her awakening as being "like an out-of-body experience." It would appear that during this period of her prayer life as a young adult Anne had experienced both prophetic and mystical prayer. But the tragic loss of her nineteen-month-old daughter (she was killed by a tractor driven by Anne's sister), her spiritual and sexual abuse by a pastor who sought to "comfort" her in her loss, as well as the sexual abuse of two of her sisters and her preteen daughter by this pastor, all seemed to diminish the frequency and intensity of feeling the loving presence of God which she had previously experienced.[16] Consider this discussion, from Matthew's interview with her:

ANNE: Because now I am weighed down with the loss and the grief and the questions and the loneliness and the "Why"? All of a sudden, I felt lost. I went from that to this. I felt lost. I just didn't understand why, at that time, how can this be? I can be on the mountaintop and in this despair? Where is God? He's not working for me. I mean that's very foolish to think that way, but I did. This is not working for me.

MATTHEW: And the feeling of the Spirit sort of stopped at that point?

ANNE: Yeah. That's what I was going to say, twenty years later sitting in my pastor's office the thing that makes me feel more guilty than anything is that I just cannot pick up my Bible and read and I cannot pray like I did. I mean, yes, I was praying all through these years, I prayed but those were prayers of, I mean, I don't know, prayers of when you just cry out to God for him. There was no fulfillment; it was just, "I need you, God," desperation prayers for twenty years.

MATTHEW: And not getting that sense of presence or that sense of peace or things that you used to receive.

ANNE: No. So it was a very dark and a very long time for me and when I told the counselor that she said, "Well, why would you want to pray?" I said, "Because it's the right thing to do." She said, "Well, if you get into a relationship with the Lord like that again and you find yourself joyful and filled with the Spirit, what do you think is going to happen to you? Are you afraid that if I [Anne] ever go back there, that I will lose again?" And I tell you, I will never forget that. I wept.

Anne's "dark night of the soul" coincided with several tragic experiences, on the one hand, as well as a business accomplishment that represents the pinnacle of the American Dream, on the other. During this time, she continued to pray and she knew that God existed, but she did not *feel* a divine presence in the same way or to the same degree. She had lost the sense of peace that had accompanied her earlier experience of a baptism of love.

A careful reading of Anne Beiler's autobiography *Twist of Faith* suggests that Anne's awareness of God as a partner would surface at times during her emotional and economic struggles as well as through emotional healing and material prosperity. The portrait of Anne that comes through her story is of an Amish-Mennonite girl with an eighth-grade education who becomes a successful businesswoman, whose Auntie Anne pretzels are known widely to those who patronize food courts of suburban malls and airports. She is an active, take-charge, successful woman with, as she confesses, a love for "butzing" (a term her Amish mother used for "staying busy at an almost frenzied pace").[17] Yet in the midst of even seeming hyperactivity, the voice of God would break into her life either during personal prayer or sometimes through prophetic words. This divine message would then often be serendipitously confirmed through the wise counsel of her husband, a family member, or business advisers. Her cultural background, where religious experiences were personal and not for sharing even with family members, seems to leave her more incredulous about prophecy than those who are deeply involved in pentecostal Christianity, where the custom of sharing personal testimonies is prevalent. Anne cannot be accused of clinging blindly to prophetic words that came her way. Yet prophetic senses and promises are sprinkled cautiously throughout her autobiographical accounts.

For example, Anne recounts sitting in a warm bubble bath as she reflected on her life sometime after she and her family had moved from Lancaster, Pennsylvania, to Texas. Her husband, Jonas, who worked as a car body repairman, had just received an unexpected job offer that doubled their income, leaving Jonas free to pursue his dream of devoting more of his time in providing psychological counseling to others without charging a fee. Anne writes:[18]

> Amazing! Yet sitting there in the tub, I was still too close to that event to see the larger significance it held. As the steam rose around me, I whispered quietly to God, "I'm willing to do whatever, I mean *whatever* you want me to do. I don't know what it is, but I am willing. You've given me so much, restored so much of my life that I thought would never heal. Let me give back, if possible."

Although Anne says she did not receive an answer to this prayer immediately, within the next several weeks restlessness seemed to stir within her as well as Jonas, "as if a time had come to move on." After a visit to their family in Lancaster, they both felt a call to "move home"—a sense of calling that filled Anne with "conflicting emotions" because of the great pain they had experienced before they moved from Pennsylvania to Texas. They began planning and packing for their return "home." Just as they were about to leave for Pennsylvania, a friend came by and gave them a prophetic word:

> "You may not believe what God just told me, but this is what He said: He will restore every broken relationship, He will give back to you more than you ever had before, He has a plan for you that you don't know about yet, but He will show it to you." Then he stopped and looked down, shaking his head as if he couldn't believe what he was about to say. "I just see so much for you guys. And it is not just a spiritual blessing. It's, well, you think this house is beautiful? And don't get me wrong, it is. But I see God giving you things that you wouldn't believe: I see houses, I see land, I see cars, I see, I just see all that stuff. God is going to give it all to you. And you're going to start some sort of business. I don't know exactly what kind, but that's the key. And it's going to happen within the first year of your arrival in Pennsylvania."[19]

Anne sat listening to the prophecy in disbelief. The part about spiritual blessings sounded possible, but not about the land and the cars and the houses: "The only response," she said,

> was to laugh: not a laugh of happiness or even amusement, but one of total disbelief. Everything we owned was in that truck! Couldn't he understand that? I was thirty-nine years old without life insurance policies or a plan for retirement. In the way of cash, after taking out the money we would need for gas and meals on our journey, we had an astronomical $25 left![20]

So it was. Within a year after Anne and Jonas returned to Pennsylvania in 1988, Auntie Anne's Soft Pretzels was being birthed with the help of a $6,000 loan from Jonas's father. From a small nondescript farmer's market stand, Auntie Anne's Soft Pretzels soon would be launched into the malls of America and eventually into the international marketplace. By 2003 their business would have 700 domestic locations and 119 locations in twelve foreign countries.[21]

Anne's autobiography includes many other simple accounts of hearing God's directions, having strong impressions and senses that were seemingly from God, including the resolution of personal problems and guidance in dealing with family crises as well as critical business decisions over the years. The stories are simple but hardly Pollyannaish, seasoned as they are with pain and struggle. The path to godly love has not always been smooth for Anne, but it has been an ongoing and important part of her life story.

Teaching Prophetic Dialogue

Steve Witt learned about prophetic dialogue from his mother, whom he described as a "mother who heard from heaven." With his characteristic wit, he goes on to share what it was like growing up with her:[22] "Imagine being a teenager with a mom who hears from God! You can't get away with anything! God would always use her to 'arrest' me if I was starting to get off track. Her keen sense of discernment spared my life many a time." Steve's most significant experiences with prophetic dialogue can be found in the account of his spiritual transformation found in the last chapter, including his being led to Canada from Cleveland and then back to Cleveland ten years later. Although his call to ministry has always been seemingly clear, it was not unwavering as reflected of the following narrative about his prophetic mother:

Once, when I was away at college, I had come to a point of frustration and decided to give up. I cleaned out my room and packed my car, ready to abandon my vision and direction. My final act of evacuation was to glance into the tiny window of my school mailbox—where I saw a letter.

Curious, I opened the letter, immediately recognizing it as a note from my mom. It was hand-printed in capital letters on a legal page. (This was typical of my mom when she would write something that was from God. Apparently God speaks in capital letters!)

It began with "DEAR STEVE... THUS SAYS THE LORD..." I perused page after page of encouragement and reminders of what had been said over me in the past. Phrases such as "From your mother's womb..." and "Have I not told you..." were sprinkled about. I remember chills running down my back as if this was coming directly from above. How did she know what to say? How could the timing be so exact? I folded up the note and proceeded back to my room, eventually completing my education.

Steve not only continues his own deep involvement in prophetic prayer, but he is intent on providing sound instruction to others through conferences and his book on the topic. He often has said that he wants everyone who belongs to his growing congregations to have a "PHD"—by which he means he wants them adept in "prophecy, healing, and deliverance" ministries so that they can effectively serve others through the use of these God-given gifts. For Steve what may appear to be paranormal—prophecy or hearing from God, healing of physical and spiritual maladies, deliverance from forces of evil—should be normal for Christian believers. Common vehicles for God's voice are many, including "dreams, visions, impressions, words, demonstrations, art, actions, parabolic events, etc."[23] An important part of Steve's calling is being a spiritual life coach who teaches others how to listen for God's voice on a regular basis, how to trust and discern it, and how "to put heaven's voice into practical action."[24]

Cultural Grids, Benevolent Outreach, and Prophetic Dialogue

Both Steve Witt and Paul Alexander grew up in traditional Pentecostal churches and graduated from Pentecostal Bible colleges. Both have committed themselves to changing the world for the better through practical action— Paul as an educator and social justice activist and Steve as a church pastor with a vision to train church members to facilitate the transformation of Cleveland. Paul's family has deep roots in Pentecostalism, while Steve's mother converted after she experienced a divine healing through the prayers of a Pentecostal neighbor. Yet the two ministers operate in different cultural grids. Steve is one of the interviewees who represents the Renewal/Revival category of our benevolent outreach typology—one who seeks to revitalize the larger church through a renewed vision of the coming kingdom of God that will bring notable changes not only to personal lives but to surrounding communities. As the son of a leader of a large labor union, Steve's vision includes strategic planning, but his significant decisions seem to be more grounded in receptivity to prophecy than in his organizational skills. His giving priority to the prophetic over the programmatic can be seen in his planting of Bethel Cleveland Church when he returned from Canada to Cleveland. Steve knew the rules for church planting—he had already established four churches—and they did not include taking out a radio spot inviting people who "loved the Lord but were dissatisfied with church" to come meet with him. As a successful church planter, Steve "knew" that such talk would bring malcontents who were unlikely to stay with any organized congregation. He did so only with divine prompting. To his surprise, ninety-two people responded to his radio advertisements and came to the first gathering; most of these men and women stayed with him helping to establish this new church. Steve described the role of the prophetic at Bethel Cleveland as follows:

> I'd say we've had our ups and downs since we've been here but I'd say we're a matured expression, a maturing/matured expression of all the things of my mainline denominational buddies, my democratic upbringing, my union father, my experiential, prophetic intercessor mother, seminary training, AOG [Assemblies of God] and the Toronto Blessing. What we are is an absolute blend of all that right now—a people that are equipped, that value the experiential but also value good teaching and training.

Paul, on the other hand, is an ordained minister in a traditional Pentecostal denomination, a professor at a Christian university, and a peace activist. He, like others we interviewed in the social justice category (Changers; recall Table 3.1), was less likely to portray God as a dialogue partner who frequently spoke to them than were the Renewers/Revivalists. As with most other interviewees whose primary work is in trying to change social and political structures, Paul is not one to frame his story through prophetic lenses.[25] In fact, most of his answers to our questions about prayer during the interview centered on the difficulties he had with praying as he moved away from his Pentecostal faith into agnosticism or in describing how he begins his university classes with prayer. His religious language seems to be more rooted in the adage commonly attributed to Francis of Assisi than pentecostal Renewers: "Preach the Gospel at all times; use words if necessary." Prayer and social action seemed to be painted with a single brush of human effort and activity.

Although our social justice interviewees tended not to clothe their interviews with God-talk, three had written books calling for the integration of prayer and social action. Shane Claiborne and Jonathan Wilson-Hartgrove, two of our interviewees who coauthored a book titled *Becoming the Answer to Our Prayers*, made a call for busy activists not to neglect prayer. They noted in their introduction: "We live in inner-city communities that are usually known for their activism, not their prayer life. In fact, writing this book has been a discipline, as we try to listen amid all the noise of wildly busy lives, and speak nothing more or less than we hear God speaking to us." Shane and Jonathan suggest that as pray-ers move away from the "silly self-serving" petitionary prayers of childhood to the more mature intercessory prayers for the poor and needy of the world, they learn to listen and hear a call to action. For them, working diligently to create a more just world seems to be the responsibility of all pray-ers: "Prayer is not so much about convincing God to do what we want God to do as it is about convincing ourselves to do what God wants us to do."[26]

Like pray-ers with a less active and more receptive style, however, Shane and Jonathan's instructive prayer for social activists is ultimately rooted in love and in listening in silence: "Prayer is about having a romance with the Divine. The more deeply we are in love with someone, the less we have to say." They contend that social activism can only go so far—"activism alone will not sustain community life, and protest doesn't necessarily make us more loving people."[27]

The prayers of social activists share commonalities with those involved in church renewal and exemplars who were primarily caregivers in that their use of ritual opens the door for moving into dialogue with the divine. Yet at times it is apparent that they seem to be using a different grid for what they say, what they hear, and how it is confirmed. For example, activists are more likely to be anchored in particular interpretations of biblical injunctions that call for an active pursuit of peace and justice rather than in the divinely produced miracles found in many biblical stories that feed the prayers of revivalists. Social justice exemplars may recognize the importance of prayer for spiritual empowerment, but their understanding of prophecy would resonate more with the Old Testament figures who decried sin and injustice than the Pauline discussion of prophecy as a gift of encouragement as taught in Steve's church. Both groups cry out for the coming kingdom of God, but their methods and understanding of the role human activity plays in ushering in the kingdom differ. The social activists are more likely to align with the busy Martha of the biblical story who complained to Jesus about her sister Mary's failure to help put dinner on the table. The Renewers, on the other hand, have an affinity for Mary, whom Jesus said had chosen "the better part" by sitting at his feet and listening to his words.[28]

Those whose mission and ministry are focused primarily on compassionate service to others may hold a middle ground between the Renewal/Revival contemplative stance and the activist stance of social justice leaders. Karen, an ordained minister in a mainline Protestant denomination, worked as a hospital chaplain before accepting the position as a chaplain at a retirement center, which includes independent and assisted living facilities as well as a nursing home. Her busy schedule does not allow her much time to spend alone in silence; emergencies seem always to be only a text message away. An ongoing sense of a divine presence, however, seems to accompany her as she ministers to the hundreds of residents, staff, and often their families and friends. Karen has received a public award for her years of tireless service in a context of chronic illness and dying—a situation that tends to breed exhaustion and burnout. Her hours are unpredictable, especially when she is participating on a "death call," which means that a resident has only days or hours to live. Using the language of the call and its attendant duties, she explains, "When I'm called to duty, I go. In any given week it can vary from sixty, seventy, to eighty hours. I'm always 'on,' and the Lord gives me strength for that." Highlighting the energizing nature of her ongoing interactions with God, Karen commented during the interview: "I sometimes say that I am drained or tired, but the Lord picks me up the next day just as revived as I was when I first started. It's just God giving me the energy."

Not infrequently, God seems to speak through her residents—sometimes in dramatic ways. As we listened to Karen's stories of how she as one chaplain was able to deal with the needs of hundreds of people we knew that she had ears to hear God in the ordinary and everyday demands of her busy life. Over and over Karen has felt a divine leading to go to a particular resident when she was on her way to another task, only to find that that resident had been praying for her to come by. She expects God to direct her steps, and God seemingly does!

Karen listens to God speaking to her through the residents, offering words of encouragement and divine approval. On a recent occasion a man who regularly came to her chapel services (but who always preferred to talk with her about football rather than the Bible) shared with her with a dream that puzzled him. "Pastor Karen," he said, "I dreamed—although I'm really not sure if I was asleep or awake—I dreamed last night that you were driving a stagecoach. It was strange; the stagecoach was up in the sky headed for a big puffy cloud and it was filled with old people. You drove the coach right into the cloud until I couldn't see it anymore." Karen replied that he had experienced a prophetic dream/vision for her. She went on to explain, "I have prepared many here at the home to make the transition through death to heaven. The dream is an encouragement for me. Thank you for sharing it." Karen laughed at she told the story; Chuck never thought of himself as a prophetic visionary! It was apparent that Karen heard the approving "voice" of God through this resident's dream.

Not uncommonly God speaks to her through residents suffering from Alzheimer's disease and dementia. On one occasion Karen came to work a bit shaken because she had narrowly escaped a car accident. As she entered the door, one of the mentally challenged young residents ran over to Karen saying excitedly, "I see an angel—I see a big shining angel standing right next to you. He is protecting you; nothing bad can happen to you. I see an angel....I see an angel." The young man spoke as if in a trance. He paused, then continued: "Pastor Karen, do you like *High School Musical*?—I like *High School Musical*." Karen knew she had just heard a prophetic word—a word of encouragement and promise. The young man had now finished its delivery!

In sum, prayer often assumes different faces for those in different life callings. We noted this pattern we described in our interviewees with their differing primary foci that we categorized as church revival, compassionate service, and social action. It could be said, for example, that the call of social justice exemplars to usher in the kingdom of God is centered in willing workers who struggle for structural changes that will benefit the poor and/or the cause of peace, while Renewers believe the kingdom of God comes through following the Spirit-filled life of Jesus, where miracles and mysteries unfold through spiritual empowerment. It is not so much that their respective language and grids are disparate and irreconcilable as much as there are different emphases and understandings as they bring together prayer, love, and human action.

As we reviewed the narratives of our exemplars, we observed that a synthesis between the social types whom we called Renewers (who tend to be high on mysticism and lower on changing the world) and the Changers (who tend to be high on social action but lower on mysticism) is rare. These two types of ministry appear to be related (at least in the United States) to different social and political viewpoints that demonstrate once again the importance of cultural grids for analyzing religious experiences. Renewers tend to be conservative, Changers tend to be liberal, and Servers run the political gamut. Yet there are some interviewees, like Shane and Jonathan, who seek to live out an integration between mystical prayer and social action.

Another interviewee is Tony Campolo, a retired university professor, ordained minister, and well-known speaker, who often uses Catholic teachings and examples of mysticism to invite evangelicals to integrate mysticism and social action. In his interview with us, Tony describes the process:

> And I pick up on [St.] Francis [of Assisi], where he sees the poor and the oppressed as sacramental, that they become means of grace. That is where we encounter Jesus—in the poor and the oppressed. And Mother Teresa picks up this same theme. Whenever I look into the eyes of a man dying of AIDS, I have this eerie sensation that Jesus is staring back at me. The poor and the oppressed become sacramental. They become the agents of grace. It's in them that I find the living Christ. That Jesus does not come to us, zapping from above, as much as he comes to us through persons. And so that becomes very crucial.

Tony is a sociologist who understands well the social problem of poverty. He is a professor emeritus whose academic career has included serving on the faculty of the University of Pennsylvania for ten years, and serving as a spiritual mentor to former president Bill Clinton; he continues to serve as president of the Evangelical Association for the Promotion of Education (EAPE). His website welcomes those who visit with the following introduction:

> Welcome to the internet home of Dr. Anthony Campolo, speaker, author, sociologist, pastor, social activist, and passionate follower of Jesus! Over his many years of Christian service, Tony has boldly challenged millions of people all over the world to respond to God's boundless love by combining personal discipleship, evangelism, and social justice. We invite you to join those of us who have been inspired by Tony's powerful message of hope.

Tony's coauthored book *The God of Intimacy and Action* weaves together the two threads of mysticism and social action that have been interwoven in his personal life as well as his ministry. He draws from ancient Christian traditions to challenge modern evangelicals to merge active prayer practices with an open receptivity to mysticism.

Tony acknowledges that his mystic mother was the catalyst behind his calling to the ministry: "So there was never any question in my mind. Whenever anybody asks me, tell me about your call to the ministry, my response is, I never was called. My mother decided!" In part serious and in part playful, he continued telling us how his mother often shared the Bible story of Eli and his son, the Old Testament prophet Samuel, who as a youngster heard God calling to him in the night. He doesn't recall his having any early mystical Samuel-like experience, but he does remember his mother's example: "I mean, my early Christian experiences were hers and only later did they become my own." He described one of his major transformations as "just an awareness," then sharing how this "aha" moment would become central to his calling:

> And I became aware that I needed to bring people into a personal relationship with Jesus, not to get them into heaven when they died, but in order to become instruments of God to work for social justice. So I could preach a sermon on social justice, and talk about the poor and the needy and the oppressed and say we have to respond to this. God wants to use you for these things. How many of you are willing to come down the aisle and receive Christ into your life so that through you he can do his work in the world? So, all of the sudden, evangelism and social justice were not two different things. They very much fit into a single model.
>
> You come down the aisle to accept Jesus; you are coming down the aisle to involve yourself in what God is doing in the world. That was a big emphasis. The whole definition of the gospel changed for me. The gospel became, not the good news of how Jesus died and took away my sins; my definition of the gospel became a declaration, the gospel is the good news of what God is doing in the world. That was very important. This is the kind of thing you work out in the existential situation. What is God doing in the world? He's transforming people and through them transforming society. So that was very important.

This realization of God's saving love with a call to change the world that came seemingly out of nowhere has become central for Tony's influential ministry. It appears that those mystical moments tend to occur not while he is wrapped in the silence of a formal time of prayer but in lived situations that are life-changing. His conviction that Jesus is encountered mystically in the faces of the poor came through another epiphany that Tony had in 1975. During our interview, Tony recounts this story as follows:

> There was an experience that I often use in my sermons where this hit me very strongly. It [seeing Jesus in the poor] was a gradual thing but then it always comes to a point where you got this once again—*aha*, so that's what it's all about. I was in the Dominican Republic at the edge of a grass landing strip. I'd just finished checking on some of our workers and EAPE (our ministry), and I was waiting for someone to come and pick me up. And this woman comes to me with this kid that's dying, swelled belly, less colored hair.
>
> I mean the kid looks dead. And she starts begging me to take her baby. I tell her I can't do that. Even if I took it, I couldn't get the baby out of the country. I can't do this. She said, but my baby's gonna die if you don't take my baby, my baby's gonna die. The airplane lands, and I run across the field, and she's running after me, yelling, "Take my baby. Don't let my baby die. Take my baby. Don't let my baby die." I climbed into the plane, closed the Plexiglas door. She catches up with the plane, and she's banging on the side of the plane. [I] tell the pilot, "Get us out of here." So he revs up the engine, and we pull away from her and into the air.
>
> And halfway back to the capital, it dawned on me who this baby was. And I could hear Jesus saying, "I was hungry and did you feed me? Naked, did you clothe me? I was sick, did you care for me? I was that child and you did not take me in." So, that was a peak experience. This dawning on me, that this is very, very important to see. So that becomes a defining moment.

Shane, Jonathan, and Tony have written to encourage their fellow social activists not to abandon prayer, reminding them that they need divine empowerment to carry on with their work as world changers. Yet their discussions and examples of mysticism seem to have a different sound than those heard in testimonies of Renewers with accounts of healing, multiplication of food, and even resurrections from the dead. Renewers like Heidi Baker, Steve Witt, and many others we have interviewed are describing more intense and powerful mystical experiences through which "love energy" seemingly impacts laws of the physical world—stories that sound much like miracles of biblical proportions that challenge the modern mind.

Encountering the Heart of God

Based on the GLNS and illuminated by narratives, we are proposing that for most pray-ers the choreography for prayer includes three steps: devotional active praying, a more passive prophetic receiving from God that requires a response on the part of the pray-er, and a degree of mystical transcendence. As we noted earlier in this chapter, the three scales—devotional prayer, prophetic prayer, and mysticism—are highly significant in statistical tests with findings that support our observations from the narratives. All three seem to work together to account for a deeper awareness of divine love that in turn empowers benevolence. Our findings suggest that most are involved to some degree in patterns that change along the uneven path of life's journey. Some of our stories have accentuated active prayer and others prophetic prayer, with others a clear mix of the two components. Shadowy figures cast by a third element of prayer that we call mysticism can also be discerned in some of these accounts. In a short guest article for "On Faith," a joint venture of the *Washington Post* and *Newsweek*, Margaret and Matthew offered a short quote from one of our interviewees that concisely describes the importance of mystical prayer experiences.[29] "Nancy"—a collaborator in a community service ministry—explained how pentecostal experiences of the Holy Spirit deepened her Christian faith, stating, "I always had the words, but I didn't have the music." For mystics like Nancy, this music can help people choreograph a flow beyond their own personal spiritual experiences and toward a life of empowered service.

As with active prayer and prophetic prayer, experiences of mystical prayer have been reported by a majority of our survey respondents—at least on occasion. Only 39 percent of our respondents said they had *never* experienced "everything seemingly disappears except the consciousness of God," 36 percent had *never* had "an experience of God that no words could possibly express," and 33 percent reported they have *never* felt the "unmistakable presence of God during prayer." One in four respondents (25 percent) claim to experience the "unmistakable presence of God" on most days or even "several times a day." When we created a mysticism scale out of these items, only 11 percent had *never* had *any* of the three experiences.[30]

As we have seen, Tony Campolo represents someone who has been able to combine his passion for social justice with a passion for mystical prayer.[31] He follows the famed founding father of the psychology of religion, William James, in defining a mystic as "one who experiences God in trans-rational and nonempirical ways." He notes that though such experiences often defy rational description and verbal expression, they do have "a profound effect on those who have them."[32] Descriptions of the nature of his mystical experiences suggest that for Tony they are personal and yet somehow interactive:

> I have something that transcends the rational. It has exploded in the depths of my being. I feel something opening up inside of me. I feel this, this connecting with an incredible sense of the spirit that not only, and this goes along with the things that I've already told you, I feel, the question was do you feel God's presence? I feel in those moments a tremendous oneness with other people, even though I'm alone. At that moment, I feel like I love everybody. They are very important times. And when I say I love everybody, you say well, doesn't this bring you joy? My answer is, not exactly, because I feel the pain of other people at that moment as well.
>
> I also have to say this: Preaching for me is sacramental. I wish I could say every time I preach, I feel the presence of God. I never know. It happens very often though. There more than in quiet times. When I preach, there comes a point at which I feel connected with God and I just feel the spirit is there and I'm there and the people are there and we're all connected.

Writing largely for the Christian evangelical community—many of whom have been wary of all things "mystical"—Tony insists that "mystical spirituality is at the base of effective evangelism" and that it "presses us into efforts to bring this justice to all oppressed aspects of God's creation."[33]

As Stephen listened to the life stories of Tony Campolo and other spiritual activists, he was reminded of a conference that the Institute for Research on Unlimited Love (for which Stephen serves as founding president) together with the Ford Foundation cosponsored at Case Western Reserve University in 2007 that brought together social activists and social scientists for dialogue.[34] Stephen knew that spirituality in activism was not new—the Quakers provide an early example in American history—but it is often ignored by those who do not see it as a driving dynamic. In the introduction to the book derived from the conference, Stephen and his coauthor state, "The spiritual background of so much social activism is often ignored by standard histories or the media," then proceed to support their assertion by pointing to the important role that spirituality played in the activism of Martin Luther King Jr., in the life of Dame Cicely Saunders (a pioneer in the field of palliative medicine and the modern hospice movement), and in the writings of Jacques Maritain (who coined the modern notion of "human dignity"). Stephen reflected further, commenting that even this conference failed to appreciate the spiritual activism of pentecostal Christianity, with most of the young activists speaking of drawing spiritual strength from Eastern (mostly Buddhist) meditational techniques. They seemed unaware of the role that pentecostalism has played and continues to play in spiritually engaged social justice. In fact, as our data suggest, Christian spiritual activism empowered by mystical prayer is alive, well, and growing. But mysticism, it is important to note, comes in varying degrees with different experiences of the divine that often work in tandem with prophetic prayer.

Heidi Baker's mystical experiences reflect those described by Tony but take on a different quality from his as well as the ones survey respondents probably had in mind when they responded to our questions. As we saw in the last chapter, Heidi's intense spiritual experiences began as a sixteen-year-old while she was living an affluent life in Laguna Beach, California. Although her parents modeled compassion for those in need, Heidi's love for the poor would go much further than anything she saw in her childhood or even what she experienced early in her ministry. The love energy seemingly generated through her times of mystical union with Jesus—who had called her into a mystical marriage with him shortly after her conversion experience—has empowered her to move within a transformed world where the blind regain their sight, food is multiplied, and the dead come back to life. The call to serve the poor that she lived out as a missionary to Indonesia and while working in the slums of London as she earned her PhD would take on new wings after Heidi frequented the revival at the Toronto Airport Christian Fellowship (now Catch the Fire Toronto) in the 1990s. Heidi described an early vision that she had in Toronto—one that seemed to catapult her ministry to the poor of the world into the world of supernaturally empowered benevolence—as follows:[35]

One night I was groaning in intercession for the children of Mozambique. There were thousands coming toward me, and I was crying, "No, Lord. There are too many!" Then I had a dramatic, clear vision of Jesus. I was with Him, and thousands and thousands of children surrounded us. I saw His shining face and His intense burning eyes of love. I also saw His body. It was bruised and broken, and His side was pierced. He said, "Look into My eyes. You give them something to eat." Then He took a piece of His broken body and handed it to me.

It became bread in my hands, and I began to give it to the children. It multiplied in my hands. Then again the Lord said, "Look into My eyes. You give them something to drink." He gave me a cup of blood and water, which flowed from His side. I knew it was a cup of bitterness and joy. I drank it and then began to give it to the children to drink. The cup did not go dry. By this point I was crying uncontrollably. I was completely undone by His fiery eyes of love. I realized what it had cost Him to provide such spiritual and physical food for us all. The Lord spoke to my heart and said, "There will always be enough, because I died."

Although Heidi was "refreshed and ready to go back to Mozambique" after this vision, there was more bitterness than joy in the suffering she would encounter on her return to her adopted country. What she and her husband Rolland thought was a fairly solid relationship with the government suddenly broke down, and their ministry was in jeopardy. There was even an alleged twenty-dollar contract on Heidi's life, of which she wryly says: "Finding someone willing to kill me was easy, but I have always insisted that I'm worth more than twenty dollars." Heidi describes their situation in Mozambique after her intense experience in Toronto as follows:

We didn't know how to cope. We had nowhere near the food or the cooking and sanitation facilities we needed. Boxes, clothes, and suitcases were piled high everywhere. Everyone was totally exhausted; everything was in complete chaos. And more children kept gravitating to our gate. We ran out of strength, crying as we watched our sea of faces gather. I wondered seriously, even after Toronto, "Does God really care? What is he like anyway?" I never thought he would leave us in a situation like this.

It was in the midst of this dark hour that a miracle would occur not unlike the mysterious feeding of crowds by Jesus in biblical times. This multiplication of food in Mozambique was the first of other similar accounts that would be reported by those who visit Iris Ministries.[36] Heidi tells the story as follows:

I thought I was going to snap. We didn't have any big pans for cooking. We weren't prepared in any way to feed all these children. A precious woman from the US embassy came over with food. "I brought you chili and rice for your family!" she announced sweetly, with just enough for the four of us. We hadn't eaten in days. I opened a door and showed her all our children. "I have a big family!" I pointed out tiredly but in complete and desperate earnest. My friend got serious. "There's not enough! I need to go home and cook some more!" But I just asked her to pray over the food. Now she was upset. "Don't do this!" she begged. But she prayed, quickly. I got out the plastic plates we used for street outreaches, and also a small pot of cornmeal I had. We began serving, and right from the start I gave everyone a full bowl. I was dazed and overwhelmed. I barely understood at the time what a wonderful thing was happening. But all our children ate, all the staff ate, my friend ate and even our [biological] family of four ate. Everyone had enough. Since then we have never said no to an orphaned, abandoned, or dying child. Now we feed and take care of more than one thousand children. They eat and drink all they want of the Lord's goodness. Because he died, there is always enough.

Heidi's mystical experiences at the Toronto revival have changed her and her beloved Mozambique with ripple effects that have been felt around the globe. She and Rolland had already developed an intense compassion for the poor through their work in Indonesia for sixteen years. Heidi recounted an experience she had in Hong Kong where she had been preaching to crowds of thousands. After one such event, she was walking through the back alleys of Kowloon, with its huddled masses of poor humanity, when "Jesus opened my eyes." She described the experience simply in the following words: "God expanded my heart and let me feel a small part of His intense compassion. It was incredible, for it was never ending. I canceled all our big meetings and began to work among the poor, becoming friends with them and reaching them one by one. His mercy and compassion are greater than we ever imagined."[37]

Experiences of God's love would intensify during the time of the Toronto revival. Heidi noted that she was "a type-A, driven person, and God had to break and humble me."[38] She asserted that she thought she had been depending on God as she worked among the poor in Asia and England but that in reality "I depended a lot on my own abilities. Naturally, things moved pitifully slowly. It's comical to think we can do God's work for Him."[39] She had a transforming and empowering experience which not only released a new power for her endeavors but she was to see the same and greater power in others whom she released for ministry. The mystical experience lasted seven days during which she was totally helpless: "For seven days I was unable to move. Rolland had to pick me up and carry me. I had to be carried to the washroom, to the hotel and back to the meeting. The weight of His glory was upon me. I felt so heavy I could not lift my head."[40] Heidi describes those seven days at the Toronto church as "a most holy time," during which she "learned more in those seven days than in ten years of academic theological study." As God promised her hundreds (which in reality have become thousands) of churches being planted in Mozambique, he spoke to her "about relinquishing control to Him" and showed her "the importance of the Body of Christ." Even her dislike for much seemingly self-centered Western Christianity dissipated with her divine encounter, and she eventually began to accept invitations to speak to gatherings throughout the world with her message of divine love that empowers benevolence. Heidi writes:

> After that transforming experience, everything in my ministry changed. He brought me to a place of utter dependence on Him. When I returned to Mozambique I began releasing people in ministry. I began to recognize potential ministers even in children as young as eight. I began relinquishing control and delegating responsibilities. The Lord started bringing missionaries from many nations to help us. Young men and women were called into ministry from all over Mozambique. I saw that it wasn't important if I spoke, but that I could release others to fulfill their potential in God. As I became less and He became more, the ministry grew at a phenomenal rate.[41]

Heidi is a wonderful storyteller; on conference stages, from church pulpits, in print, on the Iris website, and on YouTube we find many phenomenal, miraculous accounts. Some reflect her personal journey but many include stories about the African men and women she has released and empowered to serve. One of her visions that remains impressed on us as we write this book is one that preceded her ministry in a massive garbage dump outside Maputo. Heidi writes:

> And then I had a vision of Jesus and me dancing on the garbage dump in Maputo. In the vision Jesus was calling people to Himself. He was gathering youth and children dressed in festering sores and bloated bellies. As we touched each person one by one, they were completely healed. Their bellies became flat. Their sores were cured. They were made clean. As He and I stopped for each one, He would put beautiful robes on them. Each one was different—red, blue, purple, gold and silver. We began to lead them in a dance out of the dump to the wedding feast. It was the most

beautiful place, pure and clean, filled by his presence. He took each child by the hand and sat them at the head table.[42]

This vision has stuck with us in part because of the circumstances in which she lived out its implications. "Because of that vision," she says, she went to the Maputo dump repeatedly, to reach out to starving children and their families in a place of extreme "filth and nauseating wretchedness."[43] But she saw it as "one of the most beautiful places on earth" because deep relationships with Jesus are forged there. As we will see in our next chapter, people like Heidi who partner with God are able to perceive good in every situation and see beyond immediate, material circumstances—which may be quite dreadful—to embrace the much deeper and eternal reality of God's love that is always present. This is perhaps the ultimate end state of a life of prayer, in which the separation between life and prayer dissolves and one's actions become the prayer. In this context, miracles become normal. According to Heidi, when she first arrived at the dump, some of the youth "vowed to slit our throats."[44] But after telling them about her vision, they "fell to their knees in tears and were saved."[45] A visit to the dump years later was recorded for the film *Mama Heidi* and captured footage of one of these young men, initially an attacker, now smiling and hugging her—grateful for the dramatic life change he had experienced thanks to her vision and his subsequent spiritual transformation.[46]

Conclusion with a Caveat on Mysticism

As we have demonstrated through GLNS findings, the vast majority of Americans engage in active devotional prayer. Talking to God, whether or not God answers, is something that nearly nine out of ten Americans still do, a consistent figure after over sixty years of survey reports on the frequency of prayer. A clear majority of pray-ers continue on the prayer journey toward prophetic prayer where they hear God, at least on occasion, speaking to them, giving them directives that empower benevolence. Many, albeit fewer in number, have experiences of union with God as reflected in our survey questions on mysticism. American culture is probably not a good breeding ground for mysticism, particularly for the intense level of prayerful union with God that appears to empower Heidi Baker's phenomenal ministry. We became aware of the skepticism that many have of mysticism during our very first interview for our research. Roger, a Pentecostal minister who believed his calling was to revive the church by stirring up a fresh passion for God, has had a painful vocational history despite the outward appearance of being dedicated and successful. He broke into tears several times during the interview (not unusual for Pentecostals), but cautioned us against reading too much into the tears. He said he was in the midst of a bout with clinical depression at the time of the interview and he never knew whether the tears came from God or from depression.

Like Sheri, Roger was raised in a traditional Pentecostal family at a time when Pentecostalism was at odds with American culture and the upbringing of its children was exceptionally strict and stern. Roger describes this period as follows:

> Faith was always a huge part of everything that we were a part of. In a very simplistic way, very legalistic way, highly legalistic church—where the love of God was not stressed but rules and Old Testament theology and always seeking to keep the saints whipped into shape with a lot of fear and guilt. If our pastors were sitting here today, they would never say that. But that is just the way it was in the middle '50s and '60s. They believed that we needed to really walk a sanctified life and [they stressed] a lot of the rules rather than relationships.

Roger experienced beatings from his Pentecostal father, who, like many fathers of that time and culture, may have equated what today might be called child abuse with loving parenting. Roger's father was very unlike Sheri's mother, who modeled the love of God for her daughter and who modulated the potentially negative side of a mid-twentieth-century Pentecostalism as described by several of our exemplars.

Roger is swimming upstream to combat the negative influences of Pentecostalism that he experienced as a child. After being raised in a family that stressed discipline over love, in a denomination that shunned other Christians and in a southern community that was openly racist, Roger became a bridge-builder who actively works for unity among Christians in his community. His most powerful experiences of God's love have not come from mystical experiences that were also part of his Pentecostal heritage but rather from relationships within his family, with friends and collaborators, and through creation. Roger began his final statement in his interview with Matt and Margaret saying simply, "It is in other people that I feel the love of God."

Early in his interview, Roger expressed his wariness about mysticism as he commented on the questions that would become the mysticism scale for the GLNS. "I don't have Holy Ghost orgasms!" he said half joking but with animation. There have been times Roger has felt what he calls an "anointing"—

as when he is preaching and he felt "the manifest presence of God so strongly on me that I sensed I was speaking far above my intellect or my oratorical ability." Even when he has fallen to the ground during times of public worship—what old Pentecostals called "going under the power" or being "slain in the spirit" and pentecostals now refer to as "resting in the spirit" or colloquially as "carpet time"—Roger says he has always been conscious (even embarrassed) and very aware of what was going on around him. He says he has a difficult time with mystical experiences:

> I have a very difficult time—I mean I know that there's rare exceptions where [the apostle] Paul's caught up into the third heaven and Moses gets the Ten Commandments on Mt. Sinai and [the apostle] John's caught up into the, you know [the biblical book], Revelations. But I have a real hard time with this idea that somehow this person is just in another world and they are totally and only in touch with what God's showing them and speaking to them. [Roger then added,] Do I believe it can happen? Yes, I do. Do I believe it happens? [He hesitated and then continued,] Yes, but I think it happens more in other parts of the world because they are more conscious of spirit stuff. We are so European, so rationalistic; we're so impacted by the Enlightenment that it's hard for us to get into that.

Clearly some of our exemplars are more mystic than others—and some, like Roger, would speak of spiritual experiences but disclaim any mystical encounters. Yet mysticism—on some level or another—is important for a great many of Americans who participate in godly love. It can, as we will see in the next chapter, be the cup of joy that has empowered exemplars to drink of the cup of suffering with which joy is often intermingled.

6

The Cup of Suffering and Joy

DIVINE LOVE AND HEALING

SUFFERING IS AN inevitable fact of life that has been recognized by founders of all great religions of the world. The possibility of redemption from suffering is also a dominant theme in literature, drama, and film, as well as the scriptures. Certainly this is true of Christianity: Jesus's crucifixion is front and center in its theology. Jesus's suffering and death are trumped, however, by his resurrection and stand as an archetype of an ongoing dialectic between suffering and joy. The scriptures teach that suffering will end in joy, tears will be turned into laughter, and sorrow will give way to rejoicing. The biblical accounts found in both the Hebrew and Christian testaments leave little room for a Pollyannaish denial of suffering; rather, they seek to assure that trust in God can bring joy into even the worst of situations. American Christianity—particularly the "prosperity gospel" variety—has often paradoxically created a pop-cultural theology that severs the integral relationship between joy and suffering, one that denies suffering a role in strengthening character, deepening faith, increasing human compassion, and fostering abiding joy.

It is therefore not surprising that exemplars were reluctant to single out stories involving periods of deep suffering in response to our invitation to share accounts of the most significant events that had shaped their lives and core identities. Nonetheless, pain and suffering can be found lurking close to the surface in almost all of the narratives, including those of our five primary exemplars. Perhaps the reader already has been struck by shadows of pain cast by some of the stories and is wondering how suffering can be reconciled to faith in a loving God. What is it about the long-term pain brought by the tragic death of a child that halted the mystical experiences of Anne's early adulthood; the frustration with being a people pleaser that underlies Steve's joyful experience into a "baptism of 'I don't care'"; the theological unrest stemming from religious injustice that led Paul to abandon the faith of his childhood; and Herb's struggle against racism that had inflicted pain on him and his family as well as on countless African Americans throughout history? Each person has had a unique experience with suffering and each followed a different path beyond it, but there is a common plot: a spiritual transformation rooted in divine love is integral to overcoming hardships and making the switch from self-interested goals to a life of serving others.

The reader may also be taken aback by the gruesome account in the previous chapter of Heidi's mystical vision in which Jesus asked her to drink of "a cup of suffering and joy" that came from the wound in his side. Yet this vision undoubtedly has had a dramatic effect on Heidi's life and ministry. Having lived most of her years outside the United States with the poorest of the world's poor has given Heidi a perspective on joy and suffering that takes her beyond affluent America's Pollyannaish culture. Ten years after her dramatic encounter with a vision of Jesus at the Toronto revival church, Heidi would write a short article titled "A Cup of Suffering and Joy." She noted how her joy increased whenever she experienced God's provisions. Iris Ministries had gone from caring for 320 children in Mozambique to over ten thousand, as the number of churches exploded from "a few churches to over ten thousand in 17 years."[1] Her joy increased as the ministry flourished, but so did the suffering. Heidi addresses her understanding of this "cup of suffering and joy" that she willingly embraced in her vision of ten years earlier with the following graphic account written in 2007:[2]

In the last few days I have learned more than I ever imagined about the cup of suffering and joy. Our nation Mozambique has been hammered with floods, cyclones and monster waves. Pemba, Cabo Delgado, was hit with cholera. Finally a few kilometers from our Zimpeto children's center in Maputo, a large ammunitions dump blew up, spraying mines, missiles and shrapnel for thirty kilometers around. Hundreds of people were killed. Houses were leveled leaving the victims crushed beneath the rubble. I have never seen such suffering as I have seen in the last thirty days. As I stood in the ruins of a house leveled by a missile and held a weeping women in my arms, I drank of His cup of suffering. As I embraced Marcelina, 14, Edwardo, 15, and Carvalho, 12, orphaned by the blasts, I drank His cup of suffering. After driving all day through the mud and potholes of Zambezia to minister and deliver food to a distant village devastated by floods, I rocked a tiny, starving baby in my arms and tried to find milk to no avail, and I drank the cup of His suffering. After arriving in

Caia, a town with a refugee camp on the flooded Zambezi River, I spoke to the director of a large non-governmental organization as he was evacuating his workers and helicopters because he could not get past all the corruption and red tape. I drank of the cup of suffering knowing those very helicopters could have fed many precious people stranded in the flood zones starving for weeks. I opened my eyes wider still to see and drink the cup of suffering.

I also drank the cup of joy. God opened the door for us to provide food for fourteen refuge camps in Zambezia Province. I drank the cup of joy watching my Mozambican son, Norberto, lead the relief effort for the province. I drank the cup of joy seeing the faces of hopeless, desperate people run to meet King Jesus and thank Him for saving their lives. Worship of our beautiful Savior reached heaven in Zimpeto when the children, co-workers and missionaries gave glory to God for sparing their lives as missiles and bombs flew in every direction above them and from the streets thanking Jesus for holding them in His arms as the terror of the blasts continued all around them. Pastor José spoke of the amazing opportunity God had given all of them to worship in the middle of the frightening chaos. Missionaries shared how they would gladly give up their lives to protect the children, and I drank the cup of joy. We offered a home in our center to Marcelina, Edwardo and Carvalho, and watched their tears turn into laughter. God made a way to bring the children into families. Truly we are filled with inexpressible joy knowing we dwell in the shelter of the most High God. We rest in the shadow of the Almighty. He is our refuge and our fortress. We put out trust in Him. He covers us in His wings of love and we find safety in Him. We have opened our hearts to Him and He is our dwelling place. He loves us, He rescues us and commands His angels to surround us. We have called on Jesus. We have acknowledged Him. Trouble has come to our nation, and we have opened our eyes and seen the pain. We have opened our ears to hear the cry of the desperate, and so we drink His cup of suffering. We drink His cup of joy knowing we can be His hands extended in the midst of it all, and knowing He died that there would always be enough.

In this article Heidi exemplifies a Spirit-led pentecostal worldview that has been described as living in the subjunctive—the "as if" mode—that includes unlimited spiritual possibilities. In other words, the real world—the world "as it really is"—which so often seems utterly devoid of love, can be transformed through religious experiences and rituals into a sacred space in which Heaven seems to invade earth, at least momentarily. This is important for motivating people like Heidi, who are not blind to the often brutal realities that cause suffering but are instead able to see past the deficits of the immediate and live in the eternal moment of love. Our interviews suggest that this ability is an important source of hope that a better world is possible.[3] This blend of reality and transcendent vision represents a process that we have called "seeing beyond circumstances."[4]

Seeing beyond Circumstances

Heidi Baker, arguably an exemplar among exemplars, is willing to be reduced to the "simplicity of love" in a way that has made her "God's little fool."[5] *Compelled by Love*, the title of the book in which she described how to change the world through the "simple power of love," well reflects her life calling and ministry.[6] Through participating in a loving relationship with God, Heidi has learned how to "see beyond circumstances,"[7] as recounted in the above narrative when a nongovernmental organization (NGO) departed in fear and failed to distribute their resources to the starving masses. Heidi's response to the call to benevolent service is simultaneously self-sacrificial and self-affirming. Hers is a sacrificial "cup of suffering" in the sense that Heidi has repeatedly exposed herself to personal harm in the form of violence, life-threatening diseases (which she continues to contract quite frequently), and material poverty. Paradoxically, her ministry is also self-affirming in that her sacrificial risk taking in the service of a higher cause has allowed her to taste of the "cup of joy" in ways that few of us can begin to imagine.

We see in Heidi's story a central finding of our study which differentiates our attempt to get at the heart of religion (i.e., the experience of divine love that fosters benevolence) from other studies of the external shell of religion, or its structural patterns.[8] Knowing God's love is a powerful force for most of our respondents that can transform the pain of suffering into peace and joy. Their sense of life's meaning and purpose, as discussed in an earlier chapter, is intimately intertwined with their experiences of a loving God. If they had a strong feeling that they should pursue one particular course of action over another and they attributed this feeling to a calling from God, then any suffering resulting from faithfulness to the call can be radically redefined. They are indeed "compelled by love" and thus empowered by a subjunctive worldview to see joy even in the midst of human suffering and sacrifice. But more than simply seeing reality in a different, more hopeful, light, such people believe that they can draw on God's power (rather than their own abilities) to do the impossible. As Bill Johnson, another one of our exemplars, puts it, "It isn't until we break into the realm of impossibilities that we give an accurate demonstration of God's power."[9]

Examples of the compelling force of knowing God's love in response to difficult situations run throughout our interviews. One comes from a pastor we call Ben, who told us how he wept in the parking lot of the university he was attending when he yielded to a call to ministry. He realized that God's call on his life was so overwhelming that he could not put it off until after he completed work on his PhD, a degree that he had coveted for so long. Another exemplar (Nate) had a compelling encounter with Jesus at the foot of his bed, instructing him to get involved in ecumenical work despite the fact that this was prohibited by his particular denomination. He obeyed—initially at great personal and professional cost—but ultimately he found himself on a gratifying path toward a new sense of meaning and purpose. The people we interviewed did not escape suffering in responding to a divine call to serve others; their biographical narratives are often filled with pain that accompanied their faith-filled responses and their reliance on supernatural power to persevere. Recall Herb Daughtry's contention in chapter 3 that God would make his life "meaningful and worthwhile"—he did not expect it to be free of suffering. In fact, he knew that some types of suffering would increase, as when he was arrested for his activism.

Afflictions can be redefined when one is provided with a set of spiritual lenses with which to see beyond the immediate circumstances. This relates to a distinction that Quaker author Parker Palmer made about kinds of suffering: "There are life-giving ways to suffer. . . . If it's your truth, you can't not do it. And that knowledge carries you through. But there's another kind of suffering that is simply and purely death. It's death in life, and that is a darkness to be worked through to find the life on the other side."[10] The actions of those who participate in a sustained practice of godly love cannot be fully understood without appreciating the centrality of a divine call as a means to self-transcendence, life-giving ways to suffer, and ultimately, "truly living." When one is armed with a sense of purpose that transcends narrow interests, the unbearable becomes bearable.

An exemplar whom we call Warner provides yet another illustration. In telling the story of his best friend, who had recently died of cancer despite prayer and the best possible medical treatment, Warner explained how his response to the loss was shaped by living daily "in the love of the Father":

I think most of the struggle I get from people who struggle—whether it's financially, losing their job, house, whatever—is that you feel like you're in those things apart from God. The greater tragedy that they're dealing with is God's abandonment. And then they finally see that, no, God hasn't abandoned me, God is bigger than my joblessness. God's bigger than my cancer. God will continue to provide, to open doors. Everything about our lives is not meant to reach fulfillment in this stage; this is the path to something so much greater. When people live in that reality, even their own tragedies are not as significant because they're not alone. And God will have purpose in redefining our lives inside that reality.

Matt checked his understanding of what Warner had said by interjecting: "So really it's not about feeling less pain, it's about understanding the pain in a different way." Warner responded by elaborating on the nature of the "reality" of which he spoke:

And sharing the pain, with a greater reality. That's like Paul, when he talks about sharing in the sufferings of Christ. When something bad happens to me, I don't feel like I'm in it alone. I'm not. And he has faced this in greater ways than I ever will. That's why I'm in it with him. So, I'm good. Not always happy, not always thrilled, but I'm not alone. And that makes all the difference.

Living in a dynamic relationship with an all-loving and all-powerful God has the potential to permeate all aspects of a believer's life. It redefines common assumptions of costs and benefits from "What's in this for me?" to "How does this fit into a bigger plan?" It also has the power to transform negative self-concepts into positive ones as it imprints daily life with deeper purpose that is tied to a divine calling. As Warner argues, the realization that one is "not alone" is central for godly love as a lived experience, and this "makes all the difference." This theme that "God will take care of everything, no matter what happens," emerged repeatedly in our interviews. This sense of divine providence makes it easier to understand why many of our interviewees took significant personal risks in pursuing their vocations. For some it was in terms of risking bodily harm but more often it involved giving up financial security or a "normal" life while partaking in the cup of suffering experienced by others.

We introduced Karen, a hospital chaplain who now serves in a retirement center, in the last chapter as we demonstrated how prophetic prayer operates in her life. Karen has received a public award for her years of tireless service in a context of chronic illness and dying—a situation that tends to breed exhaustion and burnout. Using the language of the call and its attendant duties, she explains, "When I'm called to duty, I go. In any given week it can vary from sixty, seventy, to eighty hours. I'm always 'on,' and the Lord gives me strength for that....I sometimes say that I am drained or tired, but the Lord picks me up the next day just as revived as I was when I first started. It's just God giving me the energy." The never-ending suffering that surrounds her affects her tender spirit, yet it is mitigated by her ability to see beyond circumstances. In one particularly memorable example of seeing beyond circumstances, Karen described a situation involving a young woman suffering from multiple sclerosis. The middle-aged woman was brought to the nursing home after her husband maliciously knocked her out of her wheelchair, "took everything that they owned, took everything out of the bank and left her there in the middle of the floor." The circumstances of this incident are both tragic and bewildering, but Karen was able to see beyond them to imagine an opportunity for good:

> There's a lot of anger involved in it because you just want justice. Where I go is, "Thank you, Lord, for bringing her here so now we can try to take care of her and help her pick up her broken pieces." But there are moments, often weekly, that I think, "Why, God?" I do believe God's shoulders are big enough for the "why." He knows my mind is not big enough to understand everything. The Bible says, "My thoughts are not your thoughts, neither are my ways, your ways." And so I do the best with making meaning and bringing light to the situation that I can and asking God to give me that light. Another thing that is very pivotal is the heart of gratitude: being thankful for what I have and where I am and what I'm doing. God sustains me. Once I get back to the grateful part, all these other things just sort of fly away from me.

Karen's "heart of gratitude" emerges from the divine call to which she has responded, and it helps sustain her when the "why" questions get too big. Regardless of the circumstances, God is there to "bring light" (i.e., develop something good out of a bad situation) to enable her to see beyond the immediate situation. She is grateful that she has been empowered by her relationship with God to be the human face of (God's) love for people in seemingly loveless situations. In the subjunctive mode of being, God is always present despite the illusion of his absence.

Beyond Suffering: More Empirical Findings

The Godly Love National Survey (GLNS) provides some statistical clues for better understanding how experiences of God's personal love facilitate the ability to see beyond circumstances. Based on our qualitative analysis of interviews with exemplars, seeing beyond circumstances is clearly an important by-product of divine love that affects benevolent service. It sustains them when the going gets tough and the secular NGOs bail out, and it provides direction when the needs of others become overwhelming. Seeing beyond circumstances can be viewed as a major chord that makes melody with other minor chords, some of which were measured by the GLNS. These survey items reflect a model of holistic healing that Margaret and a colleague developed from a 1997 survey of pentecostal revivalists, which provided us with a framework for analyzing the healing measures used in the GLNS.[11] Underlying pentecostal healing beliefs and practices is a holistic worldview that goes beyond "curing" of illness and disease to include both physical and spiritual components. "Healing," as understood by many pentecostals and other spiritual healing groups, is thus somewhat different from and more encompassing than a common use of the term, where it is equated with "curing" medical maladies. It differs from the common usage in at least two important ways: (1) in its understanding of "healing" as a juxtaposition of the ordinary and the sacred and (2) in its holistic approach, the way it encompasses soul, spirit, mind, and body. At the center of the model is "spiritual healing"—experiences that can be conceptualized as ones of primary and secondary spiritual transformations that position the person in a "right relationship with God." Experiencing the presence and power of God is thus not only the heart of healing in many spiritual healing traditions, but it may well be an essential factor in what we call "seeing beyond circumstances." It mitigates the sting of setbacks, suffering, and other difficulties with the hope that promises God "will wipe every tear from their eyes. There will be no more death or mourning or crying or pain, for the old order of things has passed away" (Revelation 21:4).

To partially test whether there is a relationship between holistic healing and the experience of divine love, we selected three measures of healing from the GLNS and used multiple regression analysis to determine whether they were statistically related to the Divine Love scale. We also included six demographic measures—age, income, education, gender, race, and pentecostal identity—as controls. The holistic healing measures were threefold: an Anger with God scale (honest expressions of anger being part of the holistic healing process),[12] a single question about experiences of divine physical healing from a disease or injury, and another single item about inner or emotional healing from a psychological condition or damaged relationship. The results of the analysis were statistically significant. *They showed that experiencing a divine physical healing, anger with God, and inner/emotional healing all contributed to strengthening the statistical profile of those who had frequent experiences of divine love.*[13] Those who scored high on experiences of divine love did get angry with God and were likely to report experiences of physical healing and inner/emotional healing, and inner healing was the most powerful predictor. With these important statistical findings as a guide, we continue to use our interviews with our exemplars to put flesh and blood on these dry statistical bones. As we do so, a clearer picture emerges of the vital relationship between spiritual healing and knowing divine love.

Anger toward God

Our very first interview alerted us to the possibility that being angry with, disappointed in, or frustrated with God could be positively linked to a loving relationship with the divine. Roger's designation as a "pastor's pastor" mirrored success for those who know him, as he sought to bring about a greater understanding between religious groups in his community. But at the time of the interview Roger seemed haunted by his personal evaluation of his life as a failure; in his mind his efforts to follow the divine call on his life seemed futile. He was emotionally stalled by the roadblocks that had developed over the years that kept him from pursuing his perceived primary calling as a revivalist in a denomination that had lost its vitality. His being forced out of a pastoral position several years before our interview was followed by a new job as an executive fund-raiser in a denominational organization, a position that he believed would be an important step in the furthering of his divine call. Despite Roger's assertion that he had performed beyond expectations, he was summarily fired, leaving him and his wife without a home, with no job offers in sight, and living off his savings. At the time of our interview he was still trying to see beyond the loss and rejection, despite the kindness of local pastors and the financial support of a family member that allowed him to pursue a modified vision of bringing meaningful dialogue and prayer to local church pastors.

As we noted in the last chapter, Roger is wary of people who feel "fuzzy with God but it never seems to move them to do anything" and reports that he is more likely to experience God's love through people than through hours of prayer. Roger told us the story of an encounter between Lee Strobel (a reporter who converted to Christianity) and Charles Templeton (the late Christian apologist who turned agnostic and was suffering from early stages of Alzheimer's disease when Strobel interviewed him) to help us understand how he (Roger) was feeling about God. According to a story circulating in the 1990s,[14] Templeton reportedly broke down and wept as he spoke of his utmost respect for Jesus, but quickly recovered as he said "enough of that—I miss him." Roger then related his struggle to that account between Christian reporter and converted atheist: "And that's the way I feel about God. I love him, in spite of trying to make sense of all this craziness. And I always will, but I still get mad at him. And I'm sure he goes, 'That's okay; I get mad at you too.' But I do miss him."

The clear majority of our interviewees gave little indication of experiencing what spiritual directors would call a "dark night of the soul" that was affecting Roger at the time of his interview, a condition that may have been confounded by clinical depression for which he was receiving therapy. But Roger's open confession was a catalyst for our including questions about anger toward God in the GLNS. Our preliminary inquiry was fueled by the research interest of Julie Exline, a psychologist and a member of our research team. Although we were uncertain as to whether or not anger with God would have any impact on experiencing divine love, we leaned toward hypothesizing that if there were an effect, it would be negative. What we found was that a sizable minority of survey respondents (at least occasionally) felt anger toward God (30 percent), concluded that God was punishing them (24 percent), or believed that God's actions are unfair (30 percent). (Of those who admitted to such feelings, a clear majority said it happened only "once in a while.") These findings were not unexpected. The big surprise for us was the seemingly paradoxical relationship between anger and love. Those who scored higher on the Divine Love scale were also the ones who were most likely to admit having negative feelings toward God.

Our interviews with exemplars often included follow-up conversations in order to think through questions that would emerge during analysis. In light of our most interesting finding about anger and divine love, Margaret called Karen (whose story is recounted above) and asked her to meet for coffee. When Margaret shared our "big" finding and asked for Karen's interpretation, Karen showed little surprise. She waited for a moment and then replied: "See those people at the table over there?" Margaret nodded her head. "Well, I don't know them and they are unlikely to be able to make me angry. I am not in a relationship with them and I don't expect anything from them. On the other hand, my family and close friends can hurt me—and I might on occasion feel anger toward them." Karen then continued, "Getting angry with God isn't my thing. [She laughed as she demonstrated anger toward the heavens, bending her elbows and shaking her fists]: God is so big and I am like this little ant sitting up and shaking its front legs at God. He can take it, but it is pretty funny! When I have on very rare occasion gotten angry with him I felt like a big God was lovingly looking down at this little ant, asking, 'What *are* you doing?'"

Our statistics suggested that anger with God could represent a temporary block in the flow of human experiences of divine love, but once unblocked such feelings may actually deepen the relationship. Psychologist Julie Exline's recent research on anger with God seems to support this observation. When Margaret and Julie got together to talk about our findings, Julie responded to the GLNS preliminary findings with results from her own research. She said, "On the surface, it seems that those who have a close relationship with God often think that anger with God is wrong. But when you take a closer look at the data, the message is that as long as the relationship with God is not severed, then anger is okay."[15] Julie's work supports the GLNS findings that being angry with God is relatively common, and feeling anger with God and feeling the love of God are not mutually exclusive.[16] The problem comes when someone feels—often because of the negative assessment offered by a pastor or friend—that it is wrong to feel anger toward God. When friends are supportive (saying something like "I've been there" rather than rendering negativity and judgment) anger often signals a deepening relationship with God.[17] Julie went on to say: "Typically people were supportive, and those receiving supportive responses were more likely to approach God with their feelings. Those receiving unsupportive responses were more likely to report that they tried to suppress the anger, and they were also more likely to exit their relationship with God (saying he does not exist or to rebel against God)."[18] Julie then succinctly summarized her findings and those of her colleagues: "Taken together, these studies suggest that anger toward God is an important dimension of religious and spiritual experience, one that is measurable, widespread, and related to adjustment across various contexts and populations."[19]

Steve Mory is a renowned Christian psychiatrist and has learned from personal experience how anger with God can give way to a deeper relationship.[20] During an interview with Margaret, Steve described an incident that occurred when he was in his midteens, a spiritual encounter that helped to shape his life and ministry. His beloved church had just experienced a major split at the same time that his girlfriend (who would later become his wife) broke off their relationship. Steve provided the following account of the feelings and questions that welled up within him:

> I remember that I stayed up all night. I was angry. I wanted to talk to God.... Although I was angry, he wasn't angry. So if you ask if I see an angry God or distant God. No, I think in some way I knew him as a father then, although not nearly so much as I began to know him later.... And I knew that he was wise and caring and loving. I also knew that we weren't. And that was my question: "Why are we not like you? Why is it that the people teach me about the love of God (and they seem like they had it at the time) but all the sudden something blows up and they're at each other's throat? What's going on?..." Then I said, "I'm not leaving this room." (I got out of bed; I was in the corner of my bedroom. I was seventeen.) "I'm not leaving this room until you show up." And that would be an unusual thing for a person in my Baptist church to say. But somebody showed up. There was a light in the corner of the room and a figure and all the sudden I felt peace. I didn't hear any audible voice or any answers to my prayer. I just felt like he showed up. And I just felt peaceful like, oh, okay. And this felt very good, and then I just went to bed. I think I probably should've tried to talk. I didn't know if it was an angel, I still don't know if that was an angel or if it was the Holy Spirit. It was just a light, figure of light, not a face or I mean, it was just a calm of light. The peace that came to me was very real.

Although Steve describes this experience as being "very real" and "very significant," it was not one that he felt comfortable sharing until years later. "I didn't tell anybody for years. I don't think it would be part of the testimonies in the church I grew up in." This experience of an angry teenager with his loving God provided a foundation as Steve continued to grow his awareness of the role the divine presence can play in the midst of human suffering and struggle. His story provides a good transition toward taking a closer look at another healing measure used in our statistical equation, namely, inner or emotional healing.

Inner or Emotional Healing

Divine inner healing can be understood as an experience with God—directly or through other people—that leads to a lasting change in well-being and a deeper spiritual life. Although Margaret had done previous preliminary research on divine inner or emotional healing (sometimes called "healing of memories") with select samples of pentecostals where there is a clear history of the practice, to the best of our knowledge this question had not been included in a national survey until the GLNS. We once again were surprised by our findings that showed this healing phenomenon extended far beyond those respondents who claimed a pentecostal identity, with 61 percent of the total sample acknowledging that they had had such an experience. Approximately half (48 percent) of those who claimed an inner healing experience said it was a more or less regular occurrence, while the rest of those who had experienced inner healing (52 percent) said they experienced it only "once in a while." Results of multiple regression analysis that included our three healing measures showed that experiences of inner healing demonstrated a strong statistical relationship with the Divine Love scale—stronger than any demographic indicator and stronger than feeling anger toward God or reporting a divine physical healing.[21] The sparse research that does exist on pentecostals and inner healing can cast light on these findings from the GLNS.

In her study of neo-pentecostal revivalists, Margaret found that 78 percent of pilgrims to the revival in Toronto surveyed in 1995 claimed they had received an "inner or emotional" healing during their visit to the revival site. In a follow-up study of these same respondents two years later, 94 percent of those who claimed an inner healing indicated that they remained healed of the emotional trauma(s) that had afflicted them.[22] Margaret described inner healing as practiced among the revivalists as follows:[23]

> "Inner healing," also commonly known as "healing of memories" or "emotional healing," traces its recent origins to the writings of an Episcopal laywoman, Agnes Sanford in the early 1950s. Unlike many Christian counseling techniques that focus on the cognitive (especially an application of the Bible to particular problems), inner healing has been more holistic with its focus on emotions as well as cognition.... Numerous models of healing of memory prayer have developed over the years, many if not most within the larger P/C [pentecostal] community. They all stress an emphasis on a holistic restoration of the person with an expectation that Jesus Christ will function as healer and deliverer.

In another study of Pentecostals, Margaret and her colleague John Green conducted surveys that included a question on inner healing in over twenty

Assemblies of God churches. (John would later become a team member in the Flame of Love Project and play a significant role in designing and overseeing the GLNS.) Ninety-three percent of the nearly two thousand congregants surveyed claimed to have personally experienced a "divine inner or emotional healing." For 36 percent of the respondents it was an experience they had nearly daily. As with the GLNS respondents, those who more frequently experienced divine inner healing were also more likely to report stronger and more frequently senses of the divine presence.[24] Although these statistics are interesting, they are unable to provide the rich descriptions we found in our interviews. Blending his training as a psychiatrist with his personal experiences, Dr. Steve Mory has given us invaluable insight into the GLNS finding that experiences of inner healing are likely to be an integral part of the spiritual journey of nearly all who report deep and ongoing experiences of God's love.

Steve was president of the psychiatry section of the Christian Medical and Dental Association when he came into contact with a colleague who was familiar with the practice of inner healing. Steve described him as not being "from the same background as I was. I was from an evangelical background, but Lee was a Pentecostal—from an inner-city African American Pentecostal church—but Lee was also a psychiatrist, well trained." Steve told Margaret of the clinical depression from which he had suffered for years:

> It's hard to explain! And I'm a psychiatrist. But I had it treated for years with antidepressants, multiple doctors, psychiatrists. I had therapy with a psychoanalyst when I was in residency training. I had Christian counseling, Christian therapy. Everything that one would do in a bio-psychosocial and spiritual realm—I did all that I could do and knew to do, but the depression was only partially treated. It was more severe from age twenty-five through age forty. A fifteen-year period of relatively severe depression, never hospitalized and never suicidal, but enough that it probably should've disabled me. I would just come home with no energy. Certain times I would come home for a couple months and go episodic, the way that recurrent rage depression is. But, it did get healed. I would say it dramatically, powerfully healed at some point. Is that what you're asking?

Margaret encouraged Steve to continue his story, and he went on to describe what happened through the intervention of his colleague, Lee:

Lee told me, "Steve, we're doing this stuff, this inner healing. It's a lot better than only medication management psychopharmacology. It's a lot better than doing therapy, traditional and secular therapy models. And it's a lot better than even doing Christian counseling, what most people call Christian counseling which involves maybe some scripture verses to help reorient the client. This is like healing. This is like powerful. I'm getting some good results; you gotta do it." And I'm thinking, "I don't want that!"

But then Lee arranged a conference at his church on inner healing and this whole depression was so healed. I was filled with the joy of the Lord! And it's been fifteen years. There's not a shred of depression—never! I have this opposite gift now—I got almost too much joy. (But it's not a problem; I'm being a bit facetious.) But I'm glad to have the joy of the Lord and I don't mean as a giddy happiness—I mean a deep, abiding joy, the sense of his presence. He healed it. He came and he healed it, every dark place where depression was.

After his own healing occurred, Steve found that he could pray successfully for the inner healing of others. He described cathartic physical manifestations that may occur as he prays: "I blast people with the joy of the Lord! It just, they fall over, I mean it's just, the joy of the Lord just shoots out of me sometimes when I do conferences or when I pray for healing for people." Steve added that when he prays for those with depression, "not always, but frequently, depression gets healed almost instantly. It just disappears." Steve and his wife, Lorraine, speak and pray at conferences in which they teach and pray for healing, also eager to see others being become God's instruments for healing others. They call their three-part message "teaching, healing, and impartation." It is their desire "to impart to others the same gifts of healing for the whole person, to bring all into the presence of God, where there is fullness of joy."

Many other interviewees had similar stories to share with us. George, a Catholic leader active in the social justice movement, describes an embodied experience of pentecostal healing prayer that came about quite unexpectedly, rather than as part of the normal Catholic prayer ritual. This experience involved dancelike movements and, in George's words, "ended up reconnecting my spirit and my soul":

I was spinning and doing this and that. I was following the energy of God in how I was receiving what…it was coming in the way it was coming in. And I told [my wife] later, this is going to look goofy to you or crazy, but I got to tell you, and I've often said to her, "Look how much better I am, I obviously got healed there."...[This was] an inner healing of connection of self and psyche and soul and body.

George had "no foreknowledge" that this literal dance with the divine was going to occur, but he did note that his suffering was a precursor, stating, "I was vulnerable enough. I was open enough. I was broken enough, maybe broken in the sense of being able to receive." As a result, he experienced God "as a healer that was opening me back up and his energy and light were coming back into me and that I felt more alive, centered, grounded, strong."

Unlike Steve and George, Paul Alexander experienced his inner healing through another person rather than directly from an interaction with God.[25] Despite the high degree of care-love he received from his parents as a child, Paul's religious and nationalist upbringing left him "quite judgmental," with a "hard-core belief in war and profit" and "American exceptionalism." Graduate studies in theology and interactions with his wife (also a Pentecostal) would later soften his judgmental perspective. As Paul tells it, "This ongoing relationship with Deborah...that sort of expanded my understanding of [God's] grace." Although a born-again Christian since age five, Paul told us that he experienced getting in touch with God's grace and love through the compassion of his wife as being "saved":

I just got saved. I have never actually been saved until now. This is what salvation is. I'm saved. It was that big of a deal that I use that language. You just saved me, Deborah. I was filled with the Holy Spirit, spoke in tongues from twelve on up and I'd been "saved" since five, but...talking to Deborah and having this change, I *felt* saved. I felt really [he sighed deeply] delivered.

Salvation thus took on a new meaning for Paul around age twenty-one or twenty-two, which he told us shifted his conception of a judgmental God as he "gave up the God of wrath" and the legalism that ruled his youth in favor of an image of God that included greater grace and compassion. The shifting image of God coincided with his emotional healing. In other words, his holistic inner healing—which he refers to as his "salvation"—included a more compassionate way of being in the world, a new image of God, and a powerful emotional catharsis.

Relationships with significant others have profoundly shaped the experiences of inner healing for some other exemplars as well, including Anne Beiler. The forgiveness of her husband Jonas for her infidelity shattered the shell she had created around her emotions beginning with her early years as an Amish child. According to this account in the *Washington Post*, after she confessed her infidelities Jonas responded with self-giving love, telling her:

> I just want you to promise me one thing.... I want you to be happy. So promise me you won't leave me in the middle of the night with a note on the dresser. If you need to leave, we'll plan it together. I'll help you pack your bags, help you find a place to live, but you have to take the girls.

According to the article, "It was the last bit that broke through to her, Anne remembers, penetrating her own wall of self-loathing. 'I felt overcome by the fact that he thought I was a good enough mom to take the kids with me,' she says, crying hard at the memory."[26]

In his interview with Margaret, Jonas remarked that Anne's (Beachy) Amish background—her "cultural grid," to use the language of our second chapter—contributed to her inability to experience God's forgiveness, contrary to his own socialization experience as Old Order Amish:

> Beachy people tend to walk this tightrope that is steep in guilt and condemnation. They're trying to live a life of perfection, not applying a whole lot of any grace. Then as soon as they make a mistake, they're just guilt prone to the hilt....
>
> That's what kept her so guilt-ridden, because she feels like she failed and committed too many things and God's not gonna forgive her. There's no grace. Then once she understood God's forgiveness, she couldn't forgive herself. She was really not set free until somewhere around 2003 when she forgave herself.

Jonas recalls a very different background in the Old Order Amish, where he reports that forgiveness in his community was virtually a reflex. During his interview with Margaret, Jonas shared his parents' reaction to the death of his brother at the hands of a careless truck driver:

> My parents reassured him that there was no ill feelings on their part about what happened. It's just an accident and we'll make the most of

it. Out of that conversation, they agreed to meet every so often for dinner, which they did once or twice a year for several years. A few years later, this man and his family, his wife and family, opened up a greenhouse business. Every spring they would come and pick my dad up, my mom and dad up, because they're Amish and couldn't travel, and take them to their greenhouse and say, "Pick out whatever you need to get your garden going this spring, flower gardens and stuff like that and we'll give that to you...."

"Forgiveness plus," you know, but that's the way the Amish do it. They will go out of their way to make friends with the people that were a part of their disaster or unfortunate situation. So that's why when this school shooting[27] happened, people asked me how the Amish were going to respond? It was easy for me to say that they're gonna forgive.

People would say, "Is that real?" and I'd say, "Yeah, it's as real as the day is long." There's no doubt in my mind that that's real. I mean, they'll tell you that we're going to grieve and we're going to go through that process just like anybody else, but first of all we're going to forgive. And I think that did influence how I was able to forgive Anne because I watched my father forgive some heavy-duty stuff.

In Anne's telling of the story to Matt about the time she confessed her infidelity to Jonas, she described her reactions as follows:

I felt the presence of Jesus in my room that night.... I mean, I didn't know what was going to happen. Am I going to leave Jonas? I just thought, "How can you love me this way? How can you love me?"

The only response [from Jonas] that I had at that point was, "I do. I do." I just don't think that we get it. And as Jonas began to love me again, first of all through my sexual abuse and now through my affair, I don't know how to explain that kind of love. I don't know how to explain that.

For Anne, the healing power of Jonas's unconditional love was connected to a felt presence of Jesus. Years of guilt and shame were not necessarily washed away, but she perceived a way to move forward together as a couple. In many of our interviews, inner healing was closely tied to forgiveness. As the individual experienced forgiveness it became easier to forgive others. The narratives we have presented demonstrate that some experience divine inner healing without the presence of other people, while for Anne the experience of Jonas's unconditional love was primary. Regardless, the larger point is that inner healing had implications for others in an individual's social network.

Experiences of forgiveness among those respondents to the GLNS who reported divine inner healing were widespread. Nearly half (49 percent) indicated they were able to self-forgive as part of their inner healing experience. Almost as many had the experience of forgiving God for things that had happened to them (41 percent). Even more were able to forgive others who had hurt them (58 percent), had family relationships restored (54 percent), or were delivered from fear and anxiety (53 percent). Although inner healing appears to take on a wide variety of faces, it is clearly an important factor in experiencing the love of God.

Physical Healing

Nearly half of Americans believe in and practice prayer for physical healing. The National Center for Complementary and Alternative Medicine (NCCAM) has reported that the use of prayer is one of the leading complementary health remedies. For example, a survey of more than thirty-one thousand adults on complementary and alternative healing practices found that 45 percent had used prayer for health reasons; 43 percent had prayed for their own health; almost 25 percent had had others pray for them; and almost 10 percent had participated in a prayer group for their health.[28] The GLNS survey similarly found that 43 percent of all respondents said they do, at least on occasion, "experience divine healing of a physical illness." This figure aligns well with those who reported that they used prayer for health reasons (45 percent) and who prayed for their own health (43 percent) in the NCCAM survey. Belief in healing prayer appears to be even more extensive than personal experiences and practice. A 2003 *Newsweek* poll found 72 percent of Americans believing that "praying to God can cure someone—even if science says the person doesn't stand a chance."[29] This finding reflects an earlier Gallup Poll showing 82 percent of Americans believing "in the healing power of personal prayer," and 77 percent agreeing that "God sometimes intervenes to cure people who have a serious illness."[30]

Based on these survey statistics, including those of the GLNS, it is safe to say that prayer for healing is a *common practice* in America. Actual reports of divine healing, however, are more likely to be made by those who self-identify as pentecostal Christians. For example, a survey conducted by the Pew Forum found that 62 percent of US pentecostals—compared with 29 percent of the total population—claimed to have "experienced or witnessed a divine healing of an illness or injury."[31] The GLNS survey findings were similarly striking. Eighty percent of respondents who said they *never* experienced a divine physical healing indicated that they were neither pentecostal nor charismatic, as compared with only 20 percent of self-identified pentecostals.[32] Using multiple regression, we sought to profile persons who commonly experience divine healing of a physical illness by looking at common demographics, including pentecostal identity. Such persons are more likely to identify as pentecostal and to be nonwhite; they are somewhat more likely to be older and to have less annual income.[33]

Experiences of divine physical healing are encouraged and celebrated by many communities, particularly those sharing pentecostal and ethnic/racial cultural grids. Not everyone in our sample has had the benefit of this community support. For example, Pat is a Mennonite pastor who experienced a pentecostal-style Spirit baptism at a revival associated with the Jesus movement in the 1970s. This event is central to both her faith and works, but it is not fostered within her own religious tradition. She has spoken in tongues only that one time. It is unthinkable to do so in the congregation that she leads. Similarly, although pentecostals emphasize divine healing, her tradition does not. When Matt asked if she had ever experienced a divine healing, Pat initially said no. But then later in the interview she remembered that in fact she had been dramatically and miraculously healed by God after forty years of suffering with a debilitating illness! Divine healing is not talked about in her tradition, so she had difficulty recalling this striking example from her own life. Whereas some of our interviewees were clearly eager to share the news that miracles are real and can be experienced today, Pat is not. In fact, her interview centered more on religious teachings with regard to service of others that on spiritual affect. Pat seems to be experiencing religious burnout, as she has recently pulled back from a decade-long commitment as a leader of a social justice organization to focus on the comparatively solitary pursuit of organic gardening.

Bishop E. Josephus Johnson II was raised within a black Pentecostal culture far removed from Pat's Mennonite background. He had a born-again experience in which he "accepted the Lord" when he was eight years old that he described as a "dramatic" and "glorious": "The Holy Spirit knocked me to the floor and rolled me up under those chairs and pews, even though I had never heard of or seen such a thing."[34] Memories of his childhood faith would morph into disenchantment as he became increasingly troubled by the legalism and elitism of what he called "extreme Pentecostalism." As a young pastor he would abandon his Pentecostal heritage and replace it with "extreme fundamentalism" that left little room for divine healing. He became involved in a well-known largely white fundamentalist organization—one that he described as believing that "all spiritual manifestations had permanently ceased with the passing of the last of the twelve apostles." He became a spokesperson for the organization that sponsored his regional radio program. The bishop reported that he "looked at Pentecostals as mindless automatons who were merely reacting to their emotions and experiences with no biblical basis whatsoever."[35] Although his outspoken disdain for Pentecostalism fit well with this new affiliation, the relationship was strained when he experienced a secondary spiritual transformation—one that he calls his "resurrection." It would take him back to his Pentecostal roots (and cost him his position in the fundamentalist network). He calls his post-"resurrection" theological stance "Bapticostalism," a blend of cognition and affect that has once again made room for mystery and miracles. There was the important divine nudge that had Josephus seeking answers to questions about God, and also human instruments who participated in this "resurrection" (including some retired Catholic professors and a teacher on Hinduism). He summarized his reflections on his change in worldview that now makes room for divine healing as follows:

> All of a sudden, my Pentecostal background began to make sense. It never made sense before because they [Pentecostals] could never explain it. They [the Catholic professors and the Hindu teacher] began to explain Pentecostalism in terms of alternate states of consciousness. When you say *altered* state of consciousness, religious people start to freak out on you. That sounds like something that's weird, that's outside of you. But when you say, *alternate* states of consciousness, we've changed the wording because there's alternate reality and real reality. . . . Alternate reality is every bit as real as normal reality, maybe more, but we in America do not deal with alternate reality. We are a rationalistic society, and we don't deal with those kinds of things. There are other countries, the Bible, biblical countries—they deal with alternate states of consciousness just like it's normal.

Given his new cultural grid it is not surprising that Bishop Josephus is critical of what he regards as extremes, especially those evangelicals he sees situated at one end of the continuum and some pentecostals at the other. He notes that "evangelicals really don't have any place for emotion because they are scientific," going on to qualify his position by saying this is not what they would actually say but it is what is "really going on underneath." As he sees it:

There is no place for real miracles. So if something happens, I explain it away scientifically. So, for instance, people come in: "Can you pray for me?" I pray for you, you go back, they can't see the cancer anymore. "Well, perhaps the X-ray wasn't right. Perhaps something was off. You know, maybe they just thought they saw something." We're going to find a way because science says there is an explanation for this. One lady came in and she had a team of doctors look at her and said, "You have cancer. You have a mass. We need to operate." She asked me if I would pray for her. Certainly, I will pray for you. I believe in healing. I don't believe that God heals everybody; I don't believe I control it. But I believe that God heals. She went back to the doctor, and then she came back to me excited. "They can't find it. It's gone. They can't find it." Now, if it was one doctor maybe we could say that maybe the doctor made a mistake. They said, "No, no, we didn't make a mistake. It was there. We all saw it. We just can't explain what happened to it." Well, no, you can't explain what happened, that's what a miracle is. God has intervened supernaturally. The problem with that is, then we want to patent that and make God intervene every time. But we don't control when he intervenes and when he doesn't intervene. We ought to pray as if it all depends upon him and then leave it to him.

As reflected in the above statement, the bishop is wary not only about "extreme fundamentalism" but also of "extreme pentecostalism," particularly the tenets of the so-called Word Faith movement. Those involved in the Word Faith movement assert that God always cures ailments and diseases in response to prayer. Once prayed for, the sick person is believed by proponents of Word Faith to have been immediately healed and any remaining physical signs of illness or disease are illusion. All one need do to align physical signs of illness with faith is to continue to claim the healing. The physical evidence will follow if faith is rightly aligned. Bishop Josephus is wary of such teachings and goes on to say:

But that's where Pentecostals get into deep, deep trouble. I've had it in my church. I had one lady not too long ago when her husband had cancer she was going to a church that was very Word Faith. She's had visions. She's had dreams and everything that her husband is going to get well. I looked at him and I don't claim to be the greatest prophet in the world, but I think he's going to die.

But I wouldn't tell her that because she couldn't handle that. So I just walked with them. When he died, I had to literally put this family back together. Now they're angry: "I don't know why God would promise me something and not deliver." First of all, I don't know if God promised you that. I know you feel that he did, but there's nothing in the Bible that says every time you get cancer, God's going to heal you.

Bill Johnson—cited earlier in this chapter as he challenged believers to "break into the realm of impossibilities"—would agree with Bishop Josephus on the normalcy of an alternate reality. While he too would be wary of some of the tactics of Word Faith, he pushes further than the bishop does with his pentecostal possibility thinking. He teaches that if believers were really able to usher in God's kingdom on earth (as prayed in the Lord's Prayer), there would be no illness on earth, just as there is no disease in heaven. Of course, God's perfect kingdom is not yet here, but through prayerful action humans can make strides toward it. As a fifth-generation pastor on his father's side and fourth-generation on his mother's, Bill "grew up hearing of the great moves of God"[36]—stories of revival, Spirit baptism, and healing that left a marked impact on him. The revival fires that spread across the globe in the 1990s would torch his congregation in Redding, California, further convincing him that a life of miracles is a "normal Christian life." Bethel Church Redding would become a flagship for many who would seek to keep the revival fires burning not simply for individual transformation but to transform communities.

As we saw in an earlier chapter, Steve Witt's life and ministry was affected by the same revival movement as Bill Johnson's, providing the foundation for an eventual alignment of Steve's churches with Bill Johnson and Bethel Church in Redding. Steve recently changed the name of his congregations in northeastern Ohio to Bethel Church Cleveland as he joined the growing network of Bethel churches in the United States. These congregations are committed to revival, by which they mean "the personal, regional, and global expansion of God's kingdom through His manifest presence."[37] God's kingdom, for Bill and Steve, involves an alternate reality similar to that described by Bishop Josephus. Leaders at Bethel teach that a heavenly reality is invading the earth, with the potential for changing lives and communities. Health and divine healing are an integral part of this coming kingdom.

During his interview with us, Steve (skillfully blending together the pragmatic and the pentecostal) shared how his congregants were being prepared—"ready for a time that kingdom believers can emerge and advance the kingdom unlike any time before." Their preparation involves going to local events, like Renaissance fairs, country music festivals, and gatherings in neighborhood communities, prophetically praying with strangers, offering them encouraging words, and leading prayers for divine healing. Steve described some recent events where his congregants practiced operating in this alternate world of God's kingdom and power:

> We may be on the outer edges of that right now. So I want to get people ready to move broadly into the streets and into their neighborhoods. How are they gonna do that? Because they've had practice doing it in micro spots before like in the country music festival that we did last month with fifteen thousand people. We ministered to hundreds and hundreds of people—they came into our tent crying and people dying of cancer, people getting ready to have surgery the next day, marriages blowing. I mean, it's a country music festival—dogs being killed, pickup trucks breaking down [he laughed]. And we did three of those major events, went to Slavic Village [an inner-city neighborhood in Cleveland] and did one. We did one in Brunswick two weeks ago at the Johnny Appleseed festival. Very different venues and environments, but the needs were all the same—fear, doubts, concern and we're there. What's that do to our teams? Even if nobody's changed out of those hundreds of people ministered to, our teams are still OJT, on-the-job training.

There is plenty of opportunity for on-the-job training at Bethel churches. A visitor to one of the Bethel Cleveland churches is likely to find that prophetic encouragement and prayer for healing are common, as are testimonies of answered prayer. Through teaching, testimonies, and prayer, members of the congregation are invited to enter into this "alternate world" of spiritual possibilities, engaging in rituals that teach how to "see beyond circumstances." Steve has a personal story that demonstrates his ability to "see beyond circumstances." Consistent with ideas shared in the larger Bethel network, his congregation professes that the kingdom of God is in the making, and divine healing is part of that new paradoxical reality. Bethel Cleveland has declared their churches "cancer-free zones," as Steve himself lives with a form of cancer that resists treatment and could flare up at any time. Steve gave us insight into his thinking about physical healing when Matt asked him if he could give an example of when "you reached your human limits but then this experience of God's love helped you to go beyond that limitation."

There's like a whole lot of those. I know my most recent one was two years ago while I was in Toronto speaking. I received a call about some tests that I had had (it was conveyed through my wife). I was diagnosed with cancer. So in that dark hour I pack things up to come back home, even though I was scheduled to speak another time. My family was falling apart as a result of it. It was just deep and emotional. When you hear the "C word," you immediately think—"Death." So, and it feels imminent. You go through a period of time where you think, I'm dying. So you rethink all of life and all that stuff. But on the way home from Toronto, driving with my son, and somewhere around Buffalo, I just got [he paused], it was a very emotional thing. It usually is when God visits, you know, because he's—how can you stick a finger in a light socket and not feel it? So you, there's a sense of the greatness of heaven coming down upon you. And it was as if he—if I had a garment of worry, he removed it and put on a garment of hope.

Other seemingly serendipitous events would soon happen that continued to build Steve's hope. He shared how his daughter (who was then studying at Bethel School for the Supernatural in Redding, California) "was falling apart" because of the diagnosis. Steve was trying to encourage her to no avail when one of the pastors at Bethel Redding (whom Steve had just met in Toronto a day earlier) "just happened" to pull into the parking lot as the daughter was talking to her father by phone. Steve recounts how astonished he was at that happening:

A guy you just connected with and had a real supernatural encounter the night before now is thousands of miles away and he just happened to be pulling into the parking lot the very time my daughter is talking to me on the phone. He goes up, and it was as if her father was kissing her on the forehead. She just, she sobbed. She called me later on that day she said, "Dad, there was just such peace that came on me. It was a messenger from heaven." So, only God can arrange those kinds of circumstances. You know what, at every point in my life, he's been there for me.

Now I don't understand—I could argue, why did I get the cancer to begin with? Why wasn't God protecting me? Why? I've got people praying. I don't understand. I don't know why, but I know this, that I have a destiny in God. I will fulfill that destiny; and if God in some, in some cosmic decision, makes the decision that this is the point I go to heaven, we'll have that discussion in heaven later on. Why did that happen? Why this time? But, in the midst of it, he's showing me, "I've got the bases covered. I'm taking care of you through this." So, it was incredible.

Steve is far removed from old-time Pentecostalism that once condemned doctors and modern medicine as well as the contemporary blame-the-victim trap that lies in wait for many in the Word Faith movement who are sure that God will always heal if a person truly believes. Steve does teach that God *desires* health and wellness to prevail as the kingdom of God unfolds on earth. He also knows that God continues to be an ever-present reality for him, even in the darkest times. He continued to provide other examples of how divine hope filled his soul during his recent struggle with cancer:

I could go on how God has been there for me. I mean God sent somebody to give me tens of thousands of dollars for alternative treatment during that time where I went in daily and had three to six hours of IV every day for two months at the cost of $10,000 a month. It was totally paid for by someone I did not know, who heard about the situation and suggested I go. And I go down to Mansfield, Ohio, where these Korean women, who happen to be godly Seventh Day Adventists, would pray in a room daily as they were giving me treatment. I'm laying on a table getting treatment, and they're walking around me saying, "Your time is not up. God has called you. God has a destiny for you. You are going to rise up with a testimony." I mean, I didn't know these people existed in Mansfield—Korean women that are godly, fiery nurses that are doing more than just ministering to the physical body. And during that two-month period I wrote a book about hearing God's voice. I had no time to write the book before that. Now when you have an IV in your arm for six hours a day, about all you can do is type. As I'm sitting there, they set me up an office down in their clinic. They gave me computer access. It was incredible. I mean it goes on and on and on. You keep your heart in the right place, that's the most important thing. God will work everything out for good.

A Closing Narrative and Caveat for Scholars of Religion

We heard many other diverse stories about divine healing but found little in them to help with the untangling of the Gordian knot for scientists and clinicians who have tried (largely unsuccessfully) to systematically study healing prayer.[38] Nor did we seek to obtain medical records for reported healings in attempts to verify the stories we were told. Such efforts were beyond the scope of this study and beyond our areas of expertise. However, we are able to attest, based on both the GLNS and our interviews, to the widespread belief and ongoing practice of divine healing in American society.[39] Furthermore, the evidence suggests that experiencing divine healing strengthens a sense of divine love and may thereby affect benevolent outreach. We have been demonstrating a relationship between healing and benevolence, but know little about causation in this fluid and complex process. For example, it is tempting to time-order divine healing—to say that experiences of divine healing increase a sense of divine love, which in turn empowers benevolence. This may be true in many cases, but as the following account reported by Bill Johnson suggests, the Gordian knot will not easily be unraveled by either social science or medical clinical trials.[40]

As if writing a parable for what he calls "the normal Christian life," Bill Johnson recounts the story of a young couple—two of his congregants—who were working in the church's outreach program for street people. As they made plans for their wedding, Ralph and Colleen registered for gifts at Target, and "all they had put on their wish list were coats, hats, gloves, and sleeping bags." They had invited street people to be guests at their wedding and planned to give these gifts to them. Bill shared how during his prewedding meeting with the young couple, they had instructed him "to be sensitive to the Holy Spirit in case he wanted to heal people during the wedding." If Bill had a sense that God might heal, they instructed him "to stop the ceremony and pray for the sick." The wedding day came, and the ceremony proceeded as common in this congregation—an extended time of worship, an evangelistic message, and an opportunity to give one's life to Jesus—with no inner sense to pray for healing. But Bill reported that, even before the wedding began, two or three congregants came to him with "excitement in their voice." They prophetically intuited that there was someone coming who had been diagnosed as having only a couple of years to live. As it turned out, the man who would receive the healing that day had not attended the wedding ceremony. Luke and his wife, Jennifer, street people who were invited to the event, had come only to enjoy a good meal that promised to be part of the celebration. Bill continues:

> Following the meal my brother Bob and I brought them into the church kitchen, asking him [Luke] about the braces on each arm. He told us his problem was carpal tunnel syndrome. I asked him if he

would take the braces off and let me pray. He said yes. He did so, and we laid our hands on his wrists commanding the tunnel to open and all numbness and pain to be gone. He then moved his hands freely, experiencing the healing he had just received.

Luke was also suffering from physical problems resulting from "a horrible accident." Bill then described the healing of Luke's leg and the removal of "all the pain caused by Luke's accident." Bill goes on to recount the next phase of the healing prayer session that was going on in the church's kitchen:

> Next we asked about Luke's neck. He told me that he had cancer and was given a couple of years to live. He went on to explain that the brace was necessary because of the loss of muscles in his neck. The brace held his head in place. By this time a group had gathered, not to watch, but to participate. At my request he removed the brace while another man in our church, a medical doctor, safely held his head. As we began to pray I heard the doctor command new muscles to grow. He called them by their Latin names. I was impressed. When we were finished, Luke turned his head from side to side. All was restored. He then placed his hand on the side of his neck and exclaimed, "The lumps are gone!"

Bill concluded this story by saying Luke's doctor "gave him a clean bill of health," then added, "and the miracles continued long past the physical healing." Luke and Jennifer began "to serve Jesus as their Lord and Savior," and Luke got a job—"the first time he had worked in seventeen years." As if to remind the reader about the holistic nature of health, Bill added, "Jesus heals the whole person."

This is but one of countless stories that we found circulating in churches, religious publications, and media productions across the country of physical healing, often in conjunction with divine inner healing. This story caught our special attention because it occurred explicitly within the context of benevolence as a couple about to be married planned their unusual wedding celebration. As can be seen from this narrative, causal relationships are not easy to untangle. Which comes first—human compassion or a sense of divine empowerment? Where does grace end and human action begin? Or does human action create the context for the infusion of spiritual energy? We are not in a position to validate this story, and it is not clear how that might be accomplished with empirical methods. But whatever the sequence and whether explored through narrative or survey, there appears to be a link between healing and benevolence that warrants more study. And, as pentecostals often say at funerals and as the following memorial reminds us, death is the final "healing."

In Memoriam: A Concluding Reflection on Seeing beyond Circumstances

As we were in the midst of writing this chapter, one of our interviewees passed away. Cancer (diagnosed some six months after our interview) had taken the life of fifty-three-year-old Brenda Burnham Unruh, a county Common Pleas judge who was aptly described as "a woman of deep and unwavering faith in God; a woman of intense caring for others; a woman of great joy and hope; and despite the cancer that took her life, a woman of genuine peace until the end."[41] In reading news articles about her life, her death, and the eighteen hundred people who gathered to honor her memory, we were reminded why we had elected to interview Brenda.

Matt and Margaret reminisced about our delightful exchange with this "petite woman with graceful movements and a head-turning effervescence" that took place in her judicial chambers.[42] But with a surplus of rich interview data from exemplars throughout the country, we had not planned to include Brenda's story in this particular work. Her passing led us back to listening to our taped interview with her and reviewing the transcript. We were struck by Brenda's first words caught as we hastily turned on the recorder after we realized that she had begun the interview without waiting for our first question. She began by talking about the sermon of the then-pastor of the evangelical megachurch to which she belonged—a church that was founded by her fundamentalist grandfather and pastored by her evangelical father (who preached a series of sermons against the charismatic movement in the late 1970s).[43] In speaking of her pastor's recent message to the church, Brenda said: "He did a thing on the Holy Spirit and the tapes are going out the door because, there's a hunger. We're operating without the battery." We saw Brenda as a woman in the midst of a secondary spiritual transformation that would likely in time blend her cognitive evangelical faith with what we have called "pentecostal worldview." Her participation in godly love at the time of the interview seemed more scripted by an evangelicalism that is unfamiliar with the wide range of pentecostal possibilities and wary of much religious experience. Although trying to juxtapose religious cognition and spiritual affect in response to our probing questions, the weight of her testimony appeared to be on the cognitive. Her narrative portrayed a woman who was seeking "to walk out a life of obedience" in response to her understanding of biblical injunctions. Brenda described her move toward prayerful dialogue with the divine as she began to realize a personal, relational God:

> I feel like I'm in a relationship. When I was young, I think it was my parent's faith. And now I feel I have conversations with God. He puts things on my heart. I feel careful about wanting to say he speaks to me, but I always call it that he's putting things on my heart. He's prodding my heart. I feel that, I feel that so many people are missing that. I think he's doing that for all of us, it's not just me.

Studying the Bible and talking to God were more of her modus operandi for prayer than meditation or mysticism was. Later in the interview she added with sincere humility: "And it's hit me more and more, I am really short-changing the relationship when I'm doing all the talking. I'm trying to put more time in to listening. I've still got a ways to go on that."

Brenda's journey continued to unfold during the two and a half years following that interview, but we can only glean hints of it from secondhand sources. We believe her life provides an example of the power of a spiritual pathway that we have not particularly emphasized, namely Christians who consider themselves born-again evangelicals but eschew the pentecostal label. They too feel empowered by divine love, although they may come to regard their path (as did Brenda in her opening comment to us) as "operating without a battery." We see the power of the divine reflected in the tribute that Father Norm Douglas, another of our interviewees and a Catholic priest, paid to this evangelical Protestant and community leader as she struggled to see beyond circumstances during a two-year ordeal with cancer. As Father Norm described it, "She went through it from a pain-faith perspective," continuing: "On the one hand, she was hoping that she would experience healing. On the other, she trusted that however it finally turned out, God would be with her and her family through this."[44] We see it reflected in the e-mail her husband of over thirty years sent to family and friends as they all shared in the cup of sorrow:

> It feels at times that our path has led us into a lengthy desert experience—a harsh location where the "other side" of the terrain is not yet in sight. Yet the difficulty of the course of treatment, the length of time we have been dealing with this and the isolation that is necessary can impact body, mind and spirit. But, even last night as we prayed

together, we thanked God that, though we find ourselves in less than comfortable places, we do not walk alone.

"Seeing beyond circumstances" seems to hold a key for understanding the relationship between suffering and joy. Whether it is through the movingly personal accounts shared with us by our interviewees or the hard numbers of the survey, it is apparent that suffering cannot be erased from human experience. It can, however, be transformed and be transforming. Those who were in a relationship with a loving God generally seemed to reach the point of seeing beyond the immediate circumstances of their afflictions even through occasional bouts of anger with God, through psychological turmoil and struggles that are a part of daily life, and through physical ailments and even the process of dying. Seeing beyond circumstances is no magic bullet; rather, it is an experience and a process that can become a lifestyle, as seen in the cases of Ralph and Colleen's wedding and Brenda's funeral.

This is a good time to pause for a moment to reflect on our findings and major thesis. We have been telling the story of godly love that included a preliminary statistical exercise to demonstrate that experiences of divine love could empower benevolence. Higher scores on our Divine Love scale were more important in accounting for higher scores on our measure of benevolence toward the community than were any of the commonly used demographic measures of age, sex, gender, education, and income. In previous chapters we sought to understand people's perceptions of God's love: its relationship to spiritual transformation, to different types of prayer, and in this chapter, to human suffering and healing. We have not been concerned about the often-studied shell of religious organization, with its beliefs and ritual practices; rather, we have focused on lived religion as loving relationship with God. A relationship with a loving God seems to generate what master sociologist Pitirim Sorokin called "love energy" that empowers benevolence. In the next chapter we consider how this love energy might circulate through social networks led by exemplars of godly love. Such networks include God as a significant other, but other people are also important.

7

Human Partners and Godly Love

RELATIONSHIPS FORMING FLUID NETWORKS

EXEMPLARS OF GODLY love do not operate in a vacuum. This point was reiterated as we were writing this chapter when we received an e-mail update from Jonathan Wilson Hartgrove, a social justice exemplar we mentioned in chapter 4.[1] In addition to his social justice activism, Jonathan experienced a calling from God to start a Christian "hospitality house" that would both serve people in need and become a model for how to live in Christian community with others more generally. To put the calling into practice, he had to learn from Catholics and partner with many others. In the process of interacting with beneficiaries, he (like many Christians before him) came to see that he and his collaborators are "the poor." Our interviews revealed the enormous debt that exemplars owe to both collaborators and beneficiaries in terms of techniques of providing benevolent service. But more importantly, these interactions shaped their understanding of the meaning of "community," "love," and "religion," as well as their own identities as Christians and as leaders. Although not Catholic, Jonathan (who was raised Baptist and attended seminary at Duke University) and his wife founded a hospitality house called Rutba House, which they modeled on a long-standing Catholic tradition:

> Before Leah and I moved to Durham [NC] to start Rutba House in the summer of 2003, we spent a long weekend at Mary's House Catholic Worker, a hospitality house for homeless families in Birmingham, Alabama. We knew we wanted to start a community of hospitality and peacemaking, but we had *no idea how to do it*. With patience and good humor, Jim and Shelley Douglass answered our questions . . . and taught us several new ones. They showed us how hospitality can shape you

over a lifetime, and they gave us courage to *face the mystery beyond our questions*. We didn't come to Durham knowing how to live a life of hospitality, but we *knew by grace* that is was possible. (Emphasis added)

This quote reveals a great deal about how exemplars tend to view God and other collaborators as they seek to live lives of benevolent service. We see that Jonathan (and his wife, also an important collaborator) knew by God's grace that their vision was attainable, but they lacked the technical know-how. In seeking this knowledge from a Catholic Worker house, they were confronted with much more: the mystery beyond their questions about how to live this vision of God's loving grace in a broken world. This mystery is the heart of religion, which we have been attempting to capture with concepts such as godly love, or divine love more generally. Although how to live a life of love will perhaps always remain somewhat mysterious, many have tried to forge answers. And there is wisdom in working with others in following this path, rather than attempting to travel it alone.

Consider Jonathan's words from elsewhere in his update:

Our return trip [to Mary's House] each year was a great opportunity to remember our vision, to reflect on stories that inspired us, to keep asking the important questions....

But how is a Christian house of hospitality going to say no to the stranger who might be Jesus, right at the beginning of Advent?

And then, in the middle of our house meeting, a moment of honesty. One member said he felt an almost obsessive urgency to say yes to these requests. It wasn't healthy. It came from a deep need to prove something—to convince himself that he hadn't been neglecting the community, that we weren't struggling. He felt like we had to do it to prove that we were OK.

But there, in that moment, we knew that we weren't OK. We weren't taking care of one another. We were in no place to welcome someone else.

Jean Vanier says that people come to Christian community because they want to serve the poor, but that we can only stay when we admit that we are the poor. However important our work may be, our ability to do it isn't what makes us a community. We're not a house of hospitality when we figure out how to take care of everyone who's homeless. We're a house of hospitality when we learn to wait, when we learn to open ourselves to grace, when we let love transform us, one relationship at a time.

Jonathan's wisdom on this topic owes a great debt to other collaborators he worked with and been mentored by, as well as role models he may not have met. His update mentions Jean Vanier, the world-renowned Catholic human-itarian who founded L'Arche, an organization that serves people with devel-opmental disabilities. L'Arche does not provide services from afar or over the short term. It organizes communities of those with disabilities and those without who live together for decades and learn from each other in the pro-cess. Exemplars like Jonathan would be the first to acknowledge that they stand on the shoulders of giants like Vanier.

Up to this point we have been considering godly love primarily from the point of view of individual exemplars, supplemented by statistical analyses. Collaborators and beneficiaries have also appeared in the narratives we have presented, but in this chapter we pay more direct attention to these human partners. It is difficult to imagine how an exemplar like Heidi Baker could be effective without the help of other collaborators (most notably her husband, Rolland), many of whom are exemplars in their own right. In chapter 3, we presented a three-part typology of benevolent service involving *Servers*, *Renewers*, and *Changers* (see table 3.1). We introduce the topic of collaboration in this chapter by providing an example from each of these types. These cases are not necessarily "representative" of the others in their subtype, but we dis-cuss them because they illustrate different aspects of godly love interactions across the three domains of benevolence. Our aim is to provide the reader with a sense of what godly love looks like from a broader perspective than that of the exemplar. This is not to disparage the exemplars. Without their vision and leadership, it is difficult to imagine how any of the benevolent organizations we studied would have been founded or survived the early, lean years when most organizations fail. But godly love is not primarily about exemplars; it encompasses a network of interactions involving God and human partners.

Throughout this book, we have privileged the voice of the exemplar because of our methodological choice to learn about godly love by talking with this special group of exceptional people. The GLNS provides a broader picture, as do our collaborator interviews. It is sometimes difficult to draw a sharp line between exemplar and collaborator, or between these two groups and the beneficiaries. Some collaborators are also exemplars at the center of their own social networks, and many began as beneficiaries of the benevolence of others. Some religious organizations operate on the premise that the goal is not to serve people, but to empower them to become exemplars of godly love and future leaders who will, in turn, empower others to follow this path.

We conducted interviews with collaborators in order to better understand how different social networks were organized and how they functioned. Some were in supervisory positions, others were on the "front lines." We repeated the same process with a number of other benevolent networks. We interviewed collaborators with diverse viewpoints to make sure that we were not just getting the perspective of the leader or leadership team. Without exception, exemplars encouraged us to speak with as many collaborators or beneficiaries as we wished. We also interacted with beneficiaries, and we engaged in field observations in order to see how godly love unfolded in different social contexts.

Collaboration at a Community Service Center

We begin exploring our three-part typology of benevolent service by sharing a story about collaboration at a Christian community service in Canton, Ohio. Total Living Center (TLC) provides worship services, healing prayer, free meals, clothes, legal and medical services, counseling, and other forms of outreach to an impoverished local community. Pastor Don Bartow, now in his eighties, directs the organization he founded in 1991 after he retired from twenty-five years of serving as pastor of Westminster Presbyterian Church in Canton. Throughout his long ministry, Pastor Bartow has had a strong emphasis on prayer, especially healing prayer, even when the latter was still highly controversial in the Presbyterian Church. Although healing and prayer continue to be his focus, Bartow described how his vision of healing was enlarged through the unfolding of ministries at TLC:

> Although we continue to hold weekly healing services other things have also moved to the forefront. They have helped me to see I was presenting a somewhat narrow concept of spiritual healing. I have come to realize what the Bible teaches concerning other important things to do for one's healing. Also, it presents a lifestyle of healing in the Name of Jesus that involves far more than attending and/or participating in healing services.[2]

In short, Pastor Bartow says he came to realize that prayer for healing was only one of the "two principal aspects in the ministry of Jesus," the other being that he "helped the poor." Bartow elaborates on the dilemma he faced between what he believed to be a divine call on his life to heal the sick and the expansion of an array of services to the poor, as follows:

> If you have gotten this far, you may be wondering how I have recon-
> ciled the direction the Total Living Center has taken in relationship to
> my call to the healing ministry. You can imagine how Satan has tried to
> divert me from these many worthwhile ministries by telling me that
> because of them I was forsaking my calling to the healing ministry. I
> found my self in inner turmoil. I certainly did not want to forsake my
> high calling of proclaiming Christ heals today. At the same time I was
> seeing so many being helped and healed through our many other min-
> istries. Wherein was I to find an answer to my dilemma?[3]

After examining TLC's diverse services in light of biblical passages, Pastor Bartow concluded that the threefold ministry of spiritual healing, medical treatment for the sick, and helping the poor work together for total healing. He concludes with the following resolution to his dilemma:

> Now I see more clearly than ever that all we have done for the sick and
> the poor has not taken me from the healing ministry, but drawn me to
> the very heart of it. A believer is truly *"near to the heart of God"* when
> he or she is providing for the sick and the poor in addition to partici-
> pating in healing services. I ask, *"Do you want to be healed?"* I answer,
> *"Then not only attend healing services, but get involved with medically
> helping the sick and with helping the poor in every way possible."*[4]

Although undoubtedly prayer and studying the scriptures played an impor-
tant role in Bartow's evolving vision for TLC, interaction with others cannot be ignored, as we see from some accounts provided by collaborators.

Interactive Role of TLC Collaborators

We interviewed a total of six TLC volunteers, including one who served as a leader of a separate benevolent organization that she founded, and Pastor Sue, a woman who now serves as Pastor Bartow's assistant. As already indicated TLC provides a variety of services to thousands of people, ministries that Pastor Bartow sees as an integrated threefold ministry with healing at its core. TLC would not have come into existence, nor would it continue to thrive, without Pastor Bartow's ongoing visionary leadership. But the daily work is carried out by a small army of volunteers, with the financial support of the larger community. Each has a story to tell.

Like many volunteers, Rich started out as a beneficiary and in time became a volunteer, eventually taking charge of the food preparation and delivery operation and overseeing the other volunteers in this part of the organization. At the time of our interview, he was middle-aged and volunteering about forty hours per week. Like the other volunteers, he has not received any financial compensation for his work at the center. We asked Rich about the important events in his life that shaped who he is today, just as we did in all of our interviews. Although many exemplars provided lengthy responses to this question, the answers of collaborators were often less detailed. Rich's answer was perhaps the most succinct response we received: "To make a long story short, I got on welfare [taxpayer-provided financial assistance]." The rest of our conversation with him was about as concise as his first response. Rich received assistance from TLC and then started volunteering to help out. One day, a group of kitchen volunteers said to him, "Buddy, watch the food, we'll be back in a little while." As Rich tells it, "They were gone for six, seven hours [he laughed]. They come back, it was all done, I was feeding the people, and that is how I got into the cooking part of the church....Ever since then I have been in the kitchen. You know, cooking for thousands and thousands of people."

At the time of the interview, Rich was unemployed and living rent-free in his stepmother's house. He had been unemployed for a long time, and his grown children were no longer living with him, including a daughter who was involved in drugs and crime. We asked Rich why he continued to volunteer at such a high level, and he responded, "I don't get burned out on it. I keep coming back. I like the people here. You know, there are some very nice people here. The lady you just seen [referring to June, another collaborator we had just interviewed], she is another one that [volunteers] like almost seven days a week." When Matt followed up for more details, he said, "I like the people that I interact with. I love the pastor. He is one nice guy. You know? There is no one around like him. You know what I mean?" Rich went on to say that the pastor "helps a lot of people. So that is why I help, you know, the way I do."

Rich was raised Mormon, but he described himself as a largely nonreligious person, both in his youth and at the time of the interview. He was impressed by incidents of divine healing that he witnessed at TLC. He seemed to like being in an environment in which supernatural events occurred, although he did not participate in healing services. He stated that he did not attend TLC's worship services on Sunday and that "I never read the Bible so I don't know too much about the Bible." When Margaret asked if he had received healing through one of the pastor's prayers, Rich responded, "I am probably not worthy enough to go through the healing thing." We probed for more explanation for statements such as this, but Rich was generally unable to provide detailed answers. Years before, Rich's mother told him how she nearly drowned but had an encounter with God who appeared as "a bright light in front of her" and told her that "it isn't time." Margaret asked what Rich thought of that story and he replied, "I don't think anything of it. You know? You know…just…I am glad she was alive [he laughed]." Despite his seeming lack of religious experiences, Rich described his attraction to the TLC and its founder in a way that reflected its spiritual basis: "There is no place around here like this, there really isn't, nowhere in this area, you know, that I know of, that does what [Bartow] does here."

Daniel, another long-term volunteer, confirmed the importance of the godly love orchestrated by Pastor Bartow and the center he founded: "I did a lot of things I shouldn't have in my life, I'm—I guess you know I was on the wrong side of it for a long time and, I retired and I came up here to this place here, and I've been here for the last four years, and I love it here. It's changed my life a lot." Daniel was raised as a Baptist, a different denomination than Rich (Mormon), Pastor Sue (Methodist), or Pastor Bartow (Presbyterian). The center is clearly ecumenical in its orientation and operation; in fact, volunteers need not be religious at all. As for recruiting volunteers, Daniel suggested that it is not difficult. His wife serves with him, and he invites everyone he meets to join. Once the volunteers show up, according to Daniel, "they just love it, I mean it's just a, a place where you can really feel, when you go home that you've helped people, and that's how I feel when I go home." He described volunteering fifty to sixty hours per week, which he did not see as a sacrifice on his part ("I enjoy this too much [for it] to be a sacrifice of my time"). Daniel feels he has been helped as much as he has helped others, in part because "the pastor sees good in everybody." After four years of daily volunteering Daniel has learned to see others, as well as himself, that way too.

Pastor Sue has also found TLC to be a special place in her significant role as assistant pastor. Her mentor's vision for TLC is embodied in her calling and service. At the time of the interview, she had been volunteering for three years, sometimes up to eighty hours per week. She is primarily in charge of the daily operations when Bartow is out of town (he spends several months each year away from TLC). She coleads the healing prayer services with him when he is in town and conducts all services when he is away. Unlike most of the other volunteers, Pastor Sue initially became interested in volunteering at the center in part because she had read some of the pastor's books, and she agreed with his approach to ministry and prayer. Just before meeting Pastor Bartow for the first time, she had spent twenty-one days in continual prayer and fasting, during which she experienced what she describes as "the majestics of the experience of God's presence, the overwhelming love." When she met Bartow, she was unable to articulate exactly why she wanted to become involved in the center. According to Sue, because she was not speaking Pastor Bartow began to provide her with his impressions of her, which included "some of the stuff I didn't really want to hear." After the conversation, she realized that "he knows me better than I know myself," which is a hallmark of prophetic pray-ers like Bartow.

Despite this initial unforgettable meeting, Sue was reluctant to become too involved in the center, in part because the Bible college she was attending at the time was dismissive of much of Bartow's theology. But in the end she needed a place to pray and had no other options. The pastor allowed her to use a room in TLC—a request that no other pastor in the area was able or willing to grant—to pray as long as and whenever she wished. She faithfully made use of the prayer room and eventually became involved in a children's ministry. And as she read more of Bartow's writings, Sue became increasingly convinced that she had found her calling.

A number of volunteers seemed to have come to a deeper understanding of their own self-worth in their encounters at the center, including Sue, who described herself as in a "cocoon" before TLC helped her transform into a "butterfly." This process of self-transformation begins with the manner in which Pastor Bartow models what he perceives as God's unconditional and radically affirming love for all. This spirit is evident throughout the center, which gives it a very different feel than a state-run welfare office. Pastor Bartow serves as a magnet for volunteers, who are drawn to the center either because they need help themselves or because they would like to participate in the gratifying service of others that they have heard described by other volunteers, often their relatives, neighbors, friends, or coworkers. But what is the social glue that holds this network together and nurtures its growth? Don Bartow would surely point to God's love.

Pastor Bartow and His Collaborators

Bartow felt called to be a pastor at age ten. He recalled, "I didn't have to go through catechism or Sunday school, I just obeyed Jesus." After seminary, he was responsible for three churches in the Evangelical United Brethren denomination. One day when he was twenty years old, he was explaining some troubled feelings to a guest speaker at a Presbyterian church. The person in whom he confided was a bricklayer by trade, not a clergy member or theologian. But Bartow felt God work through the interaction he had with this layperson, who told him, "You live by faith. You don't live by feeling." What unexpectedly happened next, Bartow would later label as the experience that pentecostals call "baptism in the Holy Spirit," although he lacked the vocabulary at the time. He continued:

> I said, "But I don't feel right, I don't feel right." So, he said, "It's faith, not feeling." I'm sitting on a dresser and I all of a sudden realize, I didn't feel bad anymore. But I didn't feel good. So I said to [him], "I don't feel bad anymore but I don't feel good either. I guess I'm just in neutral." Now I, I'll never forget it, when I said those words, something absolutely powerful happened to me. Just like something fell upon me, went all over me, all in me and through me. And I came off that dresser shouting and crying and singing, kneeling, thanking God. It changed my life. And, I, I began to sing (and at that time I couldn't even carry a tune, but I did, that day) "Blessed Assurance, Jesus is Mine."

The memory of this experience (a secondary spiritual transformation, in the parlance of chapter 4) continued to renew Bartow throughout his life and opened him to the supernatural movement of God that would culminate in his founding of TLC after retirement.

Pastor Don Bartow's life story is as fascinating as it is lengthy. We would have to write a separate book to do it justice. For our purposes here, we are content to note that his unanticipated involvement in a healing ministry was essential to the holistic approach to healing practiced at TLC (including healing prayer, access to conventional medicine, provision of wholesome food, etc.). It was Don Bartow's involvement in an interaction with a woman in his congregation that first exposed him to the healing power of the Holy Spirit. He had just finished seminary when this woman asked him to pray for her very sick husband who was not responding to conventional medical treatment. The man wanted to be anointed with oil, a not uncommon practice in healing prayer. But this was news to Bartow:

> I don't know why she called me to anoint him. I'd never anointed anybody in my life. I was never taught how to anoint, never even taught about anointing.... So, I didn't know what to do. I didn't even know

what oil to use. I thought, you know, what would you use? I thought, you know, I could use three-in-one oil, you know, Father, Son, the Holy Spirit. But then I went to [my wife] and she had a little bottle of olive oil, kitchen oil, so I took it [and] put that little bottle in [my coat] and hid it. I didn't want anybody to see me with a bottle of oil.

He administered the oil and said a prayer for the man, with little expectation for efficacy:

> The only thought I had, if any, was I was making a fool of myself. But I had no thought, I didn't pray in faith and "God will raise you up and you'll be…" I just anointed the guy and got out of there. So, that's Saturday afternoon. Sunday morning the phone rings again. It's his wife. She said, "Dad wants you to stop by to see him before church." I thought, "Oh my God, the guy's about dead now…"

Much to Bartow's surprise, the man was completely healed of his dreadful skin condition. At the time Bartow did not know how to process the experience, and he actually requested that the man swear a solemn vow that he would never tell anyone that he had anointed him.

We have shared excerpts from our interviews with Pastor Bartow and some of his collaborators to provide a window into how godly love is actually practiced on a large scale. Some people, like Bartow, interact more directly with God than others such as Rich. Pastor Sue's hunger for a deeper prayer life resonated well with Pastor Bartow's call, so she allowed herself to be mentored by him. Some collaborators are undoubtedly closer to the exemplar than are others as they catch the vision and share the walk outlined by the exemplar. But volunteers like Rich who are former beneficiaries can be as essential to the work as leaders who emerge through spiritual mentoring. Rich does not perceive personal direct interaction with God, but he does sense something good, perhaps even sacred, working through Pastor Bartow and at the TLC more generally. For his part, Bartow was powerfully influenced by his interactions with the bricklayer as well as the suffering man he first anointed with oil. He attributes his experiences to God, but there was a human as well as a divine component to these two interactions. The fact that so many volunteers, like Rich, continue to flock to the center to help with the work illustrates that Pastor Bartow is not a micromanager. In fact, he allows volunteers to develop new ministries under the auspices of TLC, which is how most of the specific specialties of service have come into being. There always seems to be someone like Rich there to pick up the slack when others depart, or to develop new ministries. TLC itself is a space where multiple exemplars can follow their callings in collaboration with other people and God. Pastor Bartow described the uniqueness of TLC as follows:[5]

> There are thousands of soup kitchens in our land and throughout the world. To me, the uniqueness of the TLC is that we have so many tangible and helpful ministries under the same roof. For instance, where else are you going to find healing services and medical clinics under the same roof and ministry? Also, all of these ministries are handled by volunteers. So surely, from my limited viewpoint such a ministry is few and far between.
>
> The TLC is much more than groceries and meals. The remarkable thing the Lord has done is to bring them forth in the same facility, and staffed completely by volunteers, There is a *free* chiropractic clinic, a *free* clothing ministry, a *free* legal clinic, a *free* medical clinic, a *free* pharmacy, a *free* physical therapy clinic, and they are now preparing for a *free* pet clinic. In addition TLC has a Prayer and Retreat House where individuals and groups may pull apart for soul-searching and spiritual growth, a daily FM radio program, and a daily Internet radio program, and provides many *free* resources in all of these areas.

But the center would not have developed without Pastor Bartow, and the pastor would not be who he is without the experiences he has had with collaborators and beneficiaries. Don Bartow, like many exemplars we interviewed, has often felt like a beneficiary himself as he expressed his wonder at what TLC has become:

> Margaret, I am amazed at what we get done by volunteers, and most of them are from the community. This month we gave away about 80,000 pounds of groceries, and people of the community did practically all the work needed to accomplish this feat. Further, community volunteers gave toys to 1,038 kids. This totaled over 5,000 toys. That is no small task, but they did it. Did they do all things perfectly? No! But I assure you, a paid staff does not do all things perfectly and lovingly either. To me, this adventure with volunteers is much more exciting! For some reason I have become a truly "peculiar" person. I guess Presbyterians have a right to change this way, do we not?[6]

Collaboration in Transforming the Church and the Community

"God is pulling this strange allegiance of disconnected people for a bigger purpose." With these words, Steve Witt summed up his understanding of how God is raising up collaborators in Steve's growing network of churches and communities to serve northeastern Ohio.[7] Steve fits best into the Renewer category of our typology with a primary emphasis on Bethel Cleveland being a church that hosts revival for the purpose of transforming the larger community. But while Don Bartow combines a Renewer's approach (as seen in his focus on healing prayer) with TLC's primary mission of serving the poor, Steve's church engages in a variety of secondary service activities, while its primary emphasis is on training its members to infiltrate and change the larger culture. There is a decided mix of concern for the poor with spiritual renewal in both ministries, but the emphases are different.

Bethel Cleveland recently became part of a larger network of churches launched by Bethel Church Redding (California) that focuses on pentecostal revival. Although Bethel Redding and Bethel Cleveland have different histories Steve was drawn to partner with Bill Johnson and Bethel Redding by a shared vision: "Bethel's mission is *revival*...the personal, regional, and global expansion of God's kingdom through His manifest presence."[8] This banner found on Bethel Redding's website marks a vision shared by Bethel Cleveland and scores of others who have joined the Global Legacy network, a ministry of Bethel Redding, with the purpose of "connecting and encouraging revival leaders everywhere."[9]

Known as Metro Church South from its inception in 1996 until early 2011, Bethel Cleveland was birthed during a revival that began in Toronto in the 1990s, the same revival that transformed Heidi and Rolland Baker and their organization (Iris Ministries). Metro Church South was recently renamed "Bethel Cleveland" when Steve Witt allied with Bill Johnson of Bethel Redding and Global Legacy. Until this time Witt had been a charter member of Partners in Harvest, a network linked to the Toronto Airport Christian Fellowship (now Catch the Fire). The new Catch the Fire network appears to have a greater international emphasis on planting new churches than does Johnson's network.[10]

Contemporary neo-pentecostal networks such as these are fluid and relational. Creating new networks or changing affiliations (as Steve has done) represents more of a realignment than a schism. The New Apostolic Reformation (NAR), which we will discuss later in this chapter, informally provides a permeable arch over these and other networks as a forum for ongoing relationships among an array of leaders and ministries.[11] In an interview with Matt and Margaret, before Steve had given us any indication that Metro Church South would be joining Bethel's network, Steve enthusiastically described founder Bill Johnson as a leader who embodied different faces of the revival and someone he admired. Bill, according to Steve, was a "combination of [prophetic speaker and author] Graham Cooke's wisdom, the clinical approach of John Wimber [founder of the Vineyard churches], a theology of the kingdom advanced by [George] Ladd, and the openness to the supernatural of John Arnott [founder of Catch the Fire]." This seemingly unique mix of revival personalities and gifts that Steve saw in Bill Johnson aligned well with Steve's dream of the "kingdom [of God] transforming the city."[12]

Heidi Baker, whose US ministry headquarters are based at Bethel Redding, has been a speaker at several of the revival conferences Steve has organized over the years. During one such visit to Cleveland in 2006, Shara Pradhan (then Heidi's personal assistant and coauthor) gave a prophetic word which Steve shared in a sermon recently, a word given "when the church was still Metro Church South and before Bill Johnson ever visited or I ever visited Bethel Redding." Steve recounted Shara's prophecy as follows: "I feel like the Lord said this church is going to be a second Bethel—a second revival hotspot. And I saw you [directing this comment to Loren, Steve's daughter] as a bridge between Redding and Cleveland. And I feel that Bill Johnson is going to be coming here more, and there is going to be such partnering in the Spirit and with the anointing." When Steve recently reminded the church of this prophecy, he added, "Now that's important; you can't make someone want to partner with you. That's a God thing."[13] When Steve did visit Bethel Redding he felt that "they are our future; they are where we want to be." When he met Bill Johnson, Steve thought, "This is the kind of guy we want to emulate."

Bethel Cleveland thus can be described as a network nestled within a larger network interacting with still other interrelated networks with a shared vision of world-changing, ongoing revival. An important component of this vision is a collective experience of the felt presence of God that was commonly experienced during the height of the revival at the former Toronto Airport Christian Fellowship (now Catch the Fire) with the motto of "walking in God's love and giving it away."[14] The strength of different ties may increase (as they recently have with Bethel) or decrease (as with the long-term relationship with Partners in Harvest/Catch the Fire) as particular networks ebb and flow or forge in new directions. Steve fleshes out one simple description of knowing divine love and sharing it with others as filtered through Bethel Redding as follows:

> I love the focus on the presence of God. I love their love of the supernatural. I love the fact that they are transforming their city of Redding. Extraordinarily! I love the fact that they pour money out of their church into the city. That's a little radical, isn't it? They actually give money to their city to help them. Recently they took over a lease on their civic center so they can actually rent it back to the city and also allow them to hold some of their events there and using it as a church. And they are putting a lot of money to improve it so when they get done using it they can turn it back to the city—and it will be better than when they first got it. I like churches like that. That's the kind of church we want to be.[15]

Central to the day-to-day operation of Bethel Cleveland is a growing number of local congregations with members being trained to move out into their communities with "PHDs" in the supernatural gifts of prophecy, healing, and deliverance. One such group is pioneering locally in Cleveland's Slavic Village.

Bethel Invades Slavic Village

The small group of young people who live in Cleveland's Slavic Village are not a formal church—at least not for now—but Slavic Village operates as a test site for bringing the kingdom of God down to earth, Bethel-style. Slavic Village, once the home of a thriving and diverse ethnic community whose original members largely fled for suburbia decades ago, says it is "reinventing itself." Its website advertises: "With a rich history, residents who value close connections to family and church, and a number of unique assets, its future is bright. With convenient shopping and countless recreation options, there is no lack of amenities to enjoy. And we are proud of our diversity, evident throughout the neighborhood. People of all ages, races and income levels, families, young professionals and empty-nesters, call Slavic Village home." A network of young people from Bethel Cleveland responded to the invitation when they perceived a divine call to live and work with others in Slavic Village to transform this impoverished inner-city neighborhood.[16] Bethel's goal has been to develop and provide a model that might be used by other local congregations in the area to revitalize greater Cleveland. These young

church members in their twenties and thirties, equipped with the supernatural "PHD" of prophecy, healing, and deliverance, seek to release revival
fervor and its ascribed transformative powers by living in the community and
being a part of its fabric.

Steve had the original vision of spiritual revival bringing community transformation to Cleveland but was uncertain of the exact location for this heavenly experiment. Jeremy, one of his young collaborators, caught the vision,
found the location, and became a keeper of the vision. Jeremy and his collaborators work together with neighbors and community leaders as they bring
the material and spiritual resources of Bethel Cleveland's churches to bear on
the collective problems in the Village. Assisted by members of other Bethel
congregations, they host cookouts, provide Christmas stockings filled with
goodies, give students backpacks and supplies at the start of the new school
year, join in sponsoring festivities planned by the Slavic Village Development
Foundation, and otherwise support the struggling community as they live as
good neighbors with a spiritual vision. Just as Pastor Bartow wants to see beneficiaries become collaborators and exemplars themselves, so does Steve Witt
employ a model of collaboration with leaders who arise within his congregation and who in turn collaborate with those they seek to serve. They believe
this "strange allegiance of disconnected people" requires the intervention of
the Spirit to hold the network together and to empower it to do good.

The journey into Slavic Village began when Jeremy, then twenty-five years
old, was exploring the Village and stopped to peer through the window of a
foreclosed house. A man came up to him and asked what he was doing. It
turned out that this man was a developer who in turn introduced him to a
banker who grew up in Slavic Village and is now working for its restoration.
Jeremy, who was then employed by his father's construction business (a
business he now directs) began to share Steve's vision. Steve would soon visit
Slavic Village, and seven adult members of what was then the Metro Church
South would meet with the banker to talk about the church's vision and its
ten-year strategy. Steve's vision began to take on flesh.

Margaret and Matt interviewed Jeremy for the first time in September
2010, and Margaret did a follow-up interview on a Sunday afternoon in July
2011. Jeremy was especially animated during the second interview as he began
by relating what was happening in Slavic Village using the sermon Steve had
delivered in the morning church service:

JEREMY: One thing I want to tell you real quick before we begin—there was
     something real interesting this morning. Do you remember this morning

when Steve was talking about the Cloisters in England? [Steve had talked about them as places saturated with prayer.]

MARGARET: Yes; yes, I do.

JEREMY: Well, where I live—where I bought my house and now there are seven of us living in this group of town homes and it is called "The Cloisters."

MARGARET: That is the place you pointed out to Matt and me on our tour of the neighborhood?

JEREMY: Right. One by one we are buying them. We have bought two, and the third one will close on August 1. There are two more left now. So one by one we are taking them over. First it was just me and my roommate. Now there are seven of us living there. It has always been called "The Cloisters." My street is "Minster Court" and the next one us "Abbey Court." And I just remembered when Steve was speaking the time they were building my house. They told me that these were modeled after the old English churches. That is the theme of the town homes that were built. They modeled it after the Cloisters. And when you go back of the homes you will see it is all wide open, like we are all living together—the same feel of what he was talking about.

But also our vision—what we are trying to do there is to be planted—to take that land, to take that property—and turn it into that open heaven. Just like Steve was talking about where you walk down those halls and feel the presence of God. We want constant soaking, constant prayer, constant soaking stuff. That was very encouraging today. I didn't know he was going to talk about that. So I just put it together during the message. *We live in the Cloisters.*

Jeremy was excited to share all that had happened during the year since we interviewed him and toured Slavic Village. At the time of the second interview twenty young people were living in the Village, with an estimated total of thirty-five to forty who are committed to the vision. He reported, "There are lots and lots of others interested in helping; when we do big outreaches down there, hundreds volunteer—we have to even turn some away." And Jeremy said that more young people were coming from Bethel Redding to join them in making their vision of transforming Slavic Village a reality.

Steve shares Jeremy's excitement about the way things are evolving, but he realizes that the current configuration of networks is not necessarily a permanent one. As Steve puts it:

I don't see that this is something that will be here a hundred years from now. This is a loose network; we may say to some, "Cut loose and reach your city." This is more like a starfish kingdom standpoint—cut off a piece and it starts a new starfish. Let's raise up some people, get them in the incubator of training, and see what happens.

Like Don Bartow, Steve does not wish to see his collaborators or the beneficiaries in a permanent state of dependence. He seems focused on raising up the next generation of leaders from the ranks of collaborators and beneficiaries alike. According to Steve:

So suburban people have resources—education, energy, money, time, whatever. What urban people have to offer the suburban is understanding, patience, things like that. So we are finding as we are invading the urban population that suburban people—some think they are just going in to get rid of their suburban guilt. What is actually happening is that they are being transformed by the poor—as well as leaving a deposit resource, financial resources, education training, mentoring, whatever that might be. So in a humorous way, it is robbing from the rich to give to the poor.

This starfish model, with the rich and poor in symbiotic relationship, is not entirely Steve's creation. Such ideas are well traveled in Steve's larger networks, including that of Bill Johnson. In fact, when Steve aligned his church with Bethel Redding and Margaret asked him why he opted for this affiliation, Steve responded:

Well, I am a believer that rain flows down, water flows down. You get under something like that and it will trickle down. And the Lord had specifically told me to align myself to Bethel. He said, "Buy low," as in buying stocks. And Bethel stocks are now low and are about to skyrocket.

Bethel and the New Apostolic Reformation

When Steve, speaking in descriptive colloquialisms as he often does, says that Bethel's "stocks are about to skyrocket," obviously he is not referring to the S&P 500. He means that God's power is being revealed by Bethel, and this will become more and more evident as time progresses. Bethel Redding has established an international reputation in the renewalist movement, particularly in the so-called Third Wave neo-pentecostalism. Bill Johnson's network is itself loosely embedded in a larger religious revival movement known as the New Apostolic Reformation (NAR) that came to the attention of the news media during the Republican presidential campaign of Rick Perry in the summer of 2011. Reporters were trying to figure out what the NAR represented, Governor Perry's relationship with the NAR, and what all this meant for the presidential campaign.[17]

There are three major foci of the NAR that loosely unite exemplars we have interviewed from this movement, some of whom we feature in this book and others (due to space constraints) we do not. They have revival at its core as the catalyst that "brings heaven to earth" through cultural transformation under the visionary leadership of apostles. These NAR leaders or "apostles" (who may or may not accept the title) include a number of our interviewees: John and Carol Arnott (Catch the Fire), Ché and Sue Ahn (Harvest International Ministries and H-Rock Church), Randy Clark (Global Awakening), Heidi and Rolland Baker (Iris Ministries), Bob Ekblad (Tierra Nueva), Leif Hetland (Leif Hetland Ministries), Kris Vallottin (Bethel School of Supernatural Ministries), and C. Peter Wagner (Global Harvest Ministries). This does not mean that they subscribe to all of the ideas promoted by the different segments of the movement, but there is a kind of common ground that unites these individuals in thinking about the world and the role of God in it. (When Margaret asked Steve if he identified with the NAR, he retorted with a question—"What do you mean by it?")

As we understand it, NAR adherents share a core belief in the empowering nature of the revival of the 1990s that they contend has continued into the new millennium. They believe that the revival empowers Christians for service. Its fruits are not simply about the afterlife or intangible blessings, but about effects that can be observed in the here and now. With believers ushering in the kingdom of God will come the transformation of the cultural, political, and social institutions of the world, including government, education, media, business, and religion. A key component of this religious movement is its postdenominational structure. Networks are more fluid and are built around leaders (apostles).[18] As described by pentecostal scholar William Kay, apostolic networks are "collections of churches linked with each other and linked with an apostolic figure. In almost every case the networks are organized quite differently from denominations, and deliberately so, since the networks have conceived of themselves as avoiding the worse features of denominations by returning to a New Testament pattern."[19] The NAR is a different way of collaborating to advance the kingdom of God when compared to existing denominational structures and religious social service organizations. Just as the NAR seeks to renew the church through spiritual powers, so do members like Steve Witt seek the transformation of the larger secular culture, including the business and political realms. The reform of the church and society is tied to an unleashing of God's presence and power. Another exemplar, C. Peter Wagner is sometimes seen as the "founder" of the movement, but more accurately he is the person who *identified* an emergent movement. Wagner described the NAR as "the most radical change in the way of doing Christianity since the Protestant Reformation. The changes are obvious on every continent, and there are many commonalities."[20] Wagner and some others we have interviewed have referred to themselves as "apostles" who hold positions central to the NAR, although some (like Heidi Baker) would eschew the label. Yet they all share the belief that this supernaturally energized way of living out Christianity in the world can change the earth for the better. In fact, leaders of the Bethel churches insist that heaven can be brought down to earth through "supernatural" powers available to all Christians—all, not just a few who are officially anointed as apostles, can become exemplars of godly love.

There is a well-known trend for charismatic "gifts of the spirit" such as prophecy and healing to routinize into doctrine and ritual over time as new religious movements give way to formal denominations.[21] Despite this trend the NAR seeks to combat the routinization process by empowering individuals to enjoy direct experiences of God—especially prophecy, healing, and experiencing providential financial provisions. Network churches and schools of the supernatural provide a larger culture that nurtures such experiences. The NAR may be new, but the ongoing reformation of Christianity has continued for centuries. Some prophets of old (Francis of Assisi, Teresa of Avila, and others) led internal reformations within Catholicism through the establishment of religious orders (Catholic versions of new Protestant "sects"). The Protestant Reformation was in part due to the religious experiences of Martin Luther; John Wesley's "warming of the heart" experience is well known to Methodists. The historic revival on Azusa Street in Los Angeles in the early 1900s was a major catalyst in another major reformation, namely, the birth of the global pentecostal movement. The primary focus of these movements was not on doctrine but rather on religious experience as it informs and modifies the "living" Bible. The NAR can thus be seen as a contemporary neo-pentecostal branch of this larger historical movement.

Instead of a few pentecostal leaders working to change communities through their benevolent organizations, Steve Witt, Bill Johnson, and others in the NAR challenge all Christians to dream big and work with God to change the world, as reflected in the title of Bill Johnson's book: *Dreaming with God: Co-Laboring with God for Cultural Transformation.* He and other apostolic leaders are spelling out what this means and how it can be done. Thousands of mostly young people have attended the School for the Supernatural at Bethel Redding, with additional schools being part of other churches in the Bethel network (including Bethel Cleveland), to help people learn to hear God's voice and rely on God's power for transforming individual lives, communities, and Christianity.

We were surprised that during the writing of this chapter a number of our interviewees (who were not relationally or institutionally connected at the time we collected our original data) developed formal ties to each other that took their collaboration to a deeper level. We have already told the story of how Steve Witt affiliated his church with Bill Johnson's Bethel Reading. Shortly after Bethel Cleveland planted a church in Akron, Scott Souders (another exemplar, and pastor of the Church of the Holy Spirit Anglican Church, founded some twenty-five years earlier to offer ministry and service to Akron's inner-city poor) moved his congregation to the Bethel Akron campus. With its location directly off a major expressway exit and on the perimeters of the expanding University of Akron campus to the north and a poor and blighted urban area directly to the south, the Bethel Church campus provides a unique location for unusual collaboration. Another interviewee, Jeff Metzger (formerly pastor of Shiloh Church in Canton and an accomplished businessman), is emerging as a leader and teacher at Bethel Akron. It is too soon to know what benevolent fruit these new collaborative relationships might bear. What we can say in the meantime is that the process of godly love unfolding in traditional denominational structures is likely to be quite different when compared with the dynamics of the new apostolic networks.

Collaboration for Peace and Justice in Dangerous Contexts

Shifting gears from community service and revival to social justice (Changers, in our typology) can generate a very different perspective on godly love. But one theme that holds constant regardless of the type of ministry is the importance of collaboration. In this section we leave the familiar territory of the United States that has occupied most of our book to briefly explore collaboration for peace and justice in other parts of the world. Paul Alexander was a member of our extended research team in addition to serving as one of the five primary exemplars of godly love featured in this book. He and psychologist Robert Welsh have collected data on high-risk Christian activism at the site of violent conflicts in the United States and abroad. Like us, they interviewed exemplars of godly love and their collaborators. Involvement in dangerous situations marks the difference between their interviewees and most of ours. Here is a brief excerpt from one of their reports:

> Consider the story below recounted by one of our Colombian participants. It is but one account that illustrates transcendently motivated risky altruism in doing good for another motivated by a sense of a divine call.
>
> One night the Paras (Paramilitaries) took a 23-year-old mother in our church and shot her in front of her children, because the Paras thought she had killed her Para friend. The community was afraid to go to recover the body, for fear of what the Paras might do to anyone who showed sympathy to the mother. So they called me. I went that very night and recovered the body and gave her a proper funeral in our church, as a way of saying that the church was not going to be intimidated by the Paras' threats. As often happens here in this war, it was soon found out that the killing was a mistake for she had had nothing to do with the killing of her Para friend. Then, led by the Spirit, the church carried the coffin to where the Paras lived and buried the body there. This made the Paras face their awful mistake every time they passed the grave. As a result many of the Paras quit. They even had fights among themselves. And this event became the beginning of the end of the Paras' control in the region. Three years ago we could not drive this road we are on tonight for fear of the Guerrillas or Paras. They are still around, but their control of the people is greatly diminished.
>
> This story points to the theo-ethical perspective that the Spirit of God leads communities to take significant nonviolent risks in order for there to be greater peace and justice in society.[22]

The emphasis is both on the actions of the community, as well as the exemplar. Although the exemplar is clearly a leader in this story ("so they called me"), there is also a community network of support and collective action. Robert and Paul characterize this dynamic by writing that "the Spirit of God leads *communities* to take significant nonviolent risks" (emphasis added).

Their research suggests that exemplars draw strength both from God and also from their supportive communities. Some are outsiders who have come to an area to work for peace and justice. Others are locals who seek these ends in their own communities, in collaboration with their neighbors. When successful, all are beneficiaries of greater peace and justice, as when the Paras' "control of the people" is weakened.

What guides the work of these high-risk exemplars of godly love? One factor is the context in which they understand Holy Scripture. In the parlance of theology, a *hermeneutic* is a framework of interpretation—a lens through which the scriptures and lived experiences of religion might be understood and judged. A Palestinian Christian interviewed by Robert and Paul (Naim Stifan Ateek) helpfully defines hermeneutics as "the interpretation of ancient texts...[and] the development of criteria" to guide "modern readers" in this process of interpretation.[23] The content of a person's hermeneutical center is strongly shaped by social context. For example, Palestinian Christians like Naim who are involved in high-risk ministries tend to see social justice as the proper expression of God's love, whereas many of the middle-class American exemplars we interviewed tend to see community service or religious renewal as more theologically appropriate. The title of Naim's book, *Justice and Only Justice*, is strongly suggestive of the importance of standpoint, as what you see depends on where you stand. Naim argues that Palestinian Christians require the "authentic Word of God" and a "true meaning of those biblical texts that Jewish Zionists and Christian fundamentalists cite to substantiate their subjective claims and prejudices."[24] Naim argues that Christians must ground their understanding in Jesus and read the rest of the Bible through the lens of Jesus. In other words, the Bible must be "scrutinized by the mind of Christ."[25] According to this view, when the Bible portrays God as ordering the destruction of a city (as with Jericho, in the book of Joshua, chapter 6), this reflects an imperfect, human understanding of God that predates the life of Jesus.

Hermeneutical controversies continue to rage among theologians and laypersons alike. Our point here is that exemplars are shaped by their interactions with collaborators, just as Paul's thinking has been dramatically restructured by his contact with those like Naim who espouse a "Christocentric" hermeneutic. And for Paul and Naim, as for many of Robert and Paul's interviewees, *love is justice*. This makes sense in a context such as Palestine, where the Israeli military forcefully removes Palestinians from their land and the ability to secure the basic requirements of life is routinely in doubt, or in Colombia, where Paras murder the innocent with impunity. The meaning of godly love is obviously shaped by the local culture in which collaboration and interaction occur. It is in this sense that Robert and Paul write of the ways in which "the Spirit of God leads communities to take significant nonviolent risks." Exemplars are immersed in these communities, and their lives can only be understood with reference to a specific communal context. Collaborators may be those who help with the immediate work of a benevolent ministry, as well as role models and other influences from diverse religious traditions, activist subcultures, or theological schools of thought.

In one inspiring example, portrayed in a video that Paul and Bob captured while on a data collection trip to the Middle East and shared with the rest of the research team, a Muslim in Palestine joins with Palestinian Christians to protest the destruction of a Palestinian home. The home was in the path of a proposed wall that the government of Israel was building in order to secure land for Israelis that was currently occupied by Palestinians. Although representing a very different religious background, this Muslim man was moved to collaborate with Palestinian Christians because of his perception of the injustice of the Israeli action. By setting aside religious differences in the interest of working for a shared community value (stopping Israel's theft of land and destruction of property), this man serves as a role model for others involved in this struggle for justice regardless of religious background. We did not see many partnerships across such lines in our research, but collaboration in networks of godly love is not limited to those of one particular faith tradition. This example suggests that godly love is not necessarily insular, even in Palestine. Many Americans might be surprised to learn that a large Christian population resides there and, contrary to the barrage of media images about irreconcilable differences among religious groups, nonviolent interfaith actions for social justice do exist.

In March 2010, evangelical Palestinian Christians organized and hosted a conference in Bethlehem titled "Christ at the Checkpoint: Theology in the Service of Justice and Peace." The purpose was to bring together a variety of activists, theologians, pastors, and other Christians to "discuss the situation in Palestine and Israel," particularly to "motivate participants to become advocates for the reconciliation work of the church in Palestine/Israel and its ramifications for the Middle East and the world."[26] Paul Alexander and Naim Ateek gave presentations, as did Tony Campolo (another of our exemplars). Paul edited a book based on this conference; it opened with the words "This book is a work of love." Another conference participant and contributor to the book (also an exemplar interviewed by Robert and Paul) developed the idea of love as an obligation: "Engage in continuous acts of love to your oppressor. For it is *not* a choice we have as followers of Jesus to love the other and the enemy, but it is a commandment that we are to abide in." Another participant told of how he had been harassed and humiliated by Israeli soldiers to the point where he found it difficult to love them. But eventually, after praying about this issue, whenever he encountered the soldiers he would pray, "Lord, please let them stop me. Because when they stop me I can share your love with them."

The interactions of these exemplar-collaborators contribute to an international subculture in which love takes on a particular form: nonviolent activism for peace and justice. In the introduction to his edited book, Paul revises the definition of godly love that we used to guide the projects of our extended research team as follows:

> If we experiment with the definition of Godly Love a bit we could have an inviting definition of Godly Justice, and I submit that the work in this book aspires to embody Godly Justice in the world. "The dynamic interaction between divine and human ~~love~~ justice that enlivens and expands ~~benevolence~~ peace."[27]

It is not surprising that some of the participants in the "Christ at the Checkpoint" conference would prefer to speak of godly justice rather than godly love, given the pressing issues of inequality and coercive violence that they confront on a daily basis. The culture in this collaborative network is very different from what we find at the Total Living Center or Bethel Cleveland. Distinct material realities shape the diverse expressions of godly love among networks of Servers, Renewers, and Changers. Members of Paul's network reinforce a vision of divine love that stresses nonviolent action aimed at restructuring nations. The NAR network also emphasizes restructuring, but the content of their message is very different, as we have seen. Both are quite radical, but they reference different kinds of social norms. Holistic healing is the key to the radical vision at the TLC, and this represents yet another path for the expression of godly love. The possibility for unity within this diversity is explored in the next chapter.

The Diamond Model of Godly Love

In order to understand benevolence-producing networks suggested by the concept of godly love, which can be thought of as powerful incubators of service to others, it is helpful to have a model, or heuristic device, that presents a

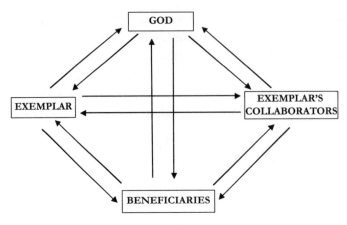

FIGURE 7.1 The Diamond Model of Godly Love

visual image of the relevant interactions. Figure 7.1 displays the "diamond model" of godly love that we have used from the earliest days of our research project to describe the relationships we are investigating.[28] The diamond shape is a starting point, but the concept of godly love is flexible enough to allow for other conceptualizations, as well as linking multiple diamonds together in a larger interactional network.[29] The concept of godly love, as illustrated by this diamond model, has proven quite helpful in *providing a framework for a dialogue* among various branches of social science and theology, which often seem to have a difficult time speaking to each other. It has had great appeal to laypersons and scholars alike, thanks to its simplicity and connection with the well-known Christian Great Commandment to love God and love neighbor as self. The concept and model continue to be developed and refined through empirical analysis and theological reflection.[30]

As displayed in the figure, an exemplar of godly love may draw strength and empowerment from a number of interactional partners, including God, collaborators, and the beneficiaries themselves. We have already seen this in the lives of exemplars like Pastor Bartow, who learned quite unexpectedly from a beneficiary that he had a gift for facilitating divine healing. Godly love interactions are the foundation of a process of learning to see beyond difficult or seemingly impossible material circumstances and are essential to preventing burnout or other reasons for desisting from a life of benevolent service.[31] No matter how bad existing conditions might be, godly love exemplars may "know" in their hearts that God's plan will come to fruition in the future and that their purpose is to help fulfill this plan regardless of the personal cost. Robert and Paul have found this in their interviews with high-risk exemplars throughout the world. And like Steve Witt, they may redefine apparent set-backs simply as "divine interruptions" that are to be embraced rather than avoided. Or they may have experiences that so fundamentally alter their conception of the world and their place in it that no perceived risk is greater than the danger of not living out God's call to love others. As Heidi Baker put it: "The moment I met Jesus I was ruined. My life was not my own. Once you see Him, there is no turning back. I have seen His eyes. Now I can never turn away. If we die, we die for Him; if we live, we live for Him."[32] This sense of meaning and purpose transcends ordinary concerns about physical or emotional well-being and financial security. In this worldview, losing one's life does not represent failure. What ultimately matters is living out a life of love, rooted in a deep relationship with God, wherever that path may lead and regardless of the secular yardsticks of success.

It is therefore appropriate that God occupies the top box in our diamond model, indicating that for the exemplar, and possibly the collaborators and beneficiaries, God is perceived as an actually existing partner in interactions, and perhaps the most important one. This has been a theme of our book, and as the GLNS demonstrated, God is indeed a "significant other" for most Americans, not just exemplars. The arrows in figure 7.1 indicate that interactions potentially flow in two directions. Any of the individuals represented in the lower triangle portion of this diamond model can interact with God, for example, by treating God as the object of their love (possibly in terms of adoration), but also by being the beneficiary of God's love. An individual may pray to God (represented by the arrow pointing to God), and God may respond (represented by the arrow pointing away from God). The prophetic dialogue that we discussed in chapter 5 is one example of such a two-way interaction with God, in which pray-ers reach out to God, wait for a response (a "sign," a feeling, or perhaps an audible voice), and then put into practice their understanding of God's will. Engaging in devotional prayer only might be more of a one-way interaction with God, as this can be more of a monologue than a dialogue. Perhaps some arrows could be made thicker than others to indicate the relative strength of a particular interaction at a given point in time; other arrows could be removed entirely or visualized with a dotted line to indicate their potential for being realized even if they do not currently exist. The latter situation would be plausible in light of our discussion of how devotional prayer may eventually lead to prophetic or mystical encounters.

In the fully specified model, all participants are involved in two-way interactions. In this case, exemplars are involved in two-way interactions with God, collaborators, and beneficiaries, and this is likely to lead to much more effective forms of benevolence than if some of these interactions were one-way or entirely absent. The whole is greater than the sum of its parts, by which we mean that the combined effect of godly love relationships understood as a whole is likely greater than might be expected by simply summing up "love energy" fostered by the individual interactions. Furthermore, by directing attention to the beneficiaries, the model serves to remind us that being involved in deep, meaningful, long-standing relations with beneficiaries can help prevent abuses associated with providing "help" that is neither requested nor effective. If an exemplar is not involved in ongoing give-and-take relationships with beneficiaries, ideally as equals to the extent that this is possible, it stands to reason that they are more likely to meet the needs of those they claim to serve and resist imposing "solutions" that are neither helpful nor appreciated.[33] We have also seen how Pastor Bartow's willingness to pray for a beneficiary's healing, at the man's request and despite Bartow's misgivings, served as a powerful learning experience that helped launch him into exemplar status, which would ultimately bring him to our attention. Clearly the beneficiary had an existing relationship with God before calling on Pastor Bartow, and this man's relationship with God in turn affected the pastor's ministry.

For the more mystical of our interviewees, supernatural miracles are central to interactions with God and an important source of empowerment for benevolence. Heidi, for example, believes that she can accomplish nothing without the power of God. Her unconditional love for others, including enemies who have attacked her, is rooted in her experience of divine power. Indeed, her love is impotent without it. When asked about the relationship between power and love, Heidi used the metaphor of needing two wings to fly:

> You can't fly with one. Power and love are very much connected. If you have this great love and compassion for the poor and have no bread, you're a very sad person. If you have great compassion and concern for the dying and the sick and you have no power to see them healed, you end up a very sad person. But the merciful love of God is that his love has teeth. His love has teeth. He doesn't give you this radical compassion so you just sob in the dirt and have no answer. He gives you radical compassion because he knows very well that any human being who would yield themselves to the power of the Holy Spirit would have the power to lay hands on the sick and they would be healed.... He does not put love in your heart without any power. That would be sick and

sad. God is a powerful and loving God, and he gives us both. So we have two wings and now we soar.

Whereas some observers have claimed that modern culture has left us "crippled in our capacities" to participate in the supernatural, for people like Heidi who have adopted a pentecostal worldview there is simply no possibility of doing her work effectively without it.[34] Participation in the unfolding of God's supernatural love in ways that bring mental, spiritual, and even physical healing to other people helps to explain why Heidi is able to persevere in the face of impossible circumstances. She claims to have experienced the divine breaking into the world, and that has radically changed her perspective and empowered her ministry when material circumstances seemed impossible.

Figure 7.2 displays another heuristic device: a four-part process that we believe captures the essential elements of participating in godly love. We developed this model to display our impression of the process of participating in godly love. Repeated religious experiences, particularly involving divine love (step 1), shift the lens through which a person understands the world, leading to an increasing focus on the spiritual over the material (step 2). This in turn impacts the quantity and quality of interactions with others and God (step 3), which are captured in the diamond model of godly love in figure 7.1. The fourth box in the model displays the outcome, as the person increasingly turns toward a life of benevolent service, strengthening the interactions in the bottom part of the diamond model of godly love and expanding their network of collaborators. If the person emerges from a social network as an exemplar at this point, it is because they are seen by collaborators and beneficiaries as especially gifted spiritual leaders, like Don, Steve, or Paul. They begin to establish durable organizations devoted to benevolence.

Many of our interviewees would describe this process as contributing to increases in the five dimensions of love displayed in the fourth box. Sociologist Pitirim Sorokin described these five dimensions in his classic work *The Ways and Power of Love*.[35] The process of participating in godly love, our interviewees would suggest, increases the intensity (power, degree), duration (amount of time), purity (selflessness), extensivity (unconditionality, extension of benevolence to more and more inclusive groups of people), and adequacy (effectiveness) of their acts of benevolent love. We have added a sixth consideration to Sorokin's original list: the content or nature of the benevolence. We have done this simply to point out that dimensions like purity or adequacy must be evaluated within a specific type of benevolence (e.g., service, renewal, social change) and that there are social, political, and

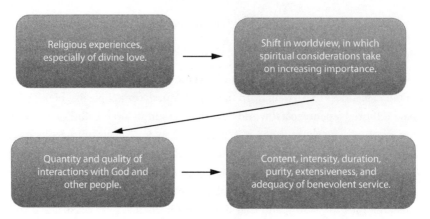

FIGURE 7.2 The Process of Participating in Godly Love

theological disagreements about the proper content of benevolence. We return to that issue in the next chapter. For now, we provide figure 7.2 primarily to sum up the process of godly love based on the material we have presented up to this point.

Collaboration in America: A View from the GLNS

Consistent with the godly love model, we asked several questions in our national survey about collaboration in the provision of benevolent service. As shown in table 7.1, almost half of all Americans work with other people when they help those in need. (The subsequent items displayed in the table are based on the 1,081 respondents who actually provided some tangible form of help to people in need, either volunteering their time or donating money.) In addition to the total sample, we also include columns showing the collaboration of the 121 respondents who experienced God's love directly most frequently ("more than once per day"), the 118 most prophetic people (those who sensed a divine call to perform a specific act on most days or more frequently), and the 262 folks who self-identified as pentecostal or charismatic. Throughout this book, we have explored the evidence that a pentecostal worldview and pentecostal experiences are important for determining the quantity and quality of divine love experiences. We have concluded that self-labeling as pentecostal (Pentecostal and/or charismatic) is less important than having pentecostal experiences such as participating in prophetic prayer. Ultimately, we might view the experience of divine love itself as a component of the pentecostal worldview, given how strongly pentecostal markers seem implicated in the experience of divine love. Table 7.1 seems to further substantiate this position, without totally discounting the importance of self-labeling, as the High Divine Love and High Prophecy groups seem to stand out more dramatically from the total sample than the pentecostal/charismatic self-identifiers, at least on some items.

As the table shows, the High Divine Love (HDL) and High Prophecy (HP) groups have higher percentages for all items than the total sample, with the HDL group showing the highest scores for five items and the HP group for two items. In three out of seven items, the pentecostal group actually had lower scores, although only marginally so. The second item on the list taps extensivity, with the highly prophetic primarily helping those outside their personal network (family, friends, coworkers) and local communities at a higher level (28 percent, compared with 23 percent for the total sample). Demonstrating the importance of religion in mobilizing benevolence, six out of ten Americans work with one or more religious groups to help people in

Table 7.1 Collaboration and Godly Love

	Total Sample (1,208)	High Divine Love (112)*	High Prophecy (118)#	Pentecostal Self-Identification (262)
Collaborate in helping those in need	45%	54%	46%	42%
Primarily help outside of personal network or local community	23%	25%	28%	21%
Work with religious group to help those in need	60%	79%	71%	73%
Work with beneficiaries to help those in need	50%	53%	64%	49%
"Strongly agree" others have shown great kindness	21%	36%	31%	24%
"Strongly agree" have received significant help	23%	35%	34%	26%
"Strongly agree" feel great joy in helping	40%	63%	53%	45%

* Feel God's love directly more than once per day
# Sensed a divine call to perform specific act most days or more often

need. It is not surprising that the figures for the subgroups are even higher, with the HDL group approaching eight out of ten. The HP group stands out in terms of working with beneficiaries to help those in need, with 64 percent indicating this, compared to 50 percent for the total sample. This was reflected in the approach of Pastor Bartow's community service center, which equips former beneficiaries to become volunteers and even organizational leaders.

We also asked respondents about the benevolence that they had received. The HDL group had the highest scores on these two items, with the prophetic not far behind. They have been shown great kindness by others and received significant help from others to a greater degree than the average American. The HDL group is also more likely to strongly agree that they feel great joy in helping others (64 percent, compared to a baseline of 40 percent). Taken together, these findings suggest those who experience a high degree of divine love or who participate in prophetic prayer are more likely to collaborate with others (and particularly those in religious groups) in helping people in need, including collaborating with the beneficiaries themselves, and they are also more likely to have received help from others and to feel pleasure in helping. This is consistent with other research that has found religious networks to be especially adept at promoting good works on behalf of others.[36]

There is some overlap between the experience of divine love and prophetic prayer, as we have already explored. Half of Americans have experienced prophetic prayer at some point in their lives, while the figure for those who have experienced the highest levels of divine love rises to 81 percent. But the two experiences are not identical. Only 26 (23 percent) of the 112 HDL respondents were also included in the HP group. So it is useful to think about these groups as somewhat overlapping but conceptually distinct. Prophetic prayer, by itself, is not required to experience the highest levels of divine love. But it is an important practice that can help foster this experience. When we assess benevolence in the next chapter, we will pay special attention to these two interesting but understudied groups.

The discerning reader may be wondering, what exactly counts as benevolent action? Is it more benevolent to prayerfully cure the soul, to give money to charitable organizations that feed the hungry and give medical service to the sick, or to lobby the government to change the social system to provide for all in need? Does saying a prayer or writing a check count as benevolence? Is divine love related to all of these activities? Does benevolence require a certain degree of personal sacrifice, hardship, and pain? There are no simple, agreed-upon answers to such questions, but these and other issues surrounding benevolence are our primary focus in the next chapter.

8

Benevolence in the Eyes of the Beholder

EFFECTS OF SOCIAL FILTERS

UNCONDITIONAL LOVE DOES not come naturally to humans as a species. As with all other relatively complex animals, evolution has endowed us with the innate capacity for reciprocal altruism but not for unconditional love. Doing good for beloved family members is one thing; extending familial love beyond kin is the material for a warm fuzzy story to cap the daily news. Indeed, we are quite adept at keeping track of those who wrong or help us, but sacrificing for our enemies makes little evolutionary sense. In other words, we do not seem to be "hardwired" for selfless love—at least not beyond immediate kin. Six years ago, Matthew designed the first university course on "the sociology of love" that deals with diverse types of love (parental, altruistic, spiritual, and romantic). He has noticed that the idea of unconditional benevolence is a difficult concept for students to accept. They are deeply skeptical of the practical value of selfless love at the beginning of the course, and roughly half remain unconvinced at the end of the semester, even after being exposed in detail to the works of benevolent leaders like Martin Luther King Jr., Gandhi, and Mother Teresa. For these young skeptics, unconditional love expressed beyond one's immediate family remains in the ethereal realm of the saints whose benevolence is dismissed by both religious and secular students, albeit for different reasons. Catholic students, whose tradition includes the canonization of saints, may insist that saints are somewhat different from most mortals, uniquely chosen by God for the role. At the other extreme, secular students have been known to contend that self-sacrificing saints are in fact mentally ill.

In previous chapters we used survey and interview data to describe the personal relationship that many Americans have with God. This relationship often includes a reportedly divine call to some special service to others that went beyond family and friends. A loving relationship with God and a divine call to action, however, are only part of the story of godly love; the other part is assessing whether experiencing divine love in fact facilitates actual benevolent service to others. There are those who would say, with little empirical evidence to back their claim, that religious experiences may be personally beneficial but have no social consequences. They would concur with this popular saying attributed to nineteenth-century Supreme Court Justice Oliver Wendell Holmes: "Some people are so heavenly minded that they are no earthly good." Another familiar nineteenth-century quote, this one by Henry David Thoreau, goes even further to express wariness about benevolence: "If I knew for a certainty that a man was coming to my house with a conscious design of doing me good, I should run for my life."[1] Holmes's concern that religious mystics might be so caught up in their own spiritual experiences that they withdraw from the needs of a suffering world is perhaps overshadowed only by Thoreau's fear that they might actually try to alleviate some part of this suffering and do real damage in the attempt! So readers have cause to question the guiding thesis of this book. Is it really possible that for many Americans religious experiences are a catalyst for benevolence that is actually beneficial to the recipient?

The relationship between personal experiences of God's love and actively demonstrating love for others beyond kin is one that we are able to test statistically through the GLNS responses. We found that those who professed to experience divine love were also likely to be more benevolent as measured by six different items and scales. Statistics, however, can tell only part of the story. By using lived-out examples provided by interviewees, we are able to illustrate the complexities of identifying and evaluating benevolence. Benevolence is more than an abstract concept; it is defined, given, and received in permeable social contexts. What is deemed benevolent action in one group may in fact be dysfunctional in another context. Using accounts provided by our interviewees to explore the efficacy of benevolence, we describe its relationship to spirituality as well as to the norms and social contexts in which benevolence appears.

Religion and Benevolence in America

As we have demonstrated throughout this book, the dynamic model of godly love takes experiences of God seriously. For the people we have interviewed, God is a collaborator in human acts of benevolence. Our finding that religious people are more benevolent than the nonreligious is not new; what is new is that we trace this benevolence, at least in part, to experiencing God's love. For example, Putnam and Campbell's recent study found that the religious in America were more generous, more involved in both secular and religious causes, more civically engaged, more altruistic, and more trustworthy than the nonreligious.[2] In seeking to explain this finding, they employed the commonly used theory of social networks, identifying such networks as the most important factor in promoting benevolence.[3] Yet Putnam and Campbell did not seem totally satisfied with their explanation and went on to ask, "If religiously based social networks...are so powerful, what in turn explains involvement in those networks?" They have few answers and note that their data "can take us only a short way."[4] After acknowledging this inability to explain involvement in religious networks, they say: "Although we lack systematic information about exactly what is discussed in these religious networks, it is possible that religious friends are more likely to raise moral issues, principles, and obligations than friends from a nonreligious context and thus to heighten your own attentiveness to such concerns." While not denying the importance of social networks, we are no more satisfied with Putnam and Campbell's speculation than they seem to be. We suggest an alternative, possibly complementary, hypothesis: perhaps these networks help foster and sustain *experiences* of a loving God.

We turn to the survey data to determine whether this complementary hypothesis finds support in the GLNS. We have already demonstrated the importance of the pentecostal worldview and religious experiences such as devotional, prophetic, and mystical prayer in predicting the experience of divine love. We have also noted that more than eight out of ten Americans reported that the experience of God's love increased their compassion for others. Does this single item measure square with statistical findings linking experiences of God's love with reported measures of benevolence? It does appear to. Our analysis suggests that this self-reported indicator of God's empowering love aligns with other survey questions used to explore the relationship between experiences of divine love and human benevolence.

In the GLNS we included a variety of diverse measures of benevolence to tap reported benevolent attitudes and actions that are common measures of benevolence. In table 8.1 we display frequencies for our key benevolence outcome variables. In the first column we present the figures for the total sample. The next four columns represent select subpopulations based on two measures of religious experience: experiencing divine love and participating in prophetic prayer. The *High Divine Love* group consists of the 112 people who "feel God's love directly" more than once per day (our highest category for that variable), compared with the 210 respondents who have never experienced divine love (*No Divine Love*). The *High Prophecy* group consists

Table 8.1 Benevolence Frequencies by Prophetic Prayer and Divine Love

	Total Sample (1,208)	High Divine Love (112)*	No Divine Love (210)**	High Prophecy (118)#	No Prophecy (590)##
Gave time	76%	93%	62%	86%	70%
Gave money	73%	84%	58%	73%	67%
Gave time more than once per week	20%	41%	20%	40%	18%
Gave money: $5,000 per year or more	3.4%	7.9%	2.8%	8.7%	2.1%
"Strongly agree" bond of humanity	23%	47%	21%	29%	20%
"Strongly agree" leave world better	46%	65%	39%	58%	42%
"Strongly agree" support world causes	17%	33%	14%	27%	15%
"Strongly agree" help humanity	27%	43%	23%	35%	23%
Income^	3.22	3.16	3.46	3.16	3.41

* Feel God's love directly more than once per day
** Do not feel God's love directly
# Sensed a divine call to perform specific act most days or more often
Do not sense a divine call to perform a specific act
^ "3" is $36,000 to $53,999

of 118 respondents who claimed they "sensed a divine call to perform a specific act" at least on "most days," compared with the 590 *No Prophecy* respondents who have never had that experience.

The general trend is readily apparent: those who scored high on divine love or prophetic prayer experiences were more likely to give their time and/ or their money to help others; they were also more likely to report benevolent attitudes, indicating the importance of bonding with and helping the larger world. The pattern is somewhat more pronounced for divine love, as those who experience divine love most frequently score the highest on all but "giving more than $5,000 per year" (the highly prophetic score slightly higher on that item). In no case is an absence of divine love (or prophecy) associated with higher benevolence.

Those who regularly sense calls from God to perform specific acts and those who experience divine love most frequently are twice as likely to give their time (more than once per week) to help people in need compared with the total sample. These two groups also report giving more than twice as much money as the total sample to help people in need, despite incomes that are somewhat lower than the average (see bottom row of figures in table 8.1). Those who experience divine love most often are also twice as likely as the full sample to strongly agree that "all people share an unbreakable bond of humanity," an attitude that has been identified as an important predictor of benevolence, and perhaps even the "heart" of altruism.[5] Based on this preliminary analysis comparing various benevolence figures, we find support for our general hypothesis that experiences of a loving God may be driving the benevolent efficacy of religious social networks. Those who frequently engage in prophetic prayer with God and those who are aware of God's love on a daily basis score higher on all GLNS benevolence measures.

Additional attention to table 8.1 is revealing. In four cases, those who experience divine love at the highest level have benevolence scores that are double those who do not experience divine love at all (and a fifth case is nearly double). All eight of the benevolence scores for the High Divine Love group are substantially above the mean for the total sample; seven of the benevolence scores for the No Divine Love group are below the mean for the total sample, and the eighth is identical to the mean. Consider this specific finding: almost half (46 percent) of all American adults feel "strongly" that they should contribute to making the world a better place, but for those who directly experience divine love most frequently, the figure rises nineteen percentage points, to 65 percent. On the other hand, only 39 percent of those who do not feel God's love directly strongly agree with this statement. In other words, there is a twenty-six-point gap in this measure of benevolence separating those Americans who are most in touch with God's love from those who have not experienced divine love at all.

Further Exploration of the Thesis

The lives of the exemplars of godly love we interviewed add important details to these simple statistics. They appear to have been empowered for greater benevolence in part through their frequent encounters with the divine. We saw in earlier chapters how these men and women experienced spiritual transformations, heard a divine call on their lives, and have been energized by different forms of prayer. They persist in their benevolence despite setbacks and suffering because they have learned to redefine the meaning of these setbacks in a way that allows them to see a bigger picture. Their personal accounts illustrate how their experiences of God's love have energized and empowered their benevolence to others outside their immediate family and friendship networks. Most people are responsive to societal norms—reinforced perhaps through biological genes—to care for those who are near and dear to them. Quite simply, we learn to scratch the backs of those who will either now (or later) be willing to scratch ours. Our survey respondents were nearly unanimous when it came to items reflecting caring for family and friends: 99 percent agreed that "when my loved ones are having problems, I do all I can to help them"; 97 percent said they "enjoy doing favors for people I know"; and 97 percent agreed that "it is important to me personally to be helpful to friends, neighbors, and coworkers."

Fewer people responded affirmatively to the questions that inquired about caring for members of their larger community or meeting global needs. When asked whether the respondent goes "out of my way to assist people in my community who are struggling" (75 percent), comes "to the aid of a stranger who seemed to be having some difficulty" (73 percent), or actively supports "causes around the world that seek to help the less fortunate" (66 percent), affirmative responses reflecting benevolence drop significantly from the near universally expressed concern for family and close friends. The decrease is even more significant if we consider those whose response was "strongly" affirmative. Only 44 percent strongly agreed that it is "important for me to leave this world better than I found it," and 26 percent strongly agreed that their efforts "are motivated by a desire to help humanity in some way." Our exemplars were definitely in the group that cared about their kin but went the extra mile in serving strangers in their midst and beyond. Using the language of sociologist Pitirim Sorokin, whose groundbreaking theory and research on love is a classic in the field, our exemplars of godly love knew a love for others that was more *extensive* than that of most Americans.[6] While nearly all survey respondents claimed benevolence toward family and to a lesser extent toward friends, the extensity of benevolence decreased with responses to questions tapping the community and the larger world.

The ethos of our modern world operates largely on what sociologist Max Weber has called "technical rationality," which tends to focus on achieving practical goals in the most efficient way. In modern societies filled with fast-food restaurants and inexpensive motels, hospitality to the stranger seems best left to formal organizations. In fact, it may be dangerous to welcome strangers into our lives. Our exemplars, however, sought to follow a complementary road that allowed them to be guided by love and service rather than solely by efficiency and practicality. They would be the first to admit that they do not live up to this ideal all of the time, or perhaps even frequently. But at important points in their lives they have responded to a calling to serve others without expectation of personal gain or success. Theirs includes a "substantive rationality" that has provided a framework for pursuing goals derived from a larger set of ethics or ultimate standards—goals grounded in a response to a divine calling to love unconditionally.[7] In the case of our exemplars, their selfless response to divine instructions may make little sense to those seeking the material rewards of a technically rational world.[8]

One memorable example can be found in Paul Alexander's social justice activism, which cost him his job at a Christian university. The university had been acting as a slumlord to disadvantaged residents by refusing to bring some of the properties it owned up to code. According to Paul, the violations—including bare wires in bathrooms—put the residents at risk. When Paul attempted to convince university administrators to fix the problems, one suggested that the university could build a wall around the properties so nobody would have to see them. The university ultimately decided to demolish the properties, thereby displacing the residents. This and other similar conflicts would eventually force Paul out of the university. But out of this early attempt at activism, Paul has developed a worldwide ministry of peace and justice. The refusal to go along with the morally expedient but financially efficient practices of his university resulted in the short-term loss of a career path, but in the long run it fortified his vocation.[9]

Whether or not Paul's actions qualify as self-giving benevolence, however, depends on how that concept is defined and the context in which the benevolence is enacted. As we will continue to demonstrate, these "social filters" make a difference. The notion of social filters implies that reality is neither "given" nor perceived in monolithic terms. Instead, cultures and subcultures provide different resources for constructing meaning in distinct ways. Paul's example demonstrates a shift to a substantively rational way of life, one that involves an expansion of the meaning of "efficiency" and an enlargement of one's circle of concern. While the academic institution where Paul was employed was operating on a technically rational cost-benefit model, at least with regard to slum housing, Paul was listening to a different voice. Some degree of substantive rationality can be demonstrated in the stories of all of our exemplars as they lived out their perceived divine calling. Thus the shortest distance to a life of meaning may not be the straight line of a secure career dictated by technical rationality but, rather, a circular path in which today's obstacles and defeats become the unexpected blessings of tomorrow.

Evidence of the power of substantive rationality to pursue a life of meaning is not only found in individual lives but may also be embodied in the organizations guided by leaders who can adeptly blend a pragmatic technical rationality with ethical substantive rationality. Steve Witt is such a leader. His fascination with the world of business and the economy that is arguably the epitome of technical rationality became readily apparent in our interview with him; it is reinforced as we listen to his Sunday sermons streamed through the Internet. He commonly develops a technically rational plan that reflects business principles to expand his cluster of churches, but he is also in tune with a divine voice that may call him to modify his plan as he takes on a seemingly unrelated task. Steve describes this juxtaposition of a well-developed plan and a divine detour as follows: "I've got a plan [for my ministry], but along the way you see a lot of needs. Like the good Samaritan, you stop, put them on your donkey." Moved by the substantive rationality of love, which flows from his experience of God's unconditional love, Steve does not lose sight of immediate needs as he looks toward his larger vision of planting one hundred churches to facilitate the spiritual and social transformation of northeast Ohio. (With the establishment of a fourth congregation under way, Steve looks beyond the present, as he jovially announces, "Only ninety-six more to go!") One example of a seeming detour from his larger vision began unexpectedly while Steve and his family were vacationing in the Bahamas. There they met the pastor of a Haitian church whose partially constructed building was without a roof and unusable for congregational gatherings. Although the Haitian pastor's problem was not in line with either a restful family vacation or relevant to his vision of transforming his hometown community, the church without a roof was put on Steve's donkey. Meeting this need took nearly two years of working through bureaucratic red tape, raising $100,000 to cover the unexpected high costs of building on the island, and providing the labor and expertise needed to put a roof on the church—"divine interruptions," in Steve's words. If the timeline for achieving his stated goals is pushed back, Steve and his collaborators believe that they are still doing God's will and living out an unconditional love of neighbor. They see beyond the technical and give meaning to their acts in terms of the substantive, an ability we have discussed elsewhere as "seeing beyond circumstances."[10]

Steve Witt does not operate in a vacuum. He has taught his church to appreciate the blurred boundaries between the spiritual things of heaven and the material reality of life on earth. Bethel Cleveland is part of a growing network of churches whose leaders and congregants believe that heaven (at least in some degree) can be brought down to earth—although there are undeniably competing visions about the form of heaven brought to earth and the means used to bring it about. Some critics outside the Bethel network, for example, might contend Steve would have done better to work for structural change in the poor Haitian community—perhaps providing food, better education, or medical services—rather than a church roof. Those in Steve's interpretive community understand the sense of being divinely directed to stop and place a particular need on the proverbial donkey—a need that might be assessed differently by those not in the community. Benevolence, as we will see, often lies in the eyes of the beholder, shaped by interpretive communities that may see the world through different lenses than those offered by a technical, rational culture. Readers might disagree with substantive religious values reflected in the lives of exemplars like Steve, whose personal relationship with God often directs his choices and frames acts of benevolence. This relationship with the divine was of primary importance in the lives of our exemplars. Many if not most, when asked to identify the most significant events in their lives, would begin with an account of how they came into a relationship with God. This relationship with the divine was regarded as central to personal lives as well as in their choices about how best to work for the betterment of the world.

Is Religion Relevant for Understanding Benevolence?

Based on the diverse measures of benevolence we used in the GLNS, we would answer this question affirmatively yet with caution. We recognize that our various measures of benevolence are hardly exhaustive. Furthermore, they reveal little about benevolence as it exists in the eyes of the beholder, that is, about its social and interpretive facets. It would appear that "religion," that is, beliefs and ritual practices, is clearly less important than "spirituality" as measured by the Divine Love scale in accounting for benevolence. Multivariate statistical analyses tested for six different measures of benevolence provide clear and consistent evidence that experiencing divine love plays a significant role in benevolence. Whether it is giving time or money, or helping at the family, friend, community, or world level, the experience of God's love has a positive and significant effect, even after controlling for six common demographic variables and four other contextual measures.

Statistical Findings for Six Benevolence Measures

Time as Benevolence

Respondents were asked how often they gave of their time "to help people in need during the last twelve months." Demographics played a small role in accounting for differences: men, younger people, and those with less income were slightly more likely to give their time to help someone in need. They were also slightly more likely to be involved in helping others through a religious network. But the leading descriptor of someone who gave time to help others was someone who frequently experienced divine love.[11]

Money as Benevolence

Not surprisingly, demographic variables played a bigger role in the amount of money "donated to help people in need during the past twelve months." Having a greater income, having a higher level of education, and (to a lesser extent) being male and older all impacted the amount of money donated. Those who gave more money to help those in need were likely to be politically liberal. Another statistically significant descriptor of those who give money to help the needy is scoring high on the Divine Love scale.[12]

Familial Benevolence

Respondents tended to strongly agree with the three questions we asked to tap benevolence directed toward their families. They were likely to "make a special effort to be kind" when someone in the family was upset and to do all they could when "loved ones are having problems," and they felt they were good "at figuring out ways to help my family." Women and those with higher incomes were more likely than men and those with less income to score high on familial benevolence. Those who scored higher on the Divine Love scale were also more likely to score high on familial benevolence, as did those who had a higher spiritual affinity for others (the "belief that all people share an unbreakable bond of humanity").[13]

Benevolence toward Friends and Coworkers

The items used to measure benevolence toward friends, neighbors, and coworkers asked whether the respondent made "a special effort to visit them when they are sick"; whether they enjoy doing favors for them; and whether it is "important to me personally to be helpful to friends, neighbors, and coworkers." The two leading predictors were spiritual affinity and experiencing divine love.[14]

Community Benevolence

Respondents were given three statements that made up the Community Benevolence scale: "I go out of my way to assist people in my community who are struggling," "I have often come to the aid of a stranger who seemed to be having difficulty," and "I regularly provide financial support to local charities." The leading descriptors for those who scored high on community benevolence were acknowledging a spiritual affinity with all humanity and experiencing divine love.[15]

World Benevolence

Our final benevolence measure asked respondents to think globally—"to think about people beyond your community" and "to consider the world." Statements included the following: "It is important for me to leave this world better than I found it," "I actively support causes around the world that seek to help the less fortunate," and "My efforts are motivated by a desire to help humanity in some way." Demographics were found to play no role in helping to describe those who scored high on the World Benevolence scale. The best descriptors were a person's self-identifying as an ideological liberal, indicating a high spiritual affinity with humankind, and scoring high on the Divine Love scale.[16]

Contextualizing and Summarizing the Statistical Findings

In chapter 1 we mentioned the work of political scientist Kristen Monroe, who, based on her research, concluded that religion is "irrelevant" for altruism.[17] She acknowledges that a "spiritual feeling of closeness to others" is important and concludes, "This finding appears to trouble some scholars from religious schools or departments of religion. I can only remind them that these are simply my findings, which I must report honestly."[18] Not only was religion irrelevant in Monroe's assessment, but there was no room in her discussion for a spiritual feeling of closeness to God. Our research suggests that there is much more to the story about religiosity and altruism.[19] The GLNS included a question that tapped Monroe's "spiritual feeling of closeness to others" by asking whether a respondent shared "an unbreakable bond of humanity" with all others "regardless of their situation." In part, Monroe's thesis is correct; spiritual affinity is an important predictor for four out of six of the benevolence measures, and in three of the cases, it was the most important predictor of benevolence. Furthermore, Monroe may also be correct about "religion": beliefs and rituals are not particularly good predictors of increased benevolence.

What is new in the statistics we have presented is the importance of experiencing God's love for empowering benevolence. Not only does the Divine Love scale appear to have direct effects on benevolence, but experiencing divine love may be indirectly affecting a feeling of a strong bond with all humankind. As shown in table 8.1, spiritual experiences—prophecy and knowing God's love—are related to the GLNS measure of spiritual affinity. Whereas 23 percent of the total sample scored high on identifying with all of humankind, the figure rises to 29 percent of those who score high on prophecy, and 47 percent of those who score high on divine love. In considering Monroe's spiritual closeness or affinity in light of our model, experiences of the divine and human continue to work together.

These findings about divine love and its impact on benevolence are consistent with the work of sociologist Pitirim Sorokin, particularly in his discussion of "love energy."[20] According to Sorokin, "love can be viewed as one of the highest energies known," and he contends that social scientists can study "the channeling, transmission, and distribution of this [nonphysical] energy."[21] Although his focus was primarily on the love energy produced by human beings, Sorokin did acknowledge the "probable hypothesis" that "an inflow of love comes from an intangible, little-studied, possibly supra-empirical source called 'God,' 'the Godhead,' 'the Soul of the Universe,' 'the Heavenly Father,' 'Truth,' and so on."[22] Although strictly speaking we have not proven Sorokin's observation, his description of a probable "supra-empirical source" of love is insightful for interpreting our surprising findings.

What surprised us is that the experience of God's love was the only variable that significantly predicted all of our dependent variables for benevolence. Whether giving time or money, or helping at the family, friend, community, or world level, the experience of God's love has a positive and significant effect, independent of controls. In the two of six models in which political ideology is significant, it is liberals who are more benevolent; younger people are more likely to give their time, while older people are more likely to give money or help their community (age was not significant in the other three models). Men are more likely to give time and money; women are more likely to help family and friends. Race is never significant, income is significant in four models (higher income predicts more benevolence in three, but the relationship is negative in one), and education is significant only once. Religious helping networks are significant in the expected positive direction in four of six models, church attendance is never significant, and sharing a bond with all humanity is positive and significant in four models. It would appear that spiritual affinity, religious helping networks, and experiences of divine love are important factors in accounting for differences in benevolence. It also appears that the effect of these factors depends on the measure used to tap benevolence. But there is still another important issue to consider in unraveling the multifaceted phenomenon we call benevolence.

Evaluating Benevolence

We have established through the GLNS that people who report more frequent experiences of divine love also report engaging in more benevolence, as tapped by six different measures. But the survey does not tell us much about the content of specific benevolent acts. To do this we will need to go beyond the survey trends and use our interview data to examine concrete actions of real people in their social and political context. This is important because abstract discussions of love and benevolence provide little guidance in the confusing circumstances of the real world. It is easy to set up a binary opposition between good and evil in the abstract and exhort people to love their neighbor, or even their enemy. But actual social issues almost always involve multiple competing goods and evils—shades of gray rather than simple dichotomies—as well as substantial disagreement or uncertainty about basic facts. Sociologists have demonstrated the distinct ways in which different groups understand social problems, tied to the fundamentally different worldviews and conceptions of reality associated with diverse subcultures. Making moral choices about doing "good" is much more complex and less certain under such conditions.

Tribalism and Benevolence

Sorokin's work on love has provided a theoretical foundation on which our project was built. Yet in the postmodern era, where diverse voices compete to define reality, there are limitations in that work, such as the hagiographic terms Sorokin used in discussing benevolent leaders like Gandhi.[23] The temptation to gloss over criticism of saintly figures is strong, but as the subtitle of one recent article puts it, perhaps "saints should be judged guilty until proved innocent."[24] Sorokin's typology of five dimensions of love remains a useful tool, as we have demonstrated in discussing the extensity of love from familial to global. It also helps us to make distinctions about expressions of love that are more or less intense, of short or long duration, pure or free of selfish motives, and adequate or effective in achieving the goal of helping the other. Of particular interest for assessing the mixed effects of benevolent actions is

Sorokin's insight on tribalism. He believed that much benevolence was "tribal," directed to the in-group at the expense of other out-groups, and therefore inadequate in the long run for fostering a better world for all. As we will demonstrate, the tribalism of in-groups helps to interpret the sometimes conflicting messages that we heard from our exemplars of godly love.

Spiritual experiences and their relationship to benevolence cannot be assessed apart from their "tribal" social contexts. Tribal perspectives differ, and these differences matter. For example, what counts as a divinely inspired vision for those who believe in the possibility of being visited by Jesus, Mary, or angels, for example, may be viewed as being demonic for Christians who believe spiritual visitations ceased with the apostle John on the Isle of Patmos. And secularists in the mental health profession who are likely to believe in neither angels nor demons, past or present, may interpret them simply as a natural product of psychopathology. To use another example, emotionally powerful visions of God associated with involuntary convulsions and shouting have been historically constructed by some groups of Protestants as "enthusiasm," or purely physical responses naively attributed to God. Other groups of Protestants resisted such secular explanations of what they saw as authentic spirituality—at least when experienced by members of their own group.[25] Such interpretations can be said to represent different "tribes" or different "interpretive communities."[26]

Contemporary religious responses to homosexuality and same-sex marriage provide another good example. In some communities the appropriately "Christian" response to homosexuals is a welcoming acceptance of a God-following neighbor, while in others homosexuals are seen as sinners in need of repentance and healing. Those who oppose homosexual practices and especially gay marriage on biblical grounds perceive homosexuals as sinners in violation of immutable divine prohibitions against same-sex relationships. Clearly for them it is a serious sin (one exemplar mentioned it in the same sentence as murder) that cannot be condoned or tolerated. Our interviewees expressed a range of opinions on this topic. Jay Bakker (son of the defamed televangelist Jim Bakker), for example, sacrificed the support of the largest financial contributor to his church when he converted it to a "welcoming" congregation.[27] Another pastor and his congregation, on the other hand, left their denomination, at great financial cost to the congregation, when it adopted a welcoming stance toward homosexuals.[28] In fact, two of our exemplars, Tony and Peggy Campolo, are well known in the evangelical community for representing different interpretive communities on gay marriage. Tony has succinctly summarized their respective positions before one of their public debates on the topic:

> First of all, I have to announce that we are two people who do not agree. We have very, very divergent views on this issue. I for instance believe that the Bible does not allow for same gender sexual marriage. I do not believe that same gender sexual intercourse is permissible if you read the Bible as I do. Peggy believes in monogamous relationships. In short, she would hold to a belief that within the framework of evangelical Christianity, gay marriages are permissible and she will try to make her point.[29]

Not only have we noted different voices representing different perspectives among our exemplars; we have also observed how changes in attitudes can occur and the role that prophetic prayer can play in such a change. The story that follows is one that demonstrates how interaction with God (and encountering members of the other "tribe") can precipitate a softening prejudice against homosexuality and gay marriage. Kris Vallotton, founder of Bethel School of the Supernatural Ministry in Redding, California, and one of our interviewees, reported his initial reaction to be one of anger when he found himself sitting next to a gay couple on a five-hour airline flight. As he watched them hold hands and "romantically embrace each other," Kris found his disgust growing—that is, until he heard from God: "As I sat there brewing, the Holy Spirit began to remind me that he loved these men. He was on a mission to draw them into the kingdom and he needed someone to show them the heart of the King." Kris tried to make small talk to break the ice with his new traveling companions, but his attempts were rebuffed. Gradually—after a humorous exchange (and sharing some cashews)—the walls that divided Kris and the two gay men, Frank and Tony, began to weaken. Kris had been reading a book about building an emotionally healthy church, and one of the men pointed to it, saying: "I don't like the Church. Those people scare me." To which Kris replied, "Yeah, they scare me too, but they pay me to work there." More humor and a long three-way conversation developed. Kris commented on the change of his demeanor, "I actually started to enjoy their company."

Kris, who is a leader in a community where prophetic prayer is taught and valued, began to get a prophetic word for Tony, and he asked if Tony wanted to hear what God had to say to him. With permission granted, Kris described "seeing" Tony in scenes where he was painting and sculpting, adding: "Tony, God told me to tell you that he has really gifted you in the arts and he says he created you to make a living at it." Before Kris could go on, the other man [Frank] was astounded and exclaimed: "Wow, that is absolutely true about Tony." Tony then replied, "I just took up sculpting and working with clay....Wow! How encouraging." A few minutes later Kris presented an equally revealing and encouraging prophetic word that was well received by Frank and confirmed by Tony. The account said nothing about sin and salvation; rather, it served to demonstrate the word of God's love for the men that God had spoken to Kris. Kris provided the following comment about his own response to this unexpected encounter: "I learned so much on the plane that day—mercy finally had a victory in my life. And Tony and Frank were introduced to the kingdom through a violent act of grace!"[30]

Sorokin recognizes that humans tend to work for their in-groups—in this case, gays for gays and conservative Christians for conservative Christians—often at the expense of those who are not part of their tribe. Yet there is little in Sorokin's framework that would enable us to tackle the lack of consensus about ultimate goals or "the good" implied in benevolence. In the example just provided of a pentecostal minister and the gay couple, adequacy of "the good" (such as working for laws supporting gay marriage versus supporting state constitutional amendments that condemn it) can only be understood in terms of a reference group or an interpretive community. In order to develop a fuller theoretical frame, we couple Sorokin's insight on tribalism with the work of another well-known sociologist, Philip Rieff. Through Rieff's discussion of changing social norms, we are able to better locate expressions of godly love within a concrete interpretive setting, thus giving us lenses to evaluate how well an act lives up to the stated goals of a group, as well as asking broader questions about the value of the goals for the larger community.[31]

Interdicts and Benevolence

In a posthumously published work that was assembled from fragments composed over several decades, Rieff attempted to explain, as the subtitle of his book suggests, "the gift of grace, and how it has been taken away from us" by modern ways of thinking and being.[32] He viewed the *charismatic* (which we might loosely translate as the spiritually empowered godly love exemplar) as a function of *interdicts* (i.e., divinely given cultural norms that impose limits on behavior and demand unqualified obedience). Rieff offered the example of the Ten Commandments, and the creedal order of ancient Judaism more generally, to illustrate the function of interdicts or societal prohibitions: "These interdictive instructions drew the Jews out of the welter of individual possibilities and established their corporate identity, their covenant."[33] He further argued, "It is for this reason that the true charismatic is always an interdictory figure, closing down the openness of possibility, narrowing the human passion for the infinite into a particular culture or way of life."[34]

To take a Christian example that is especially relevant to the study of godly love, the Great Commandment given by Jesus (love God and love neighbor as self) requires acute *agape*—love even to the point of loving one's enemies (see Matthew 5:44). This severe command often seems beyond the ability of mere mortals. Rieff would suggest that modernity and postmodernity cannot foster a true love of enemies. This is because contemporary *therapeutic* culture, with its tendency to provide salve for all moral discomfort just as it seeks to cure all physical pain, has undermined the divine creedal order. In the absence of a sacred order to provide binding moral rules, we are free to realize our full human potential as we, and perhaps our psychological therapist, see fit. But for Rieff this freedom comes at the price of a loss of divine grace and absolute standards of human conduct. Therapeutic culture is, at its core, a "releaser from the interdicts" that Rieff believes are essential for charisma and true spirituality.[35]

The lives of exemplars of godly love suggest that Rieff's pessimism about the lost "gift of grace" does not apply to all sectors of modern society. For many of our interviewees, whom we have called "pentecostal" with a lowercase *p* to signify their participation in the gifts of the Spirit, and for other "saints" like Gandhi and Mother Teresa, benevolence cannot be understood apart from divine commands, at least as they conceive of them.[36] If Gandhi and Mother Teresa were political reactionaries or friends of poverty rather than the poor, as some critics claim, this fact was inseparable from both their faith and their benevolent works. Their lives make little sense except as creative attempts to live within the demands of religious interdicts and commandments.[37]

Such imperatives and prohibitions, however, are not frozen in time, as we have seen in our example of perspectives on homosexuality; they are subject to evolving interpretations by communities. Margaret has shown how the seemingly fixed interdicts of the Catholic Church regarding religious life that governed Mother Teresa and her community have changed since the Second Vatican Council in the last half century.[38] Although the interdicts of Catholicism are likely to be formulated as church laws, Protestants have grounded their interdicts directly in the Bible. Their interdicts, however, are no less confusing, contradictory, and ripe for change than those of Catholicism. Christians in recent history, for example, have used the Bible to condone slavery, to support wars, to limit the rights of women, to prohibit interracial marriage, to support laws against the use of contraceptives, and to prohibit divorce. During this same historical period, other Christians have used the Bible to argue for abolition, for equal rights for women, and later for civil rights.[39] Currently select biblical passages are actively being employed to promote legislation to abolish abortion and to block legislation to guarantee the civil rights of gays. (Paradoxically, the same Christians who are protesting changes in the name of "family values" seem to have little interest in trying to repeal legislation that permits divorce—even though Jesus was quite explicit in his condemnation of divorce.) We are not prepared or equipped to explore all of these confusing contradictions of biblically based demands and interdicts, but it is apparent that changing social contexts do matter when evaluating benevolence.

Based on findings from the survey data and observations from exemplar interviews, however, we do have insight about how religious experience may help with interpreting biblical interdicts. Experiences of divine love have been found to play a significant role in benevolence, and we suggest that experiencing God's love—especially through prophetic prayer—is a factor that can change expressions of benevolence for individuals and perhaps their subcultures. Kris Vallotton's experience on the plane and the "lesson in mercy" derived from his prophetic interaction with the gay couple provides one example. Not only did this encounter mark a spiritual transformation for Kris; he has also included this account in a published work. With thousands of others reading it, Kris's story can have a ripple effect with his readers as they too may be struggling to be more accepting of homosexuals. The law of love has the potential to trump the interdict against homosexuality, just as it has in recent history trumped laws that blocked racial and gender equality. In this sense, love may be moving toward the status of master imperative that trumps all others. Love may serve as a lens through which the Bible is read and reinterpreted differently across generations. Another key to understanding how the Bible may continue to be perceived as a source of truth even while its interdicts are changing may be found in the differing ways the Bible is approached by believers.

Despite the fact that nearly three-fourths of Americans (74 percent, according to the GLNS) claim to believe "that the Holy Scripture is the word of God, true, word for word," this does not mean that the majority of Americans actually are literalists. The scriptures, many would argue, can be treated purely cognitively and/or filtered through experiential lenses. A modern Christian understanding of the Bible often distinguishes an affective

"Rhema" from a more cognitive "Logos." Increasingly in populist Christian (especially pentecostal) theology, Rhema "is called 'a word from the Word,' referring to the revelation received by the reader from the Holy Spirit" that accompanies the literal printed word. This distinction reminds the believer that Jesus is the Word of God (Logos) and the Spirit must be the interpreter (Rhema) in ways that reflect Jesus.[40] Believers are commonly reminded that the triune God is not "Father, Son, and the Bible" but that, rather, the third person of the Trinity is an active Holy Spirit who empowers followers to live lives of love. There arguably has been an increased emphasis on the Holy Spirit (and on the command to love) in American Christianity over the past half century. This may be due in part to the "pentecostalization" process where by the pentecostal worldview (as described in chapter 2) has filtered into evangelical and mainline churches, including the Catholic Church.

Paradoxically, this freedom to not only read but also interpret the Bible has always been a Protestant legacy, but it is one that has splintered Protestantism into countless sects and denominations. To use Sorokin's term, there are many Protestant "tribes" with different biblical interpretations and different interdicts, and they have become a house divided. Although the theoretical concepts of tribalism and its interdicts do not explain the dynamics or resolve the issues associated with conflicting "benevolence," it does provide a frame for demonstrating the importance of divine love. Knowing the love of God and hearing God's voice, suggests our data, can be a factor in better understanding this complex issue. We now turn to accounts from our exemplars for lived examples of divergent interdicts that were found in different social contexts.

Divine Calling, Changing Interdicts, and Ongoing Spiritual Transformation

The exemplars of benevolence selected for our interviews were involved in three broad types of service: community service (outreach to people in need, such as a homeless shelter); renewal/revival (revitalization of the larger church especially as guided by a vision of ushering in the kingdom of God on earth); and social justice (actions taken to effect changes in social and political structures).[41] We refer to people engaged in these three types of ministry as *Servers*, *Renewers*, or *Changers*, respectively. Particularly in the case of Renewers and Changers, we noted early in our interviews how they were drawn to focus on a particular kind of benevolence and that benevolence was rooted in a particular social context that reflected different political orientations. Thus

Renewers and Changers generally belonged to different political tribes, with the former leaning conservative and the latter liberal. In the section that follows, we examine the "benevolence" of two of our primary interviewees (Herb, Paul), who are both leaders promoting social justice, as well as one social network (the New Apostolic Reformation, henceforth NAR) in which a number of our Renewer interviewees were embedded. We have deliberately chosen conservative (NAR) and liberal/radical (Herb, Paul) examples to demonstrate the chasm that can be created by different "tribal" affiliations and conflicting "interdicts." As we will see, interdicts and commands are often bound up with implicit political implications even when an attempt is made to sidestep divisive ideologies. Some of our interviewees feel a divine calling (and divine empowerment) to work for justice for the oppressed. Others seek to meet the material needs of those who lack such things as food, shelter, clothing, education, or job skills, and they see this work as divinely inspired and blessed. Still others emphasize renewing the church according to inter-dictory standards that have gone unheeded. Why the difference? We suggest that interdicts do not come to people through divine revelation alone but are also mediated by the social groups in which they are embedded. Godly love can be seen as an expression of interdicts, but it is the social group that helps to filter this love, thereby shaping the content and character of this expres-sion. This is not to suggest that individuals are cultural dopes—that their behavior is entirely determined by their socialization—or spiritual dopes blindly following interdicts. They have all been influenced by other people and institutions, while at the same time they exercise some degree of creativity and "free will" (social scientists generally prefer "agency") in charting their own course through life.

The New Apostolic Reformation (NAR)

As we write this section, the NAR has been making the news because of the ties of some leaders to Republican politicians, particularly the campaign of former presidential candidate Governor Rick Perry of Texas.[42] British Pentecostal scholar William K. Kay observes that the NAR began in the char-ismatic movement of the 1970s and developed steam during the Toronto Blessing revival (1994–2006), a revival that affected both North American and British Pentecostalism. Kay (2007) notes: "They believed that the kingdom of God was going to advance against all opposition and that the kingdom had an earthly and political dimension and was not simply a distant spiritual benefit or an internal blessing to be invisibly enjoyed by the believer."[43]

C. Peter Wagner (one of our interviewees), who arguably has been called the "founder" of the NAR, has described it as "the fastest growing cutting edge of worldwide Christianity in our times…the most radical change in the way of doing Christianity since the Protestant Reformation."[44]

This amorphous movement is driven by a conception of "the good" that proponents see as consistent with the will of God. But as with most bold new movements, not everyone—not even everyone who has self-identified or been identified with the movement—would agree with all the propositions attributed to the NAR.[45] One media report offers the following observation:

> But what makes the New Apostolic Reformation movement so potent is its growing fascination with infiltrating politics and government. The new prophets and apostles believe Christians—certain Christians—are destined to not just take "dominion" over government, but stealthily climb to the commanding heights of what they term the "Seven Mountains" of society, including the media and the arts and entertainment world. They believe they're intended to lord over it all. As a first step, they're leading an "army of God" to commandeer civilian government.[46]

Sermons and teachings about how to accomplish the goal of bringing heaven to earth generally steer clear of overt partisan politics; instead, they focus on learning to listen for God and allowing God to empower believers in whatever is their life destiny.[47] Whether in the realm of business and finance, education, administration, or the arts, the message is to rely on the Holy Spirit to direct and empower the worker to bring a piece of heaven to the situation. Having said this, some leaders of the NAR have become overtly political with militaristic language seasoning news reports that would make the uninitiated reader wonder whether the NAR is taking lessons from radical Islam.

We first encountered the NAR firsthand in the summer of 2008 at a conference at the Global Awakening's (GA) sprawling Apostolic Resource Center in Mechanicsburg, Pennsylvania. GA is an organization founded by healing evangelist Randy Clark, commonly known in neo-pentecostal circles as the one who launched the Toronto Blessing revival in 1994.[48] During one of the first sessions NAR leader Peter Wagner explored the relationship between truth and power, arguing that in the old system power was a function of truth. In other words, if you conformed to God's truth, you gained power; truth was predefined by your denomination. In the postdenominational era the situation is reversed: power defines truth. The prophet or apostle is the source of interdicts, to return to Rieff's central construct. No longer beholden to a denominational hierarchy, prophets in the NAR use their charismatic power to redefine the truths that limited the imaginations of the previous generations. In fact, this process occurs in denominational structures as well. But in this context the pace intensifies, new possibilities are opened up, horizons are expanded. Wagner also discussed church finances, arguing that pastors should be given more authority to dispose of budgets as they see fit, in keeping with their role as apostles or prophets, rather than answering to a board, elders, or other overseers. The speaker noted that a church he had attended had a multi-million-dollar budget and that the pastor, as the one anointed by God, had complete control of it.

As sociologists, Margaret and Matt could easily imagine the potential for abuse in such a free-flowing institutional context. Indeed, the troubling case of Lakeland revivalist Todd Bentley was just beginning to unfold while this conference was going on. In midsummer 2008 Peter Wagner, Bill Johnson, Ché Ahn, and John Arnott—all of whom were both interviewed for this project and part of the NAR—were playing the role of self-proclaimed apostles within Bentley's soon-to-be-defunct revival ministry.[49] Although Bentley's role in the Lakeland revival would come to an end, a divorced and remarried (and reportedly repentant) Bentley would be back in the revival business three years later.[50] Bill Johnson's letter of endorsement of Bentley makes use of passive voice, stating that "Todd's marriage imploded" and "We grieved especially for Todd and his family, who would suffer from the choices that were made." But Johnson concludes:

> *In conclusion, I recommend Todd to you, believing that you will be blessed and encouraged by his ministry.* But perhaps even more important is the fact that Todd will be a reminder to us that it is possible to stand after such a great fall. We all live by grace, and only by grace. We desperately need examples of those who have walked in integrity all of their lives. But when there is sin, we need examples of restoration to bring hope to the broken people, many of whom are in our congregations. *God will use Todd to be a message of restoration.*[51] [Emphasis in the original]

What is truth in such tangled circumstances? Bentley's life suggests that truth, like benevolence, is in the eyes of the beholder. If truth is largely a function of power derived from reportedly divine appointment to the office of prophet or apostle, then those without power (and the designated office), such as Bentley's wife and children, are clearly at a disadvantage to answer this question. This seemed to us to be a particularly problematic aspect of the benevolence associated with the ideology of the NAR, whose leaders assert that the church was never been meant to be a democracy.[52] On the other hand, Johnson's endorsement can be read as an expression of the radical forgiveness at the heart of the Christian faith, a grace extended to transgressors who may not seem to merit it through the lens of a secular worldview. The contest over defining reality always starts with such social filters, which shape the ways in which facts are deployed in making sense of ambiguous situations.

As we discussed in chapter 3, one type of benevolent service that we studied relates to revitalizing the church. This is the primary focus of the NAR, although the movement also aims for radical social changes as well. Steve Witt is affiliated with the loosely structured NAR network, as reflected in his decision to align his churches with Bill Johnson's network of Bethel churches. The mission of Bethel churches has been identified as "revival"—"the personal, regional, and global expansion of God's kingdom through His manifest presence." Steve and his four Bethel churches in northeastern Ohio, as we have illustrated, provide an example of how NAR churches do ministry, namely with what they perceive to be supernatural empowerment.[53] It is important to note that there are also many ministries involving the meeting of material needs by those involved in the NAR. A primary difference between the NAR and the outreach of most other church groups is the role that a divine nudge and divine serendipity can play (as we illustrated through Steve Witt's putting the Haitian church on his "donkey") in the benevolence process.

But clearly some apostolic leaders are more confrontational and aggressive than others as they seek to bring the kingdom of God down to earth. This can be seen in the ministries of NAR apostle Ché Ahn and his longtime collaborator, prophet Lou Engle. As Ché discussed in a videotaped interview with the British show *Revival Fires*, an overarching NAR purpose is to translate the "revival" (church revitalization) into "reformation" (reform of civil society). To make his point, Ché compared his leadership in fighting against gay marriage in California to the abolitionists' fight against slavery.[54] It is not enough to renew the church; for Ahn and others in the NAR, there must be a related impact on the wider society. For Ché this influence must flow from upholding God's interdicts, especially those against abortion and gay marriage.[55] As we noted earlier, homosexuality is a topic that came up repeatedly and one that seemed to serve as a proxy for conservative politics. For Ché Ahn and his collaborators (e.g., Lou Engle), the call to renew the church and the world includes fidelity to the interdict defining marriage as involving one man and one woman.

We returned to Pennsylvania in the fall of 2008 in order to attend the annual GA-sponsored Voice of the Apostles conference and to conduct more interviews. This time a larger auditorium was needed for the crowd, so a large, modern-looking church near GA's Apostolic Resource Center was used. The historic election of Barack Obama as the forty-fourth president of the United States was just three days away, and the energy level at the conference was high, in part because of opposition to his candidacy. Speakers and attendees appeared to overwhelmingly support the John McCain and Sarah Palin ticket. While we were conducting an interview with a Global Awakening collaborator in a quiet side room, we could hear loud cheers coming from the main auditorium, where hundreds of attendees were responding both to the apostolic/pentecostal messages of the speakers and to political appeals to pray McCain into the White House. (Ché Ahn would lead a prayer meeting at an evening session of the conference that would pray specifically for Obama's defeat.) The background tension of the politically charged atmosphere was palpable as Margaret and Matt conducted the interviews.

Although Matt and Margaret share with most other sociologists a liberal/ radical political perspective, Margaret has long been a participant observer at revival gatherings. This was the first in which Margaret experienced naked politics being openly touted. Perhaps this was because of the upcoming presidential election. Or perhaps it was because we were behind the scenes doing interviews that gave us a particular vantage point. We both struggled to remain open-minded at this particular event as political differences surfaced between us and our interviewees. At one point during one of our interviews the implicit tension in the setting became overt when the interviewee brought up the campaign by NAR mainstay Lou Engle and others to shut down abortion clinics. Margaret interjected that this work was "not very loving, from my position," and the interview became a bit contentious. As the interview was winding down, Margaret corrected statements the young interviewee had made about Margaret Sanger. Seemingly uninformed about Sanger and the unique role she played in making contraception acceptable and legal as one of the founders of Planned Parenthood, Margaret questioned the interviewee's connecting Sanger with "racism" and "euthanasia." Commitment to the methods of values-free social science sometimes gives way to reasoned debate about social reality.

Our purpose in bringing a bit of our vantage point into the discussion of the NAR is to remind the reader—and ourselves—that religion-based benevolence sometimes unfolds in a political context and must be evaluated as such. We will see that in our next example, albeit from a very different political and cognitive vantage point. The interdicts at the heart of the NAR are constructed through a conservative political reading of the Bible, or what theologians would call a conservative "hermeneutic," or interpretive lens. Herbert Daughtry has a very different hermeneutic, but it is also a lens with a specific focus.

Herbert Daughtry

If the NAR interpretive lens is framed in the universal (if politically conservative) terms of transforming the world in the image of the kingdom of God, Herb's hermeneutic seems more concretely grounded in the local experience of the black community and is therefore more politically radical. It is perhaps easy to see why this kind of "tribalism" (again to use Sorokin's pejorative term) might permeate Daughtry's thinking and the culture of his ministry. As we discussed in chapter 3, Herb's "theme" is that the black community "must organize ourselves and act with self-interest" in order to deal with the concrete reality that its members are "being beaten and killed because we are powerless."[56] When Matt (along with research team member A. G. Miller) conducted the interview with Daughtry, his was the eighty-ninth such interview collected by the project. But even before it began, Matt told Herb that the specific expression of "social justice at this particular church is really unique among all of the other interviews." Herb sees this work, as we have noted, as a "covenant with the Almighty—a covenant that said if we did our part—that is to say if we worked with and struggled for the people—that God in turn would make our lives meaningful and worthwhile."[57]

This vision of his role helps explain why we labeled Herb a Local Planner in table 3.2. His benevolence is directed to the black community rather than outward to the wider world (hence "local"), and he articulates comparatively few pentecostal experiences, making him more of a Planner than a Mystic compared to others we interviewed. Recall from chapter 4 his description of his religious conversion in jail: "And I can't say that I got hit by fireballs or that angels tapped me upside the head. But deep down, within my very being, I knew that a change had happened, and I would never be the same."

As we have noted, Herb has spent his whole life "at the point of pain." That is where he believes that the servant of God ought to be, partly because that was the concrete example of Jesus. According to the Gospels, Jesus devoted much effort to liberating the oppressed (both the materially poor and the "poor in spirit"), he spent a great deal of time with despised individuals, and he was crucified for transgressing the norms of the dominant groups.

We have avoided much discussion of theology up to this point, but recent work in black theology might be helpful in understanding the in-group focus of Herb's benevolence—or, to put it more positively, its concreteness. Theologian J. Kameron Carter, drawing on the work of James Cone and others, explains that "abstraction" is the "perennial problem of white theology and Euro-American racism as a whole." This gets in the way of the white church expressing the Christian faith "authentically." According to Carter, "White Christianity does not entail concrete living, though it passes itself off as doing so."[58] In other words, it is useless at the "point of pain," where the black community so often finds itself.

Eschewing abstract and "universal" discussions of love or the kingdom of God, Herb and other Local Planners confront specific problems of racial injustice. By contrast, writes Carter, "white intellectual formation is in fact a religious, cultural, colonializing, and colonizing formation" because it deals with abstract categories rather than real people and relationships. Jesus did not stand with "the oppressed" symbolically as an abstract category; rather, he engaged with specific oppressed individuals and groups in a particular time and place. He wrote no theology but instead went to the point of pain. Carter explains that:

> In other words, whiteness as a theological problem has been insufficiently treated. At its heart is a problematic vision of the human as closed within itself, sealed off from possibilities of cultural intimacy and thus reciprocity. Rather than the site of intimacy, culture becomes the site of closure and containment.

This "closure and containment" has fed centuries of colonialism and oppression, often with tacit or even explicit support of the white Christian church. Lofty sermons went hand in hand with oppressive actions. The "real" Christian, according to the perspective developed here, is on the front lines battling oppression and is embedded in tangible and specific relationships with the suffering.

Recalling the civil rights struggles of the mid-1960s at one point in our interview, Herb provided an illustration of Carter's theological point:

> In Selma, you know when they had the clash there, [popular evangelist] Billy Graham had this great big meeting in the stadium. Black and white folks together, and this was supposed to be a symbol of Jesus's love for black and white people, and all you needed to do was clean up

your heart. They had everybody join hands. Blessed be the Lord, we all love Jesus. But when they all left, they all went back to their segregated patterns. All went back to an unchanged society. They all patted themselves on the back, how much Jesus loves us. But Jesus didn't seem to love them enough to make them want to change the systems that were destroying people.

Herb went on to discuss another conflict he had with different white Christian groups in that era, saying, "I mean, I'm saved. I'm filled with the Holy Ghost. I speak in tongues. I'm a mighty burning fire. I'm as conservative as anybody, I guess, theologically. But we have to struggle with the application of this conservative theology in the streets of Brooklyn. We have to struggle with our people in the penitentiary." The struggle with applying theology to the situation of blacks in a particular time and place is central to understanding Herb's benevolent service.

The context of white Christianity to which Herb was exposed in this era was very different, as he explained when he joked with us that "these white evangelicals got some beautiful retreat centers." When Matt asked whether Herb had seen "any progress in the white church since that time period on this issue," he responded, "I've not been that close. As I said, I pretty much kept my distance. I'm very suspicious of white evangelicals in terms of their social commitment, social justice commitment and their concerns for African liberation." He later offered this conclusion: "I haven't seen any significant movements within the evangelical circles that either verbally or in action fight for, struggle for, human rights and self-determination, particularly for people of African ancestry." When Daughtry was invited by white Christians to a dialogue at a small Christian college a short drive from Margaret and Matt's university that focused on "the application in social, political areas" of theological principles, his remarks were not well received, and he "never got any more invitations."

This discussion serves to underscore how the interdicts might look very different to a prophetic figure like Herb compared with the apostles and prophets of the NAR. This helps us understand the prophetic and interdictory tone in Herb's letter to the mayor of New York City in 1978, which ended all possibility of dialogue: "Let me repeat, with all the emphasis I can command, THE ONLY PLACE I LOOK FORWARD TO SEEING YOU IS BEFORE THE JUDGMENT SEAT OF GOD." Another part of the letter made the following accusation: "You, sir, seemed set upon a course that has been described by others as a 'war against the poor and against Black people.'" Herb concluded

the letter by quoting Robert Kennedy, writing, "Those who make evolutionary change impossible, make violent revolution inevitable."[59] Are such
sentiments benevolent? Are they examples of godly love? The answer depends
entirely on one's standpoint and hermeneutic. In this letter, Herb seems more
in tune with the Jesus who brings a sword (Matthew 10:34) than the Jesus
who is perhaps better known as the Prince of Peace (Isaiah 9:6).

It is easy to imagine how such an approach might lead to further conflict.
Herb has been accused of being anti-Semitic, a charge that prompted him to
write *No Monopoly on Suffering: Blacks and Jews in Crown Heights (and
Elsewhere)*. In the late 1970s, the *New York Post* even ran a picture of Daughtry
with "a portrait of Hitler superimposed over my face."[60] Earlier, the *Post*
printed a picture of him with the caption "We will get the Jews and the people
in the long black coats."[61] The latter is a reference to Hasidic Jews. Herb writes
in *No Monopoly* that the *Post* misquoted him and that what he really said was
"When we organize our patrol, when men meet men, we will see then what
the people in the long black coats will do."[62] In an interview with the *New
York Times*, Daughtry explained, "We're not looking for a confrontation. But
Blacks have been assaulted by the Hasid patrols, and we think our own patrols
will reduce, not increase, tension."

Herb has played leadership roles in specific conflicts like this one, participating in countless boycotts and protests over the years, but he is also involved
in more long-term planning. He was the founder of the National Black United
Front (NBUF) and served in a leadership capacity in many other organizations and community groups. The NBUF started as a local group with five
"Principles of Unity," among them a call for the "re-distribution of the
resources and wealth of the nation to provide abundantly for all citizens."[63]
His confrontations are by no means limited to economic and political issues.
As he said in our interview, referring to his postconversion time in jail when
he was reaching out to other prisoners, "This is one of the things that always
ticks me off about white evangelicals. I just can't…they're either inconsistent,
hypocritical, but they couldn't understand what we were doing." Disagreements
led to Herb boycotting a prayer meeting with other Christians.

It is easy to see why the godly love of Herbert Daughtry has a different
content from that of the NAR when different socialization experiences are
taken into consideration. According to A. G. Miller, Herb's jailhouse
conversion to Christianity in the wake of his arrest for armed robbery, assault,
and weapons possession "brought him some sense of clarity about his need
to accept his punishment and submit himself to God."[64] This profound
experience in the context of the criminal justice system shaped Herb's

subsequent ministry in important ways; such formative experiences were not typical for the middle-class whites who serve as leaders of the NAR. Herb wrote a document in prison that would serve as a road map for his vocation after his release that focused on the specific problems associated with the fact that "the colored races have been inequitably treated, cruelly oppressed and maliciously misinformed about their history, and about themselves."[65] One of the most pressing issues related to the need to "eradicate crime among youth"—the title of the third section of this visionary document.[66] Herb stresses that "Jesus has a black past, an African origin," which is part of his overarching approach to understanding theological and social reality—and which often brings him into conflict with whites.[67] He writes:

> Blacks should say to whites, We have found the real Jesus, and He has set us free. We do not hate you. But we do love ourselves, and because we love ourselves, we are more inclined to love you, for we understand that he who truly loves himself cannot hate another. We are not against you, but we are against exploitation and oppression and we are determined to struggle against these conditions.[68]

Paul Alexander

Amid the deafening explosions of sound grenades, the cry of "Salaam, shalom! Salaam, shalom! [Peace!]" emerges from the group of nonviolent Christian and Muslim protesters being attacked by the Israeli military in Bait Jala, Palestine. At first, the plea fails to prevent another salvo from endangering the lives those in the crowd, but then the firing finally stops. It is March 18, 2010, and Paul Alexander is participating in this peaceful demonstration in this predominantly Arab-Christian town in the West Bank.[69] His involvement is part of his ongoing theological and social scientific research into high-risk ministry, funded by the Flame of Love Project. Paul is a long way from his home, which at that time was in southern California, where he was employed as a theology professor at a small Christian university. He has also, figuratively speaking, traveled a long way from his former self. As we discussed in chapter 3, when we first introduced Paul, he described himself in his formative years as not simply "anti–social justice" but "pro–social injustice" and enthusiastically pro-military.

But now as cofounder of Pentecostals and Charismatics for Peace and Justice, Paul shares Herbert Daughtry's deep concern for social justice—although the content of this concern differs, as does the venue in which it is expressed.[70] For Herb (a Local Planner in our typology), the focus is justice for the black community in the United States, and his attempts to work toward this laudable goal have resulted, intentionally or not, in significant friction with Jews and others in his community. Paul is a Global Planner in our typology—low on pentecostal worldview but high on extensivity. Yet his abiding concern with justice for all perhaps inevitably has also put him at odds with some of those who have the power to oppress—in Paul's case, Jews in Israel and others elsewhere who support the militarily enforced oppression of Palestinians.[71] It is this issue that has drawn Paul to Bait Jala, a small town in the West Bank, where the Israeli government—with the help of its armed forces—is constructing a large "Berlin-style" wall through a Palestinian Christian neighborhood. Paul and the other protestors were marching to the Christian-owned home that stands in the way of the construction in order to draw attention to the community devastation that has been backed by the violence of the state of Israel.

Paul is traveling a very different path from that of his youth, when his religious faith coexisted with a fierce militarism and nationalism. His days were filled with Rush Limbaugh's virulent brand of conservative ideology and a total lack of concern for peace and social justice. Had he remained in this frame of mind, it is likely that he would not have run into problems with his future employer at a Christian university in Texas. He was a typical "good kid" who "did everything right," but he did not perceive "the greed and the racism and the sexism" in his society. For sport he engaged in hunting practices that resembled shooting fish in a barrel: "You know, killing eighteen or twenty snowbirds in the snow....I'd throw out the feed and I'd hide in the garage and snipe them. That is, violence toward animals, it did go along with very much of a willingness to kill people in war." His attitude was in line with the social norms in his religious community and in his small Kansas town. The focus was on issues of personal sin, such as smoking or premarital sex, but not structural "sins" like poverty or institutionalized violence.

He refers to his life through college as his "precritical time," meaning that he simply accepted the practices of his social group without reflecting on them. At this point in his life, the thought of benevolent service to oppressed groups like the Palestinians in Bait Jala simply did not enter his mind. His relationship with God did not require the additional step of loving neighbor as self, or if it did the definition of "neighbor" was narrowly circumscribed. It certainly would not have included Palestinians. After a phase of spiritual darkness in which he lost all faith in the pentecostal religion of his childhood, he rediscovered God through his historical/theological research in graduate school and his encounters with the Mennonite tradition. But his image of God became very different from the one he held in his youth, and interdicts took on a new meaning: Paul's God became a God of peace. He found pacifist role models among the Mennonites, and he learned that leaders of his own pentecostal tradition had initially been staunch pacifists as well. His new orientation is informed by a renewed focus on the life of Jesus. Paul argues that this takes violence "off the table" and that he has "caught a vision of God, of the God who is love revealed clearly in Jesus with concrete implications for the way I live my life." He now reads "the Old Testament hopefully, through Jesus's eyes, the way Jesus read it.... I try to stay pretty close to Jesus." Staying close to Jesus is his method of becoming a Christian peacemaker.[72]

Paul's nonviolent, justice-seeking conceptualization of Jesus brought him into increasing conflict with the university where he was employed and the political inclinations of the denomination with which it is affiliated.[73] In the wake of the terrorist attacks on September 11, 2001, the university president called a campuswide meeting to respond to the violence. Paul recoiled at the nationalistic and promilitary message he heard being spoken from the podium and felt a compulsion to respond in a way that he believed that the example of Jesus required. He explained in our interview that he "needed to say words of reconciliation and peace" without worrying about "the repercussions institutionally." In Paul's book *Peace to War*, he described himself as "squirming" and "feeling a definite 'leading of the Holy Spirit.'"[74] He elaborated on this sense of being led as follows: "But there was just a real feeling, I don't want to say compulsion, but a real drawing, pushing, pulling of needing to say specific, I knew exactly what I needed to say. Who are we? We're followers of Jesus."

In the aftermath of his speech on 9/11, with its call to self-examination instead of retaliation, Paul's teaching contract was not renewed. Of this speech Paul writes, "I have no idea if what I did or said was good or right. I just know that I had been reading a lot of Frank Bartleman, Arthur Booth-Clibborn, the early Assemblies of God peace witness, John Howard Yoder, and Jesus." The experience of writing his book *Peace to War* on pacifism in early Pentecostalism "created such a monumental change in my life that I was compelled (I think led by the Holy Spirit)" to found the activist organization Pentecostals and Charismatics for Peace and Justice (PCPJ).[75]

Paul was compelled to speak because he had developed a strong commitment to nonviolence and the peaceful pursuit of justice applied to all people. This commitment was derived in part from his experiences in studying theology and his exposure to Mennonite writings, but also because of his contact with his wife and other Christians who espoused these views. During its hundred-year history, Paul's religious denomination has moved from an early stance of biblically justified pacifism to its current position as a denomination with congregants who overwhelmingly support U.S. military actions.[76] Paul has argued that his interpretive lens (hermeneutic) is "Christocentric," which means that he reads the Bible through the eyes of Jesus. In Paul's reading, Jesus acted nonviolently and in favor of liberating the oppressed, leading Paul to accept an interdict against war that his denomination does not share. But Paul is not alone in his convictions. In 2007 Paul addressed over six thousand Mennonites, a denomination known for its pacifism, at their biannual national convention.[77]

Where other speakers at Paul's university on 9/11 were fanning the flames of nationalism and militarism, Paul felt compelled to remind everyone that they were followers of Jesus, who demanded that they love their enemies. Whether his actions that day are seen as benevolent or not depends on the interpretive lens through which they are viewed. In terms of religious experience, Paul speaks softly about such issues, occasionally ascribing his actions to a "leading of the Holy Spirit" (his speech on 9/11) or more tentatively as "I think led by the Holy Spirit" (his cofounding of PCPJ), but more often referring to the example or words of Jesus from the Bible, rather than direct experiences of a pentecostal nature.

What's Love Got to Do with Benevolence?

As clearly demonstrated in our survey findings and reflected in our select accounts from exemplars, experiencing God's love is one of the driving forces of benevolence. Our interviewees felt a divine mandate to give their lives for the betterment of others. They would be the first to agree, however, it is not always clear when God stops speaking and they begin pursuing an agenda that may not be divinely directed. It is not always easy to be sure that one has heard from a benevolent God—or whether one is simply dancing to the drumbeat of one's own particular tribe. We deliberately focused on ministries—changing society, reviving primal Christianity, and serving the needy—that could be impacted by different political forces as they pursued sometimes countervailing goals. It is unlikely, for example, that the social activist Herb Daughtry and the revivalist Ché Ahn would feel comfortable working together to pursue a common course of benevolent action. Herb's seeking justice for poor blacks and Ché's $30 million church in a Pasadena landmark are on different radar screens (despite Ché's international network of churches with "mercy ministries" to serve the poor).[78] As we have argued, tribalism and chosen interdicts can make a huge difference in evaluating benevolence, as can the often unacknowledged "tribal" affiliations of the evaluators and their guiding values. Perhaps it is easier now to see why Thoreau said he would run for his life if he knew someone was coming to his house with a design of doing him good!

Focusing on two political extremes allowed us to demonstrate tribal faces of benevolence as exemplars identified with the specific tribes and accepted particular interdicts. But our discussion also has pushed care-love (which we labeled as service) into the background. Most exemplars who have the primary ministry of serving others—providing food and shelter for those in need, safe haven for prostitutes, care for the sick and elderly—were less concerned about partisan politics than were most social activists and many revivalists. Clearly Paul Alexander and Herb Daughtry have similar views about the "prophetic truth-telling" of the "black church pulpit," but their version of truth-telling is very different than the truth-telling of the largely white NAR and its coming kingdom of God. Both are grounded in religious experience but shaped in different social and political contexts. Where Rieff might speak of interdicts and Sorokin might speak of love in timeless and absolute terms, the godly love exemplars we have reviewed here remind us of the importance of contextualization and interpretive communities in assessing the dimensions of benevolence identified by Sorokin.

It would seem that there is little hope of realizing Sorokin's dream of moving beyond tribalism, as people generally fail to understand perspectives of those outside their own tribes. We judged, however, that our exemplars commonly did move beyond their tribes, at least more than most people do—or they would have not been selected for inclusion in our study. Furthermore, recognizing their limitations and willing to share their shortcomings, few exemplars would have felt comfortable with the label "exemplar of godly love." Although sometimes unable to see beyond the vision of their respective tribes, our exemplars seemed to be faithfully pursuing lives of benevolence, doing what they could to make the world a better place based on the divine calling they believe they have received.

One of our interviewees seemed to stand out among the rest as she consciously works to transcend the divisions she encounters and to deal with tribal demons as they arise. For Heidi Baker, "radical love equals radical obedience"—obedience not to existing interdicts or to any particular group but to the ongoing call of God. Ever since her conversion on a Native American reservation when she was sixteen years old, this petite but dynamic woman who was raised with the comforts of an affluent California beach community has sought to give God whatever she believed he was asking of her. In response to a shared call on their lives, Heidi and her husband, Rolland, have always worked with the "poorest of the poor"—first in Indonesia, then Hong Kong, then with the homeless in London, and finally in Mozambique. They came to be widely known in American pentecostal communities during the revival at the Toronto Airport Christian Fellowship (now Catch the Fire Toronto) in the mid-1990s, when Heidi began receiving invitations to speak at churches and conferences. At one point not too long ago Heidi confessed that she had been judging "rich Americans." She came to this awareness when God spoke to her and told her that she did not love him. Her heart was torn apart as she questioned him for details. The answer came that she was judging Americans. She will still occasionally ask the relatively affluent white audiences who pack churches and conference halls to forgive her for the way she once judged them. Heidi has come to see God's unlimited love for all—even rich Americans.

More recently she came to recognize that she was judging the "apostles" of the NAR, a network to which her name is often linked. She was attending a meeting at a large and affluent church in California where fifty or so apostles were being "anointed." Apparently uncomfortable with this ritual, as she told this story, she confessed to being grateful that she was not the speaker that evening. About that time, she was called on to lead the prayer for the apostles. It was then that she had a vision of an awkward, pimply faced young bride wobbling down the aisle in high-heeled shoes. She knew this bride represented the Church and was impressed by how much God loves the Church despite its imperfections.[79] Then her vision changed as the awkward teen becomes a "radiant bride" made perfect through the love of Jesus. Heidi repeatedly understands and enacts "love" in a way that is as contagious as it is challenging. Although obviously frustrated by the "blue T-shirt bunch" (the apostles were all wearing blue shirts to signify their set-apart status), Heidi sensed that God was telling her not to criticize but to be obedient to radical love. Perhaps this approach represents an alternative to tribalism and divisive interdicts. She eschews the political in her attempt to follow the inclusive command to love the one God has put before her. In our concluding chapter, we attempt to make sense of the disparate approaches to godly love that we have documented throughout this book.

Conclusion

CULTURAL GRIDS AND BIBLICAL HOLES

Love never fails. But where there are prophecies, they will
cease; where there are tongues, they will be stilled; where
there is knowledge, it will pass away. For we know in part
and we prophesy in part, but when completeness comes,
what is in part disappears. —1 Corinthians 13:8–10, NIV

IN THIS CHAPTER, we reflect on the lessons we have learned from our
research on godly love in light of the "big questions" that we raised at the
beginning of the book. These questions involved the meaning of life, our responsibilities to other people, how to live in a conflict-ridden world, and where to
find support during our darkest moments. Such issues have been the mainstays
of religion and philosophy for millennia. We do not claim that our research
provides definitive answers to any of them. As the apostle Paul writes in
1 Corinthians in the epigraph above, we can know only in part, a description that
fits well our struggle to understand the heart of religion. Our survey and interview data, however, do help us better understand how Americans in the twenty-
first century relate to such issues in light of their experience of divine love.

Our interviews document many dramatic examples of how divine love
seemed to help people break through impossible circumstances. One of our
exemplars shared a particularly remarkable example with us off the record.
We have since discovered this story in Internet broadcasts and on blogs, but
we have kept the identities of the people involved confidential for reasons that
will become obvious. Like many of the people we interviewed, Alex's ability
to love the unlovable is stunning. It is particularly astonishing to those of us
who are accustomed to the conventional experience of conditional love
limited primarily to one's in-group, and even then most fully realized only

when loved ones meet our expectations and return our love in equal measure. Alex was giving a public talk on the parable of the Good Samaritan, in which Jesus tells the story of how two religious figures ignored a dying man on the side of the road. The man, a victim of a robbery and brutal beating, is ultimately rescued by a socially despised person. This parable answers the question "Who is my neighbor?" and illustrates a totally different approach to love than the insular perspective of the "religious" that Jesus frequently criticized. But Alex was not simply reviewing a well-known biblical story in order to exhort the audience to extend love to others beyond one's own tribe. There was a deeper lesson, and Alex referred to a more personal application of the parable: "Now some of us think that the dying man is going to be lovely and sweet and cuddly and kind....Sometimes the dying man is cruel....We brought one drug addict home...and he took our little daughter, our four-year-old daughter, and he raped her."[1]

The aftermath of such evil is far-reaching. The child was beset with nightmares—"night terrors" is more accurate—and her screaming woke the family every night for a full year. Alex was bewildered by the experience: following God's will had resulted in this terrible incident. Alex prayed to God for understanding and perceived God responding with a question: "Will you still love the poor?" Bewilderment continued as God instructed Alex to face the perpetrator and ask *him* to pray that Alex might receive more love. When Alex complied and received this prayer from the shamed rapist, the child's night terrors stopped. Jesus was adept at shocking people into new ways of thinking (and loving) with surprising parables like the Good Samaritan. Alex's story had a similar effect on us, and we were rendered speechless as we tried in vain to process what we had heard. Many questions remain, partly because the power of this story prevented us from asking follow-up questions, such as whether the perpetrator was ever prosecuted for the crime (it appears that he was not). The perennial question of theodicy (reconciling a loving God with the presence of evil in the world) appears answered to Alex's satisfaction as a result of the supernatural connection between the prayer of a rapist and the cessation of night terrors.

If we remain baffled by this story, it might be good to explore why. Alex's world is filled with the love of God, despite the coexistence of suffering and death. Participation in supernatural miracles and in ongoing interactions with a God who is perceived as both real and engaged in a personal, loving relationship has helped Alex reframe the tragedies of life. They become temporary setbacks on the path to realizing a divine plan that we can only dimly perceive with our limited understanding. The human response to a terrible crime is to demand justice in the here and now, or even to exact vengeance oneself. Yet Alex's response to this tragic, incomprehensibly horrific attack epitomizes the potential of divine love to help people see beyond the worst circumstances of their broken lives to find a deeper meaning in a love that knows no bounds. If such a love seems superhuman, that is the point. Therein lies the heart of religion.

The Centrality of Divine Love in American Experience

In chapter 1, we discussed the popularity of the novel *The Shack*, which was on the *New York Times* best-seller list while we were conducting our research. As with Alex's updating of the parable of the Good Samaritan, *The Shack* is about resolving theodicy, loving the unlovable, and seeing the world through the lens of divine love. In the novel, the main character's daughter is brutally murdered and the father comes to grips with this tragedy through a vivid encounter with a loving God in the shack where the murder occurred. In God's presence, the run-down shack is transformed into a warm and inviting home. For the author, W. Paul Young, we all have a metaphorical "shack" where we house our deepest pain:

> The setting of the darkest, deepest blackness creates a backdrop in which grace becomes most evident. If I went back to my shack and knocked at the door and no one answers; there's no hope. But when I knock at the door, God comes flying out, wraps me up and says, "I've been here the whole time." [Young:] "But I thought You hated me." [God:] "That was you that hated you, it wasn't Me." And so, that's our hope.[2]

The idea that God loves us and can transform our pain into joy runs deep in America, as evidenced by the popularity of *The Shack* and countless other cultural products that convey the same message. And as we have discussed, the contemporary notion of a loving God reflects a revolution in Christian theology since the middle of the twentieth century that has promoted the experience of a God who desires a deeply loving *personal* relationship with every person. Although Alex's story is difficult to fathom, the experience of God's love reframing suffering and empowering human love (even of the unlovable) does resonate with millions of Americans. In *The Shack*, God helps the protagonist to see the murderer as God sees him. This is not a primarily cognitive process. Instead, it involves an experience of empathy previously inaccessible, unlocked by God's love.

We had completed over one hundred interviews with exemplars of godly love by June 2009, when Matt was able to join Paul Young for lunch. Paul was in town to speak to a large audience about the story behind *The Shack*. There was no time to schedule a formal interview, but the lunch conversation was enlightening. Paul, you may recall from chapter 1, had experienced a "death of innocence" akin to Alex's daughter. This, Paul told Matt, is symbolized in the novel by the murder of the main character's daughter. As Paul described it, "Deepest pain asks the best questions." So it is with the big questions that motivated our research project and framed the beginning of this book. Learning that enemies are neighbors too and worthy of love, how to find meaning and purpose in a conflict-ridden world, or where to turn in one's hour of desperation does not come easy. Not for Paul, Alex, or the protagonist in *The Shack*. Such lessons involve suffering, as many of our interviews reminded us. But not pointless suffering. The feeling that God participates in our suffering and thereby redeems it is a strong theme implicit (and often explicit) in our interviews.

Matt asked Paul to define "love," a question that he asked many of our interviewees. After a short, thoughtful pause, Paul responded, "Relentless commitment to the good of the other." *The Shack* is a meditation on this theme in the context of a loving relationship with God. Its enormous popularity is not surprising in light of our research. Our survey found that the vast majority of Americans have powerful experiences of God's love, including perceiving this love as the strongest force in the universe. Those who experience divine love more frequently, according to our survey, do report more benevolence toward others. Our interviews provide us with strong clues about the reasons why. It seems that powerful experiences of divine love are an important part of spiritual transformations that are associated with what we have called a pentecostal worldview—a worldview that encourages believers to live in a world of supernatural possibilities. This pentecostal grid helps to move prayer beyond devotional activities to a love affair with God, transforms suffering into joy, and fosters benevolence toward an expanding circle of others. This can become a kind of virtuous circle that feeds back into additional spiritual transformations, more encounters with divine love, even deeper experiences of prayer, and heightened participation in benevolence.

"Relentless commitment to the good of the other." In a culture that often seems confused about the meaning of love—from the "love" of ice cream to the temporary infatuation experienced by those who feel they have been struck by Cupid's arrow, we have found infinite ways to apply the term—Paul Young seems to have boiled love down to its essence. His wisdom has come at a price, as his biography demonstrates. And there is simply no way for us to assess how well Paul might live up to this ideal in his own life, based on one lunchtime encounter. But it is interesting to compare Paul's understanding of love, in light of his definition and the content of his novel, with one recently penned by Stephen:

> The Institute for Research on Unlimited Love defines love as follows: The essence of love is to affectively affirm as well as to unselfishly delight in the well-being of others, and to engage in acts of care and service on their behalf; unlimited love extends this love to all others without exception in an enduring and constant way. Widely considered the highest form of virtue, unlimited love is often deemed a Creative Presence underlying and integral to all of reality: participation in unlimited love constitutes the fullest experience of spirituality.[3]

Stephen is founder and president of this institute, Matt serves as vice president, and Margaret is on the board of directors. We shared a common passion, albeit at times rooted in differing cultural frameworks, as we explored together the possibility of unlimited love for all others in a world of conflict and divisions. Our research on godly love has left us guardedly optimistic. From Paul Young's inspirational fiction to Alex's inspirational ministry, to the daily prayer lives of millions of Americans, striving to live up to the ideal of "unlimited love" or a "relentless commitment to the good of the other" would seem to be an important part of the American experience. To this point, it has not received the scientific study that it deserves.

Of course we have confronted plenty of examples of the behavior of people falling short of the unlimited love ideal. As chapter 8 demonstrates, the good of the other is often in the eye of the beholder. For example, it was obvious to us that all was not well between Paul Young and another of our interviewees (Wayne Jacobsen, publisher and contributing editor of *The Shack*). In their relationship, conflict seemed to prevail over commitment to the good of the other. This situation did not surprise us. One of Margaret's earlier books documented a benevolent ministry seeking to help the poor and homeless in which godly love interactions were abundant and that provided much-needed services. But there were fundamental problems—cracks in the foundation, so to speak—that inevitably led to the undoing of the entire ministry. In reference to Sorokin's dimensions of love that we discussed in chapter 7, the duration and adequacy of this outreach did not live up to its potential given the spiritual and material resources it possessed. In other words, to quote a famous line from Yeats, "things fall apart." The problem was easy to see in hindsight, as the "helpers" and "beneficiaries" were sharply demarcated within the structure of the ministry, which limited the possibility for a genuine community of equals to emerge. Given the cultural and structural divides in the wider society, a ministry that reproduces such inequalities is perhaps doomed to fail to realize its vision of dramatic personal and communal transformation.[4]

The American experience of godly love has its shortcomings, but it is a central aspect of religious life and continues to empower and to organize much benevolence in this country. This book is part of an emerging body of scientific research and theological reflection that, taken as a whole, represents an initial statement on the topic—not the final word. What we have attempted to do here is to establish that godly love is highly prevalent and consequential in the United States and to document some of its diversity and applications. In addition, we have outlined a plausible understanding of the process by which people encounter divine love and, working with others, seek to express this love to others in benevolent ways.

Prayer is central to the relationship between divine love and benevolence, as we have discussed at length in chapter 5. Although nearly 90 percent of Americans say they pray, social scientists have tended to portray it as an undifferentiated concept. Through our survey statistics and stories from our interviewees, we have painted a nuanced and dynamic picture of prayer as progressing from active (devotional) toward an increasingly receptive stance (prophetic and mystical). Pastor Don Bartow, whose Total Living Center community service ministry was described in chapter 7, nicely summarized a model of prayer that is more widespread in America than previous scholarship has captured:

> If you quiet your spirit...quiet yourself...that's when his power is released, I believe. And it's what sustains me. And I believe prayer is having relationship with the Father. Prayer is not verbalization. Prayer is intimacy.

Power as used by Bartow and most other exemplars is not synonymous with might and force or even strength and authority, all common descriptors of power. It is more like spiritual energy—Sorokin's *love energy*—that empowers the pray-er to live a life of benevolence through intimacy with God. This intimacy is attained not through devotional acts but as a result of more receptive listening and being in the divine presence. Pastor Bartow, like many Americans, feels that he is sustained in his benevolent work by the power that flows from intimacy with God. For them, divine love is the door to a life of benevolence and prayer is the key that unlocks it.

What about Jesus? Cultural Grids and the Christian Life

Although our discussions of theology have been largely implicit up to this point, theological considerations have shaped our research project from the very beginning. Our research proposal promised to integrate theology and social science, and we developed our research instruments out of a multiyear dialogue between scientists and theologians, as well as interactions with those involved in the production of benevolence. As a theologian, Stephen had made important contributions to the topic of divine love, including playing an instrumental role in bringing Sorokin's classic *The Ways and Power of Love* back into print.

So our question was not "Does godly love matter?" but, rather, "How does godly love matter?"—specifically, how does it matter for followers of Jesus? Using the GLNS, we sought to answer this question on a national scale. We acknowledge that there are other ways to frame the study of love, and certainly other religious groups on which to focus. We believe that our study has provided a starting point for a broader conversation among scientists and theologians about the role experiences of divine love play in the Christian life, especially with regard to benevolence. It is our hope that this conversation will expand to other faith traditions as well.

Christ, Love, and Culture

Because the Flame of Love Project was conceived within a Christian theological tradition, it takes "God is love" as its first theological principle.[5] Although some might question whether "God" and "love" are mere synonyms, few would question whether love is central to a Christian understanding of God. Most Christians profess a personal God who loves affectionately and responds affirmatively to human expressions of love, as well as human suffering. For them religion is more than a "head game" of cognitions and beliefs. It is a lived experience of love, often expressed as affection for God and others, compassion, encouragement, support, and supernatural empowerment. But we would be remiss if we did not point out that in one of the twentieth century's most influential works of theology, *Christ and Culture*, H. Richard Niebuhr took issue with the identification of God with love. For Niebuhr, different groups of Christians had elevated one of God's many attributes to preeminent status, always the one that fit with their own cultural grid: "Interpreted by a monk, he may take on monastic characteristics; delineated by a socialist he may show the features of a radical reformer.... The virtue of Christ which religious liberalism has magnified beyond all others is love."[6] Contesting these and other constructions of Jesus, Niebuhr asserted that "it was not love but God that filled his soul" and that all of Jesus's extraordinary virtues (love, hope, obedience, humility) were "due to that unique devotion to God and to that single-hearted trust in Him which can be symbolized by no other figure of speech so well as by the one which calls him Son of God."[7] Thus all other characteristics of Jesus flowed from his devotion to God. Niebuhr put it this way: "Any one of the virtues of Jesus may be taken as the key to the understanding of his character and teaching but each is intelligible in its apparent radicalism only as a relation to God....It is better...to take them all together."

Niebuhr argued that this holistic understanding of Jesus, with his single-minded devotion to God, was the obvious role model for the Christian life. Few who call themselves Christian would argue with him on that point. The problem is that neither Niebuhr nor our exemplars—or the authors—are capable of doing more than "seeing in part." Agreement may be actually limited to the realm of theory rather than lived experience. We are cognizant of the jumble of different understandings of who Jesus was (and is) by diverse interpretive communities with different hermeneutical lenses (see chapter 8). So it is not surprising that different styles of Christian engagement with "culture"—a "fallen world" in contradistinction to the perfect "kingdom of God"—are also extrapolated from the scriptures. Indeed, Niebuhr argued that "Christian perplexity in this area has been perennial" despite the conviction among Christians that Jesus "as living Lord" provides a definitive answer that "transcends the wisdom of all his interpreters yet employs their partial insights and their necessary conflicts."[8] In other words, Niebuhr claims that there is an answer to the question "How should a Christian engage the world?," although the ability of an individual or group to perceive this correctly and completely will always be limited.

Niebuhr and others who followed him have developed a variety of schemes and labels to describe the different styles of Christian engagement with the world. It seems to us that there are three overarching approaches: standing in opposition or separating from the mainstream (what Niebuhr called "Christ against culture"), accommodating or assimilating to the world ("Christ of culture"), or attempting to change or reform the culture ("Christ the transformer of culture"). It is obviously possible that the same individual or group could embody all three approaches with regard to different issues. To take a hypothetical example, one could withdraw from the mainstream economic system by living "off the grid" on a collective farm, but continue to accommodate mainstream culture by reading secular novels, while attempting to transform the world by speaking prophetically at political protests. Leo Tolstoy, the well-known Russian novelist, activist, and Christian anarchist we briefly discussed in chapter 1, renounced material wealth for the sake of following Jesus by giving up his estate. This is "standing against" culture. Yet Tolstoy continued to live on the estate, which represents a partial accommodation, because this facilitated his agenda of transforming culture in Christian ways.[9] One's understanding of Jesus will impact both the selection of problems to be solved as well as the style of engagement with culture.

Engagement with culture is also related to the different faces of Jesus reflected in our typology of Serving, Changing, and Renewing (see table 3.1).[10] The particular path modeled by each, we contend, is in part tied to experiences of being divinely called to a particular mission or given vocation. This divine call is a lifelong process, often with twists and turns, but commonly marked by epiphanies that guide and encourage along the way. We even find a dim reflection of this process in the staid statistics of the GLNS, where experiencing divine love was found to have a positive impact on having a strong sense of meaning, purpose, and destiny in life. The importance of experientially knowing God's love in accounting for a strong sense of existential well-being has been shown to be statistically significant and positive—a relationship that holds strong even after controlling for demographic variables.[11] Although these statistical findings cannot detail the journey, the interview narratives do add valuable insight pointing to the significance of cultural contexts—with somewhat different faces of Jesus—for interpreting and living out the call.

As two of our research team members (Robert Welsh and Paul Alexander) have argued, "All followers of Jesus interpret him through a contextual grid and emphasize particular aspects of his birth, life, teachings, death, or resurrection over others." The "high-risk" activists for peace and social justice (Changers) that they studied tended to teach about "the ministry of Jesus to the poor," but they also emphasized the call to identify "with those who lived under the first-century Roman occupation, and are inspired by the times Jesus challenged the oppressive structures of occupation."[12] Ministries are often an amalgamation of two categories, one of which is more dominant than the other, but the focus of the ministry is shaped by the face of Jesus it embraces. Servers and Renewers often appeared to accommodate themselves more to the existing culture than the Changers did. Servers, for example, were more likely to focus on the Jesus who instructed his followers to give food to the hungry and drink to the thirsty, favoring the meeting of immediate needs over long-term ideological and structural changes. Renewers, on the other hand, emphasized parallel universes of the coming kingdom of God and a fallen world, with a focus on transforming the culture into an image of the perfect kingdom. Central to this transformation is divine empowerment, with its supernatural "signs and wonders." Renewers seem to be following Jesus's admonition to wait in Jerusalem for the Spirit to come from on high, the Holy Spirit who would supply the spiritual power to "make disciples out of all nations." Most of our Servers and Renewers, despite varying populist theologies, seemed to accept the dominant culture for what it is and accommodated their work within its parameters. Only a handful ever even bordered on rejecting American culture. With Jesus they would "render to Caesar what is Caesar's and to God what is God's."

With that important qualifier, there were significant differences in cultural grids on select items of culture. Changers, particularly those who have been sensitized to the injustice found throughout societies, were more likely than Servers or Renewers to find fault with the dominant culture, moving closer to a stance that Niebuhr called "Christ against culture." We see this illustrated through Jim Wallis, popular author and founder of *Sojourners*, a magazine that focuses on social justice. Reflecting the radical stance that could be found in the youth culture of the late 1960s, *Sojourners* had been originally called the *Post-American*. The name change signaled the modulating of the radical stance that began when the group moved from Chicago to Washington, DC, where Jim and his colleagues hoped to have an influence on politics. For over forty years *Sojourners* has critiqued a view of Jesus that has been wedded to American capitalism, nationalism, and the unrealized American dream that has eluded the poor. As Jim sees it, the Bible that Americans profess is one that is "full of holes."

The Christian Life ... with a Bible Full of Holes

Jim Wallis is an influential advocate for the poor and has counseled presidents and a host of other political and economic elites. He is also a best-selling author (e.g., *God's Politics*) and frequent participant in media debates involving faith. The organization he cofounded (Sojourners) grew out of an intentional community and continues to take as its mission the articulation of a "biblical call to social justice, inspiring hope and building a movement to transform individuals, communities, the church, and the world."[13] For decades Jim has been drawing attention to the ways in which some groups of Christians have followed what he sees as a partial understanding of Jesus based on a "Bible full of holes." He brings to life Niebuhr's discussion of "partial insights" about Jesus as he shifts attention to the fact that some Christian groups are ignoring Jesus's mission to the poor. As Jim tells it, years ago one of his collaborators

> took a pair of scissors in an old Bible and began to cut out of the Bible, every single reference to the poor. It took a long time. And when he was done, the Bible was in shreds, in pieces, it was falling apart. It was full of holes. I would take it out with me to preach. I would hold it high in front of congregations and I would say, brothers and sisters, this is our American Bible. It's full of holes. Our Bible is full of holes.

But fixing one "hole" by focusing on justice for the poor, as Sojourners has sought to do, often leaves others. For example, the intentional community that birthed Sojourners was spiritually enriched by contact with a Catholic charismatic (pentecostal) community in Chicago that focused on renewing the church. But after moving to Washington, DC, Sojourners shifted its focus away from both charismatic spirituality and eventually from an emphasis on communal living as it became recognized as a political force. Their mission patched some of the holes in neglected biblical teachings on poverty and social justice. However, the pentecostal side of Jesus that was the message of the Catholic charismatics—the Jesus who changed water into wine, walked on water, multiplied food, healed the sick, and promised that his followers would do "greater things" than he had done—was downplayed if not silenced. This was illustrated when Matt asked Jim about the lasting effect of charismatic context out of which Sojourners had grown. Jim, again implicitly making Niebuhr's point about partial insights, replied:

> In the history of church there are these renewal/reform movements. Sojourners is part of that great tradition. They often think that they have the whole answer. Most reform movements think they have it. They usually have part of the answer. God has raised them up to fill the vacuum or some lacking or some hole. They need to listen to each other.

Despite the influence of the Catholic charismatic renewal on Sojourners' early history, Jim seemed reluctant to embrace the pentecostal label today. In talking to Matt about the feelings of inadequacy he sometimes experiences when "speaking at the World Economic Forum to CEOs and heads of states about the moral values of the market economy in an economic crisis," Jim confessed "feelings of 'What am I going to say to these people?'" He then shared how "you just pray that if this is something that is of God that you'll find the words, be given the words." He concluded, laughing, "I don't want to be too pentecostal here."

It makes little sense to ask whether or not Jim is a pentecostal, although we do note that he seemed to accept our broad definition when he agreed to be interviewed. Dichotomies like "pentecostal" and "non-pentecostal" can be helpful for discussion purposes, but lived experience is generally much more nuanced and better conceptualized along a continuum. Jim is pentecostal to some degree (as were most of our interviewees), but is hardly a Renewer. In the parlance of table 3.2, we would consider him a Global Planner. His last remark (and laughter) suggests that he does not want to self-identify as "too pentecostal." He also seemingly distanced himself from freely talking about his personal prayer life by using the pronoun "you" rather than "I." Jim, like most Christians, synthesizes apparently incompatible aspects of his lived experiences in a process that integrates disparate religious and cultural resources. Our typology of Changer, Server, and Renewer is a useful device, but one that does not always capture the creative work of biblical cutting and pasting of Jesus's teachings reported by our interviewees. Their stories are often complex, and in the final analysis, everyone's Bible has some holes. Old ones may be patched, and unwittingly new ones are created. This impacts the character of religion-based benevolence. Our statistical findings from the GLNS and the lived accounts of our interviewees help to cast additional light on this dynamic process.

Cultural Grids, Spiritual Experiences, and Benevolence

Cultural grids, laden as they are with different biblical "holes," do matter. The qualities of love described by Pitirim Sorokin—especially extensity, intensity, and duration—differ even for religious grids that claim the primacy of love. Servers and Renewers, for example, are often blind to the prejudice, social inequities, and injustice that pierce the hearts of Changers as they display tribal instincts to preserve the interests of their own groups. That is not to say that Changers are immune from tribalism. Like Herb Daughtry, who is admittedly focused on the black community and is largely indifferent to what is going on in the white community, Changers too can put the object of a specific cause above a more inclusive common good. And as Margaret found in studying a now-defunct community where service was combined with renewal, love can develop for an ever-changing abstract utopian vision that supersedes the needs of the people reportedly being served.[14]

Furthermore, cultural understandings are not static; they are subject to many social forces as well as changing perceptions of divine guidance and direction. Increasing contact with disparate groups has been a factor leading some interviewees to expand the lenses through which they see the world—or at least to modify them. Paul Alexander's life story, told earlier, provides a good illustration in his transition from militarism to pacifism and in his blending of a Mennonite passion for justice and the poor with a pentecostal passion for encountering the Holy Spirit. As he pursued his research on those who risked their lives to share the love of God with those in blighted areas of the United States and especially his face-to-face contact with war-torn Palestinians, we noted his benevolence becoming more radicalized—or, in Sorokin's terms, his love has become more extensive and intensive for groups that he once knew and cared little about. Still an ordained minister in the Assemblies of God and a theology professor, Paul seeks to touch another generation of students with his love for faraway Palestinians as well those suffering the effects of poverty and injustice in his homeland. Cultural frameworks, as we discussed in chapter 8, do play an important role in the way we access and assess acts of benevolence.

Expanding Cultural Grids

The cultural frameworks that circumscribe benevolence can be malleable and permeable; they are not cast in stone. Furthermore, spiritual transformations—especially those involving a personal divine call to a specific work as discussed in chapter 3—were often significant catalysts for changes for exemplars. We were reminded of the power of religious experience to expand cultural grids when Margaret received a detailed e-mail update from Cecil M. (Mel) Robeck Jr. as we were writing this section. Mel, one of our interviewees, is professor of church history and ecumenics and director of the David DuPlessis Center for Christian Spirituality at Fuller Theological Seminary. Like Paul Alexander, he grew up in the Assemblies of God (AG), now the ninth-largest American denomination and one of the largest denominations in global Pentecostalism.[15]

Until the 1970s the AG was dismissed by most scholars of religion as a small sect hardly worthy of note. Founded in 1914 by men and women who had experienced the Azusa Street Revival (1906–9), the denomination was more concerned with end-times and intense missionary activity than in changing the larger culture. (The seeds sown in missionary activity throughout the world bore fruit for the international network of AG churches, with an estimated membership of 64 million, including over 3 million members and adherents in the United States.)[16] The prevailing culture of the AG for the first half of its existence is best characterized in terms of Niebuhr's "Christ against culture." The AG, with its prohibitions and proscriptions, was clearly countercultural and critical of both mainstream Protestantism and Roman Catholicism. As its American followers experienced upward mobility during the last half of the twentieth century, the denomination slowly acclimated and accommodated to the larger culture. Prohibited "worldly" practices— like men participating in and patronizing sporting events; women cutting their hair and wearing makeup and jewelry; visits to movie theaters and other such entertainment; pursuit of higher education and even divorce and remar- riage—gave way as a growing number of affluent members embraced much of what had been rigidly proscribed. Most members, however, still continued to see their church as part of the elect, and many to this day deliberately distance themselves from all but evangelical Protestantism.

Mel Robeck grew up during the transitional period when the AG began to acclimate and accommodate to the larger culture. Yet the AG remained (and still remains) wary of Christians in different sectors of American Christianity, with many leaders and members still being unwilling to coop- erate or dialogue with either mainline Protestantism or Roman Catholicism.[17] Mel reported a most unusual experience of an unexpected divine call to promote ecumenism that altered his cultural lens and changed his life—a vision of Jesus himself. Mel had already discerned the call to attend semi- nary and to become involved in teaching, but exactly when, where, or how this call would take form was still emerging. From 1975 until 1985, when he earned his PhD, he was heavily involved in administrative work at Fuller Theological Seminary—administrative work that would continue through the 1980s. During that time Mel was elected president of the Society for Pentecostal Studies for the 1982–83 year, a tenure that would involve his presenting a presidential address. Mel was troubled by the persistent fac- tionalism that then existed in the organization, and he prayed for months for divine direction in preparing the lecture. An answer was soon coming. As Mel reported in an interview with us:

At that time our meetings were in November, and I think it must have been about August that I was asleep and then all of sudden I was awake. I saw the Lord standing at the end of my bed. He said, "I want you to talk about ecumenism." I said, "I can't do that. I don't know anything about it." I went back to sleep. I don't know exactly when but it seemed like a few minutes later he woke me up again. He was standing right there. He said, "No, I want you talk about ecumenism." I said, "Lord, I can't do that. I am going to get into trouble. Don't you know the Assemblies of God have bylaws that say I can't do this? Don't you know David DuPlessis?"

David DuPlessis, the late AG minister for whom the center Mel now directs is named, was a pioneer Pentecostal ecumenist. While living in his native South Africa, a prophecy given to him in 1936 foretold "a new wave of Pentecost coming to the earth through mainline denominations" and that God intended "to send you [DuPlessis] to these denominations."[18] When this second Pentecostal wave began its roll over American Christianity in the late 1950s as prophesied, DuPlessis (who by this time had moved to the United States) became affectionately known as "Mr. Pentecost" by the neo-pentecostal Protestants and Catholics alike. For his efforts at bridging walls between Pentecostalism and mainline Christianity, DuPlessis was defrocked by the Assemblies of God in 1962 and would not be reinstated until eighteen years later. Despite this reinstatement when DuPlessis died in 1987, his death would be largely ignored by the AG. Mel would write at the time of his death: "His life was prophetic, as he straddled the ecumenical, charismatic, and Pentecostal worlds, and predictably, he entered somewhat into the prophet's fate."[19] Mel was not eager to suffer the same fate, but he knew he had heard God and he decided he would obey, regardless of cost.

A longtime scholar of Pentecostalism, Mel had shelves and files filled with "this wonderful collection of Pentecostal literature going right back to the beginning." Just as Paul Alexander would years later search for pacifism in the history of early Pentecostalism, Mel searched for signs of ecumenism:

The word "ecumenism" doesn't show up there [in the old literature]. So I thought, oneness, unity, John 17:21. Let's see what I could find. Holy cow, it was everywhere. Charles Parham says, "The Lord has anointed me to be an apostle of unity." I looked at that and said, "How could that be?" Then I would go to the Azusa Street papers, and it says "We believe in Christian unity" everywhere. I thought, "I never heard this all my life in the Assembly of God church."...I thought that it would be interesting to trace this history out, and maybe I'd get some answers. To make a long story short, I think it was when we identified with the evangelical movement that the evangelical enemies became our enemies. We did that for the sake of our acceptability.

As did DuPlessis before him, there are times that Mel has shared in the prophet's fate in the hands of his denominational leaders as he patched some of the holes in his Bible, particularly those dealing with the unity of all Christians. While DuPlessis suffered an inquisition because of his involvement in the World Council of Churches, Mel would pay a price for his dialogue with Roman Catholicism.[20] The AG has changed in recent years, and for the most part, Mel is now left free to follow his call. He has been successful in transcending his initial cultural lens in an important way: expanding it to include respect for and dialogue with Catholic leaders.

Over the decades Mel has represented pentecostalism in countless interfaith gatherings in Rome and remains a preeminent face and force for pentecostal interfaith dialogue. As Mel wrote to us about his October 2011 visit to the Vatican, he has seen the fruit of his expanded grid:

> I was one of 80 people selected to sit on the platform with His Holiness. Those of us who sat on the platform were selected because we are considered to be "heads of delegations." Since I was the only Pentecostal to attend, it was my honor to be so selected to represent all Pentecostals. I am very much aware that for 25 years I have simply served as a place holder until such a time as some Pentecostal leader takes it upon himself to take the risk to attend one of these kinds of ecumenical functions—but that is another story. I have no official position. I have no intrinsic authority. It is all a matter of grace![21]

Mel could not have imagined when he first responded to a divine calling for ecumenism that his journey would eventually result in joining Pope Benedict XVI and five other top religious dignitaries at the head table. This is one of the many examples of inexplicable and unexpected—perhaps impossible— outcomes that have given the lives of our exemplars deeper meaning. It illustrates an overarching theme from our interviews, best articulated by Anne Beiler, that God can "make a way" in impossible circumstances. And although he longs for the day when he will be replaced by an official representative from the AG in ecumenical dialogue, in the meantime Mel's religious lens has expanded to a remarkable degree as he has sought to plug a biblical hole (lack of Christian unity) in response to the divine call on his life. Being given a place of honor next to the pope is a particularly memorable example for Mel of God's love for his faithful servant.

Mixing and Matching in Cultural Grids

Critical reassessments of Niebuhr's mutually exclusive forms of engagement with culture have pointed out that Christians may accept some aspects of culture (e.g., medicine, farming techniques) while rejecting others (e.g., consumerism).[22] And in fact, none of our interviewees rejected American culture entirely in an attempt to create a separate counterculture. Herb Daughtry seems to come the closest in his preference for the black community and lack of concern with white culture. For the most part, however, there has been considerable mixing and matching of elements that reflect a style of engagement that might be termed "Christ in culture." For example, Paul Alexander remains strongly engaged with his denomination as he attempts to influence some of its theological and sociopolitical positions toward openly advocating changes in the dominant American way. He does decry violence, militarism, and consumerism, along with sexism, racism, and many other detrimental social ills that he sees as inherent in American culture, but he has not founded a separatist community. In fact, he enjoys a solidly middle-class life. But he does speak a prophetic voice confident that he is closing some of the holes in his Bible through his Christocentric hermeneutic of the scriptures.

Anne and Jonas Beiler provide perhaps our best example of exemplars raised in a countercultural community, and they too have largely acclimated to the prevailing American culture. Through life's tragedies and successes, values that are very important to the Amish—serving others, forgiveness, and community—remain part of their calling. When we interviewed Anne in 2008, she was putting the finishing touches on the speech she had been invited to make at the Republican National Convention. Although seasoned with the appropriate patriotic and partisan comments, within the talk can be found examples of her Amish heritage that modeled hard work ("My values and my heritage helped me to grow from this little girl of poverty to this woman of prosperity") and giving back to the community through service to others ("With prosperity comes responsibility"; "This life is about others"). In fact, Jonas believes God had given them unbelievable success with Auntie Anne's Soft Pretzels so that they would have the resources to establish the Family Center at Gap, which promotes community and service. When Anne asserts that "true prosperity is a richness of heart and spirit," she shares a lesson she learned as part of her Amish heritage.

Anne began her employment at the little market that led to Auntie Anne's Soft Pretzels because the family needed money. Jonas was spending more and more of his time counseling those in need, time that took away from his gainful employment. His many years of counseling, however, sensitized him to real problems facing families in modern society. During his interview with us, Jonas shared how he observed the stress that plagues many families and how he felt God gave them the understanding and the resources to do something about it:

> Most people can't take off work, can't lose that much time, because that affects their pay. I'm watching these families and everything that strains them, that makes them lose valuable work time, that makes for less money in their pay. It's all important stuff—they have to do it. See, that's what God helped me to understand. That we can bring at least some of these services together.

Jonas's years of counseling would also give him a national platform as a spokesperson for the Amish community on forgiveness when a gunman in Pennsylvania murdered five young girls in a one-room schoolhouse before killing himself. The eyes of the world were on the Amish parents who reached out to the family of the dead gunman with care and forgiveness. As Jonas has noted in an interview for his book on the Nickel Mines Amish school shooting, "Forgiveness is woven into the Amish culture."[23]

Anne and Jonas Beiler's goal of meeting the spiritual, psychological, and material needs of their local community does not seek to replicate an Amish culture of their upbringing. They have embraced and experienced the American dream with its promise of material prosperity, but they have tempered it with lessons they learned as children growing up in the Amish culture. These lessons are at the heart of the center's mission statement: "The Family Center exists to help families thrive by providing a hub of interactive services which offer a healing presence, foster healthy relationships and model community cooperation."[24]

Transposing Grids in the Coming Kingdom

Our typology presented in table 3.2 (see chapter 3) has divided exemplars along an axis we label Planners and Mystics. Based on both the statistical findings of the GLNS and our qualitative interviews, we observed that some exemplars were more likely than others to be grounded in a worldview of supernatural possibilities—an "as if" world in which prophecy, healing, and miracles played significant roles in their lives—and we identified these exemplars as either Global or Local *Mystics*. The other half of our fourfold typology of Global and Local *Planners* accounted for respondents who may be deeply spiritual but less influenced by what we have called the *pentecostal worldview*. Some, such as Jim Wallis, Paul Alexander, Mel Robeck, and Anne Beiler, had tasted of the supernatural worldview of pentecostals, but their Christianity has acclimated in varying ways and degrees to the post-Enlightenment modern world that is wary of miracles, mystery, and magic. Like Jim Wallis, planners would not want to sound "too pentecostal," although many had tasted of pentecostal-like experiences along the way of their spiritual journeys. The mystics, on the other hand, are not concerned about sounding "too pentecostal," if "pentecostal" means being a transmitter for the power of the Holy Spirit with "signs and wonders" like prophecy, healing, and deliverance. With an eschatology that professes that God wishes to bring his kingdom into the present-day world, they are less likely to talk about "saving souls" or praying for the Second Coming of Jesus than they are in proclaiming a "kingdom on earth as it is in heaven." They operate in a culture where words of prophetic encouragement, divine healing, miraculous provision, and miracles are readily available to all who believe. They seek to create a new world as the old culture is transformed by the power of the Holy Spirit before their very eyes. Instead of setting themselves apart in distinct communities as their Pentecostal forefathers did, they regard themselves as spiritual leaven being used to transform the dominant culture.

And at least for those exemplars who are linked with the growing but amorphous network known as the New Apostolic Reformation (NAR) discussed in chapter 7, the cultural realignment means transforming this world into the kingdom of God by the power of the Holy Spirit working through believers. They challenge believers to expect a divine response in accord with the Lord's Prayer that petitions "thy kingdom come, thy will be done on earth as it is in heaven." While Servers and Changers would undoubtedly have a different hermeneutic on the kingdom, the focus for Renewers is a call to recognize that supernatural experiences are normal Christianity in a world where God's kingdom is in the process of unfolding.

Thus, the NAR has called not for a rejection, separation, or withdrawal from the dominant culture (as did early Pentecostal forefathers and mothers), but for a transformation of the existing culture. Although their emphasis has been on the use of supernatural power, like their predecessors the NAR members combine what Grant Wacker, a historian of pentecostalism, has called "primitivist and pragmatic impulses."[25] As they endeavor to usher in the supernatural "signs and wonders," they are seeking to integrate these spiritual experiences with pragmatically defined strategies derived from their selective reading of the Bible. Of particular importance for many is the reinstating the fivefold ministry (especially the offices of prophets and apostles, adding them to teachers, evangelists, and pastors) for church renewal and the transforming the seven mountains of culture (business, education, government, media, arts and entertainment, religion, and family) through divinely empowered service in the larger community.[26] In seeking a biblical guide to cultural transformation, the NAR is not without holes in its Bible, as we saw in chapter 8. At times and in some places their kingdom of God looks remarkably like a potpourri of entrepreneurial nondenominational churches, Wall Street adventures, and a Republican Party platform with promises from select passages from another Bible that has holes.

Iris Ministries, the ministry founded by Heidi and Rolland Baker, provides an example of cultural transformation brought about by the "signs and wonders" of contemporary revivals. The ministry is linked with the NAR, but due to its African location its relationship to culture is different from that of the NAR in the United States. As Rolland Baker writes in one of the Iris newsletters:[27]

> We are often asked what brings about church growth here? Is it our Bible teaching, Bible school structure, bush conferences, strategy, what? Many things might be involved but our own pastors tell us that it is miracles that brings the people. They go where Jesus heals them, loves them, and does things for them. We might say that those things shouldn't be necessary, but our people are very simple. They don't want to go where they can't feel or appreciate the presence of Jesus, even if the place is a beautiful traditional church. They don't want to exchange their powerful witch doctors for a powerless church. They want a living God involved with their lives who can be trusted in everything and who has more power than any opposition.

Rolland has identified the heart of what has been called the NAR—namely, revival in which the presence and the power of God are experienced reality. We have already provided many of Heidi Baker's experiences and suggested how they have empowered her for service throughout the chapters. For Heidi, knowing the love of God cannot be separated from revival power. Supernatural miracles are dependent on tangible experiences of a loving God for divine empowerment to serve. She believes that she can accomplish nothing without the power of God. Her unconditional love for others, including enemies who have attacked her, is rooted in her experience of the power that comes from knowing God's love. Indeed, for Heidi love is impotent without power. We demonstrated this in chapter 7, where we reported Heidi's metaphor of the two wings of power and love. As she said, "You can't fly with one. Power and love are very much connected.²⁸ If you have this great love and compassion for the poor and have no bread, you're a very sad person. If you have great compassion and concern for the dying and the sick and you have no power to see them healed, you end up a very sad person. But the merciful love of God is that his love has teeth. His love has teeth."

Although Heidi appears to have reservations about subsidiary theologies found in teachings about the restoration of the fivefold ministry and the seven mountains of culture, she is reluctant to criticize. In Heidi's social network there is a great deal of status-seeking as some are labeled as "apostles" or "prophets." She restrains her criticism of this culture because she has not been called to be a divisive voice. She personally rejects such titles (saying, "I don't understand 'apostle.' I just don't get it.").²⁹ God told her: "Apostolic—upside down—it's the lowest place."³⁰ In other words, for Heidi the apostle of God is the one who serves *all* others, not the one who basks in popularity and prestige. From some vantage points (e.g., followers of Nietzsche), this may seem like an incomprehensible "slave morality." And indeed it is perplexing, unless one has had Heidi's experiences.

And the Greatest of These Is Love?

Our differing grids of interpretation all reflect partial, context-specific solutions and diverse answers to the problems facing the world. It is often easier to see the speck in the eye of another than to see the beam blocking our own. We have tried to stay close to the stories of our exemplars, but the critical light of our training would at times shine on dark spots. Remember that even Mother Teresa had her detractors.³¹ But there is one exemplar who articulates through word and deed, perhaps more simply and clearly than any other, the awesome power of love.

The website describing the mission of Iris Ministries offers a clear picture of an organization that has affected thousands upon thousands of lives across the globe. Its opening succinct statement reflects the godly love we heard in our interview with Heidi Baker:³²

Iris Ministries is a Christian organization committed to expressing a living and tangible response to those commandments that Jesus called greatest: "Love the Lord your God with all your heart and with all your soul and with all your mind and with all your strength, and, Love your neighbor as yourself." It is our conviction that the Spirit of God has asked us to make this love concrete in the world, incarnate in all our thoughts, our bodies, our lives, and our every action. Iris Ministries exists to participate in bringing the Kingdom of God to earth in all its aspects, but most especially through our particular calling to serve the very poor: the destitute, the lost, the broken, and the forgotten.

Despite the success of Iris Ministries, her PhD in systematic theology from King's College London, and her renown as a revival speaker, Heidi regards herself as but one small person in a very large world with a simple message. Her childlike simplicity is reflected in Heidi's comment in Margaret's 2008 interview with her when she said with a smile, twinkling eyes, and a voice filled with glee: "I'm just happy; I'm a happy lover of God and lover of people. I'm very simple. As I've gotten older, I've just become more and more simple. I'm very simple. What you see is what you get. I just want to love God and the one in front of me. That's it." The website for Heidi and Rolland's ministry sums up their perceived calling as making Godly love "concrete in the world, incarnate in all our thoughts, our bodies, our lives, and our every action."[33]

Although she certainly does not lack convictions, Heidi is reluctant to criticize other people. On more than one occasion Margaret has heard her apologize to American audiences for having judged them and has heard her express reluctance to speak at American conferences because she would rather be ministering to poor children in Africa. This is because she feels that God has rebuked her for judging the faults of others. She follows the Jesus who brings peace rather than the sword. Perhaps reasonable people will disagree about the merits of this approach, but it flows from Heidi's experiences. As William James pointed out over a century ago, a particular religious experience can be quite compelling to the person who has it and equally unconvincing to those whose experience has been otherwise.[34]

Heidi's commitment to love the one before her is born of deep, ongoing experiences of God's unconditional love. For one-third of each year she travels the world inspiring others to serve the poor, but she told Margaret that this comes at "a great personal cost to me because I love being in the dirt with the poor…all the time." When Margaret asked Heidi if there was anything else that she wished to add to her interview, Heidi responded without hesitation:

> I believe that all fruitfulness flows from intimacy. So a real key for me with the love thing is you need to know how loved you are.... All of your identity is in this place where you are loved by your Father.... I just feel like Father God adores me. I'm different, but I'm his and he likes me. He likes me. He said, "Just be you. I totally adore you. I love you. I'm committed to loving you. I am in love with you." I've heard Father God say that to me. And because of that, I don't have a need to be needed, but I feel so much courage rise up.... It's no longer, "I just need somebody to feel good when I touch them." No, no, no. I already feel good. I already feel happy. I'm happy. I feel blessed. I feel full.

Thriving by serving others, loving as you have been loved, living a life of meaning. This is the path of faith, hope, and love envisioned by the New Testament. Our research with exemplars like Heidi Baker suggests that St. Paul might indeed be on to something: "And now these three remain: faith, hope and love. But the greatest of these is love."[35]

Notes

ACKNOWLEDGMENTS

1. Titles and affiliations have changed for some members in the years since we first began our work. Sadly, Clark Pinnock passed away while the research was unfolding. We remain grateful to Clark for his work. His book *The Flame of Love* provided the title for our research project.

INTRODUCTION

1. Karen Armstrong, *The Case for God* (New York: Anchor, 2009), 330.
2. One recent study found that the religious in America were more generous, more involved in both secular and religious causes, more civically engaged, had a greater "inclination towards altruism," and were viewed as more trustworthy than the nonreligious. On the other hand, they were also more intolerant, which seemed to be the "dark side" of religion. See Robert D. Putnam and David E. Campbell, *American Grace: How Religion Divides and Unites Us* (New York: Simon & Schuster, 2010), 487, 492.
3. Pitirim Sorokin's landmark study found a strong spiritual dimension to the lives of "atheistic altruists," for whom "the term *matter* often means about the same as the term *God*, for a believer; the term *life energy* becomes co-identical with that of the *supraconscious*; and so on." Pitirim A. Sorokin, *The Ways and Power of Love: Types, Factors, and Techniques of Moral Transformation* (1954; rpt., Philadelphia: Templeton Foundation Press, 2002), 146. More recent research has supported Sorokin's contention in the sense that there is a "'vertical' dimension to the altruism of the religious and 'secular' alike.... Quasi-religious experiences may be operative even for nonreligious people." Secular altruists frequently frame their activism in transcendent, religious terms, such as defending "sacred space" or combating "sin." Matthew T. Lee and Thomas L. Kychun, "The Possibilities and Limitations of Religious-Based Altruism for Solving Endemic Social Problems: Findings from a Multi-Year Research Project," in *Proceedings of the International Society for the Comparative Study of Civilization's 40th Conference*, edited by Connie Lamb and Andrew Targowski, 228–35 (Provo, UT: ISCSC, 2010), 234–35.

4. Dean Karnazes, *Ultra Marathon Man: Confessions of an All-Night Runner* (New York: J. P. Tarcher/Penguin, 2005), 155, 158.

5. Stephen G. Post, *The Hidden Gifts of Helping: How the Power of Giving, Compassion, and Hope Gets Us through Hard Times* (San Francisco: Jossey-Bass, 2011), 23.

6. Ibid., 24.

7. Ibid.

8. Karen Armstrong, *The Great Transformation: The Beginning of Our Religious Traditions* (New York: Knopf, 2006), 391–92.

9. Armstrong, *The Case for God*, 329.

10. Armstrong, *The Great Transformation*, 392.

11. Ibid., 398.

12. Cf. Philippians 4:7 and Ephesians 3:19.

13. Paul Froese and Christopher Bader, *America's Four Gods: What We Say about God—and What That Says about Us* (New York: Oxford University Press, 2010), 4.

14. Ibid., 50.

15. Ibid., 9.

16. Ibid., 15.

17. Putnam and Campbell, *American Grace*, 458. The statistical mistake Brooks made was attributing causation to a spurious relationship between conservatism and generosity. It is religiosity, not conservatism, that increases generosity.

18. In *Altruism in World Religions*, William Scott Green argues that a "reasonable scholarly consensus" of the meaning of altruism in contemporary thinking is an "intentional action intended ultimately for the welfare of others that entails at least the possibility of either no benefit or a loss to the actor." William Scott Green, "Introduction: Altruism and the Study of Religion," in *Altruism in World Religions*, edited by Jacob Neusner and Bruce Chilton, ix–xiv (Washington, DC: Georgetown University Press, 2005), xiii.

19. Keishin Inaba and Kate Loewenthal, "Religion and Altruism," in *The Oxford Handbook of the Sociology of Religion*, edited by Peter Clarke (New York: Oxford University Press, 2009), 876.

20. Robert Wuthnow, "Altruism and Sociological Theory," *Social Service Review* 67 (1993): 344–57, 347.

21. Ibid., 354.

22. Ibid., 345.

23. Ibid., 355–56.

24. Inaba and Loewenthal, *The Oxford Handbook*, 877.

25. Robert Wuthnow, *Acts of Compassion: Caring for Others and Helping Ourselves* (Princeton, NJ: Princeton University Press, 1991), 220.

26. Armstrong, *The Great Transformation*, 383.

27. Ibid., 376.

28. Ibid., 387.

29. Margaret M. Poloma and Ralph W. Hood Jr., *Blood and Fire: Godly Love in a Pentecostal Emerging Church* (New York: New York University Press, 2008). See also Christopher Hitchens, *The Missionary Position: Mother Teresa in Theory and Practice* (London: Verso, 1995).

30. Theologian Paul Alexander and psychologist Robert Welsh, with funding from the Flame of Love Project (see the acknowledgments section above), interviewed over one hundred Christian exemplars engaged in peace and social justice ministries in high-risk areas throughout the world, including war zones and occupied territories where violent death is a constant threat. Paul and Bob have also found that their interviewees acknowledge their own feet of clay, even as they achieve the seemingly impossible.

CHAPTER 1

1. This term was coined in Margaret M. Poloma and Ralph W. Hood Jr., *Blood and Fire: Godly Love in a Pentecostal Emerging Church* (New York: New York University Press, 2008). For more discussion, see Matthew T. Lee and Margaret M. Poloma, *A Sociological Study of the Great Commandment in Pentecostalism: The Practice of Godly Love as Benevolent Service* (New York: Edwin Mellen, 2009). Godly love has previously been defined as the perceived interaction of divine and human love that enlivens and expands benevolence. The emphasis on perceptions sidesteps the question of the existence of God (or human love, for that matter, which can be misperceived) and relies instead on the well-known Thomas theorem, which states that if people perceive something to be real, then this social fact will have real consequences for their thoughts and behaviors. An interdisciplinary group of scholars associated with our research project has explored different conceptualizations of godly love in Matthew T. Lee and Amos Yong, eds., *The Science and Theology of Godly Love* (DeKalb: Northern Illinois University Press, 2012). For more multidisciplinary perspectives, see also Matthew T. Lee and Amos Yong, eds., *Godly Love: Impediments and Possibilities* (Lanham, MD: Lexington Books, 2012).

2. We explored our concept of godly love with some of our interviewees after they had provided their life stories to us. We did not want our conceptual frameworks to influence them, so we simply asked them to tell us about the important events of their lives that had shaped who they are today. After we had a thorough understanding of how they made sense of their own thoughts, behaviors, and social contexts, we invited some interviewees to critique our findings or concepts (depending on time constraints, both theirs and ours). When we explained to Wayne Jacobsen that our concept of godly love was related to the Great Commandment, he challenged us to consider the New Commandment. He has articulated his perspective in his writings and podcasts. For example, see Wayne Jacobsen, *He Loves Me! Learning to Live in the Father's Affection* (Newbury Park, CA: Windblown Media, 2007).

3. See Frank D. Macchia, "The God behind the Shack: Recent Revolutions in the Theology of God." Keynote presentation on Wednesday, July 22, 2009, as part of a two-week seminar titled "The Flame of Love: An Interdisciplinary Dialogue on the Great Commandment," hosted by Calvin College's Seminars in Christian Scholarship Program in Grand Rapids, Michigan, with funding from a research endeavor called the Flame of Love Project. The Flame of Love Project provided support for this seminar via the John Templeton Foundation. The three authors of this book serve as co–principal investigators for the Flame of Love Project.

4. Jared Diamond, *Guns, Germs, and Steel* (New York: W. W. Norton, 1997), 266.

5. This quote was selected from an interview conducted by Margaret Poloma with Klaus Kugler on November 7, 2010, in Cuyahoga Falls, Ohio. It was one of 120 such interviews conducted as part of the research project described in this book. For more about Klaus's story, see Sabine Kuegler, *Jungle Child: A Remarkable Journey into the Heart of a Lost Tribe* (Munich: Droemer Knaur, 2005). A feature film on the lives of the Kugler family was released in Germany by Universal Pictures on February 17, 2011.

6. For an example of the external approach, see Robert D. Putnam and David E. Campbell, *American Grace: How Religion Divides and Unites Us* (New York: Simon & Schuster, 2010).

7. Kristen Renwick Monroe, *The Heart of Altruism: Perceptions of a Common Humanity* (Princeton, NJ: Princeton University Press, 1996). Monroe's compelling research on some forms of altruism has concluded that religion is "irrelevant" (122). Her award-winning and widely cited book notes, "This finding appears to trouble some scholars from religious schools or departments of religion. I can only remind them that these are simply my findings, which I must report honestly" (248). But how we measure benevolence affects the conclusions that we draw. Our research suggests that there is much more to the story than Monroe's findings have revealed.

8. David Brooks, *The Social Animal: The Hidden Sources of Love, Character, and Achievement* (New York: Random House, 2011), introduction, Kindle edition. In the introduction Brooks also writes, "If there is a divine creativity, surely it is active in this inner soulsphere, where brain matter produces emotion, where love rewires the neurons."

9. Leo Tolstoy, *Anna Karenina* (1877; rpt., New York: Penguin, 2004), 817.

10. "The Shack on the NY Times Best Seller List," press release posted May 3, 2011, http://windblownmedia.com/press-room/news-releases.html.

11. Craig Cable, "Author of *The Shack* Reveals Its Meaning, and Where Real Hope and Healing Come From," March 24, 2011, www.breakingchristiannews.com/articles/display_art.html?ID=8778.

12. In a public presentation on *The Shack*, theologian Frank Macchia referred to this shift as a "revolution" in theology that has transformed an impassive, neo-Platonic image of God over the twentieth century into a God who is co-present in the

suffering experienced by people and, above all, deeply involved in relationships. Of course Tolstoy's peasants, like many other laypersons, were well ahead of the theologians on this issue. Sociologist Philip Rieff, on the other hand, would no doubt have seen this as another unfortunate instance of the "triumph of the therapeutic." See Macchia, "The God behind the Shack." See also Jacobsen, *He Loves Me!*, as well as Philip Rieff, *Charisma: The Gift of Grace, and How It Has Been Taken away from Us* (New York: Vintage Books, 2007).

13. We conducted four survey efforts for the Flame of Love Project (see Lee and Poloma, *A Sociological Study of the Great Commandment*). Preliminary surveys used to develop the full national survey included (1) questionnaires distributed to over 120 exemplars of godly love as part of in-depth, face-to-face interviews conducted in 2008–9; and (2) a pilot telephone survey of a national random sample of 600 adults conducted by telephone in the summer of 2009. The third phase, a national telephone survey conducted in English and Spanish, collected a random sample of 1,208 adults in the fall of 2009 (with a margin of error of plus or minus 2.9 percentage points and a response rate of 36 percent). In this book, we refer to this phase as the Godly Love National Survey (GLNS), or more generically as our "national survey." A fourth and final survey (not discussed in this book) collected an oversample of 400 African American and 400 Hispanic evangelicals and Pentecostals throughout the United States, using the same questionnaire as the national sample and also conducted by telephone. The pilot, GLNS, and oversample surveys were conducted by the Bliss Institute of Applied Politics at the University of Akron under the direction of the three of us and John C. Green.

14. For the importance of religious friendship networks on benevolence, see Putnam and Campbell, *American Grace*. See also Robert D. Putnam, "What's So Darn Special about Religious Friends?," in *Altruism, Morality, and Social Solidarity Forum: A Forum for Scholarship and Newsletter of the AMSS Section of the American Sociological Association* 3 (2012): 1, 19–20.

15. Cathy Lynn Grossman, "How Americans Imagine God," *USA Weekend*, December 17–19, 2010, 6–7, quote on 6.

16. Lee and Poloma, *A Sociological Study of the Great Commandment*.

17. For a complete list of team members, see pages v–vi in Lee and Poloma and the Acknowledgments section of this book.

18. As reported in the Acknowledgments, we funded five subprojects at a minimum of $150,000 each through a competitive Request for Proposals, and we also supported a wide variety of writing projects, seminars, and biannual meetings of a think tank on godly love.

19. Sonnet 116 by William Shakespeare begins with these lines:

> Let me not to the marriage of true minds
> Admit impediments. Love is not love
> Which alters when it alteration finds,

> Or bends with the remover to remove:
> O no! it is an ever-fixed mark
> That looks on tempests and is never shaken.

20. Jacobsen, *He Loves Me!*, 20.

21. There are a lot of reasons why some people prefer to self-identify as spiritual but not religious. Some have had negative experiences with "organized" religion, but have had positive experiences with a creative, loving force that they may or may not call "God." Even many Christians lament the potentially harmful effects of a "dead" religion, which they seek to revitalize by creating new ritual practices or reviving old ones. So it is fashionable in some circles to decry "religion," but in general the distinction between spirituality and religion does not make much of a difference in analyses based on our survey results.

22. The following is the breakdown of figures from the GLNS for importance of religion: *extremely important* (37 percent), *very important* (25 percent), *somewhat important* (21 percent), *not very important* (7 percent), and *not at all important* (10 percent). The corresponding figures for the importance of spirituality: *extremely important* (35 percent), *very important* (33 percent), *somewhat important* (20 percent), *not very important* (12 percent), and *not at all important* (5 percent).

23. The exact wording of the question was "How often do you feel God's love for you directly?" The response categories were as follows: *never* (18.5 percent), *once in a while* (13 percent), *some days* (10.5 percent), *most days* (14.1 percent), *every day* (35.6 percent), and *more than once a day* (9.3 percent). Comparable data from the 2004 General Social Survey (GSS), another survey with a nationally representative sample, revealed that 50.2 percent felt God's love directly every day or many times per day, and 84.2 percent had this experience at least once in a while. See www.thearda.com/quickstats/qs_16.asp, accessed February 25, 2011. Phrased somewhat differently on the 2006/2007 Faith Matters survey, another national survey with a large sample, the result is basically the same: 62 percent of Americans "feel God's love 'very often'" (see Putnam and Campbell, *American Grace*, 470). The wording for both the GSS and GLNS question on feeling God's love directly derives from the work of Lynn Underwood and her Daily Spiritual Experience Scale. See Lynn G. Underwood, "Daily Spiritual Experiences," in *Multidimensional Measurement of Religiousness/Spirituality for Use in Health Research* (Kalamazoo, MI: Fetzer Institute, 2003), 11–17, www.fetzer.org/research/248-dses, accessed April 10, 2010.

24. Of those saying that religion and spirituality are very important to them, 64.5 percent reported that they felt God's love *at least once a day*. This figure fell by a factor of 10, to less than 6.4 percent, for the much smaller group of Americans who claimed that neither religion nor spirituality is important.

25. Looking at the numbers from another angle, we can say that almost half (48 percent) of the respondents who had a strong sense of purpose directly experienced

God's love at least once a day, compared with the 14 percent who had a strong sense of purpose but never experienced divine love.

26. This question is unique to the GLNS. Previous surveys, like the GSS, could be used to show the link between experiencing God's love and helping others through correlational data analysis. We are able to do this with the GLNS, but we also thought it would be informative to ask about both God's love and benevolence in a single question that explicitly links the two. We appreciate the constructive conversations that we had with John C. Green about these kinds of issues as we constructed our pilot survey and made the revisions that produced the GLNS.

27. The four-item Divine Love scale is discussed in more detail in chapter 2; see especially note 11. As the name implies, this scale measures the extent to which a survey respondent claims to have experienced divine love.

28. The adjusted R^2 (.10) with community benevolence as the dependent variable was statistically significant. The leading factor was experiencing divine love (beta = .25), with those scoring higher on the Divine Love scale also scoring higher on the Community Benevolence scale. Age was negatively related to community benevolence (beta = −.13), and income was positively related (beta = .11). The other demographics were not statistically significant. We note that a cross-sectional survey (i.e., one that is conducted at a single point in time) cannot establish causality, but it does allow us to identify the magnitude of the effect of one variable on another, independent of other potentially confounding factors.

CHAPTER 2

1. For a detailed social scientific analysis of how members of one neo-pentecostal denomination learn to walk and talk with God, see T. M. Luhrmann's *When God Talks Back* (New York: Alfred A. Knopf, 2012). Luhrmann uses data collected through interviews, an experiment, and extensive participant observation to support her hypothesis that people can train to hear God's voice through prayer practices that enable the pray-er to experience God in ongoing interactive relationship.

2. Two of the best historical accounts to trace the early historic Pentecostal movement are Cecil M. Robeck Jr., *Azusa Street: Mission and Revival* (Nashville: Thomas Nelson, 2006), and Grant Wacker, *Heaven Below: Early Pentecostals and American Culture* (Cambridge, MA: Harvard University Press, 2001).

3. Given the wide variety of terms pentecostals use to describe themselves, it is probable that the GLNS may underreport their number. For example, our 27 percent figure, although significant, is lower than the 36 percent reported by Barna (accessed January 7, 2008, www.barna.org). This notable discrepancy is probably due to differences in the questions used in the two surveys. The GLNS used two straightforward questions: (1) Would you describe yourself as a Pentecostal Christian or not? and (2) Would you describe yourself as a charismatic Christian or not? These items were recoded into a single item indicating whether respondents

considered themselves to be either Pentecostal or charismatic. Barna's comprehensive question asked whether respondents "consider yourself to be a Pentecostal or charismatic Christian, meaning that you have been filled by the Holy Spirit and believe that the charismatic gifts, such as tongues and healing, are valid and alive today." We preferred simpler questions that separated self-identification from belief in the charismatic gifts. Furthermore, we asked other questions about experiencing (not believing in) the gifts of tongues and healing.

4. See, for example, Harvey Cox, *Fire from Heaven: The Rise of Pentecostal Spirituality and the Reshaping of Religion in the Twenty-First Century* (Reading, MA: Addison-Wesley, 1995); Donald E. Miller and Tetsunao Yamamori, *Global Pentecostalism: The New Face of Christian Social Engagement* (Berkeley: University of California Press, 2007); Candy Gunther Brown, ed., *Global Pentecostal and Charismatic Healing* (New York: Oxford University Press, 2011).

5. In tracing the origins of the global Pentecostal movement, European theologian Walter Hollenweger in his treatise *Pentecostalism: Origins and Developments Worldwide* (Peabody, MA: Hendrickson, 1997) has identified five primary roots: black, Catholic, evangelical, critical, and ecumenical. The unique merging of cultures and theologies suggests that there was never a single Pentecostalism—there has always been a plurality of pentecostalisms.

6. Two of our research team members, theologian Peter Althouse and sociologist Michael Wilkinson, have surveyed a select group of pentecostals who practice "soaking prayer." Soaking prayer, a legacy of the 1990s renewal, is a particular approach to contemplative or meditative prayer in which the pray-er (in groups or alone) takes a comfortable position (often lying on the floor) and generally with music in the background relaxes and expects to experience the presence of God. Peter and Michael found that 98 percent of their 250 respondents indicated that they were "Spirit-filled" Christians. The researchers reported, however, that even for this highly particular group of pentecostals, the preferred self-description varied greatly: Pentecostal (12 percent), Charismatic (35 percent), Third Wave (4 percent), Full Gospel (7 percent), Revival (16 percent), Apostolic (11 percent), and an undesignated Other (14 percent).

7. This alternate worldview can be seen as being played out in an "as if" (subjunctive mood) world of possibilities. (It contrasts with the "as is" [indicative mood] of everyday reality.) Religious rituals are one means of creating and sustaining the "reality" of possibilities. Pentecostalism, perhaps more than any other approach to Christianity, creates and sustains a worldview of possibilities. For further discussion, see Adam B. Seligman, Robert P. Weller, Michael J. Puett, and Bennett Simon, *Ritual and Its Consequences* (New York: Oxford University Press, 2008).

8. For example, the coeditor of a collection of essays on the "future of Pentecostalism" in the United States notes that in the face of evangelicalization, upward mobility of congregants, and other social and demographic forces, "the contributors to this book seem pessimistic that there is the will or vitality left in classical Pentecostal

denominations to project a spiritually vital Pentecostalism into the decades ahead." See Eric Patterson, conclusion to *The Future of Pentecostalism in the United States*, edited by Eric Patterson and Edmund Rybarczyk, 189–209 (Lanham, MD: Lexington, 2007), 206.

9. It is important to note the distinctive relationship between evangelicalism and pentecostalism in the United States. In sum, most pentecostals would claim to be evangelicals (e.g., to be "born again"), but many evangelicals would not claim to be pentecostal. There is a tension between highly experiential pentecostals (who are open to experiences like prophecy, divine healing, deliverance, and speaking in tongues) and dispensationalist evangelicals (who deny the validity of these "spiritual gifts" for the modern church).

10. For a theological discussion of pentecostalism as a worldview, see Jackie David Johns, "Yielding to the Spirit: The Dynamics of a Pentecostal Model of Praxis," in *The Globalization of Pentecostalism: A Religion Made to Travel*, edited by Murray W. Dempster, Byron D. Klaus, and Doug Petersen, 70–84 (Carlisle, CA: Regnum, 1999). See also Margaret M. Poloma, *Main Street Mystics* (Walnut Creek, CA: Alta Mira Press, 2003), and www.researchonreligion.org/protestantism/margaret-poloma-on-pentecotalism-the-assemblies-of-god-and-godly-love (accessed January 18, 2012) for a podcast interview on Pentecostalism and godly love.

11. A reliable scale composed of multiple items to measure a single phenomenon, when available, is more robust and provides a better measure than use of a single item. The four questions used to comprise the scale to measure *experiences of God's love* include the following: feeling God's love directly; feeling God's love through others; feeling God's love as the greatest power in the universe; and feeling God's love increasing your compassion for others. The alpha or reliability coefficient is .93.

12. Multiple regression analysis, a statistical procedure that allows for the testing of multiple factors simultaneously, was performed to determine which if any of the seven independent variables—race, age, education, income, marital status, gender, and pentecostal identity—are correlated with scores for divine love. The adjusted R^2 was .15, with significant beta scores for being pentecostal or charismatic (beta = .26), being female (beta = .19); and self-identifying as nonwhite (beta = .16).

13. Margaret M. Poloma, *The Charismatic Movement: Is There a New Pentecost?* (Boston: Twayne, 1982).

14. Denominational families commonly include Roman Catholic (stands alone), mainline Protestant (e.g., Episcopal Church, Evangelical Lutheran Church of America, Presbyterian Church (USA), and United Methodist Church), conservative Protestant (e.g., Assemblies of God, Churches of Christ, Southern Baptist Convention, Presbyterian Church of America), and historically black denominations (e.g., National Baptist Convention, Church of God in Christ, African Methodist Episcopal). To this commonly used short list (see Cynthia Woolever and Deborah Bruce, *Beyond the Ordinary: 10 Strengths of U.S. Congregations* [Louisville, KY: Westminster John Knox Press, 2004]) we have added two other

rapidly growing groups, Hispanic Catholic and Hispanic Protestant. Also included for comparison purposes is the 14 percent of respondents to our National Survey who claimed no religious affiliation.

15. Cynthia Woolever and Deborah Bruce's report on the findings from the US Congregational Life Survey (*Beyond the Ordinary*), which included over three hundred thousand worshippers in more than two thousand congregations, meshes well with our general survey findings. Especially relevant is this summary statement (21): "Conservative Protestant congregations and churches in historically black denominations consistently scored highest on the Growing Spirituality Index. This was true for all of the individual elements as well as for the composite index....Mainline and liberal Protestant churches scored in the middle range. Catholic parishes made the lowest score on the index and its elements."

16. For further discussion of gender differences and religiosity see C. Daniel Batson, Patricia Schoenrade, and W. Larry Ventis, *Religion and the Individual: A Social-Psychological Perspective* (New York: Oxford University Press, 1993).

17. "Sheri" is a pseudonym. Throughout the book, we refer to some of our interviewees by their actual names and others by pseudonyms in order to protect their privacy. Out of 120 interviews, all but one gave us permission to use their names in publications, and we received approval from the Institutional Review Board at the University of Akron to reveal their identities. But we could see no good reason to do this, unless the person was a public figure. All of the primary exemplars we use in this book to illustrate central themes served as a leader of a large organization, made public statements through the media, have written books, and/or have served as public spokespeople for specific groups. Interested readers may wish to visit their websites, read their books, or get involved in their organizations, so we have revealed their identities. For others, we believe their interests are best served by remaining anonymous. We are grateful for their participation in this research and would not want them to receive unwanted attention as a result of the publication of this book.

18. Although gender differences have commonly been measured and reported in research on religion, feminine spiritualities have been treated largely as an artifact rather than a topic worthy of extensive investigation. See Mary Jo Meadow, "Current and Emerging Themes in the Psychology of Religion," in *Psychology of Religion*, edited by H. Newton Malony, 254–63 (Grand Rapids, MI: Baker Book House, 1991). Considerable amounts of scholarship have been devoted to gender discrimination (sexism) in religion in recent years, but much less attention has been paid to feminine spiritualities and what they contribute to the cultural grid of denominational groupings.

19. 2010 census figures from http://quickfacts.census.gov/qfd/states/00000.html, accessed May 31, 2012.

20. E. Franklin Frazier, *The Negro Church in America* (New York: Schocken Books, 1963), 44.

21. These religious practices range from those of black Catholics to black Muslims, with the vast majority identifying with one of the many types of black Protestantism. See Elfriede Wedam, "The Mosaic of Black Religion in Indianapolis," September 2000, www.polis.iupui.edu/ruc/newsletters/research/vol2no8, accessed August 13, 2010.

22. See Renita J. Weems, "Black America and Religion," *Ebony Magazine*, November 2005, http://findarticles.com/p/articles/mi_m1077/is, accessed August 12, 2010.

23. Ibid. Elfriede Wedam, citing social ethicist Robert M. Franklin, *Another Day's Journey: Black Churches Confronting the American Crisis* (Minneapolis: Fortress, 1997), 41–52.

24. Joseph Varacalli, *The Catholic Experience in America* (Westport, CT: Greenwood, 2006), 4.

25. It is likely that the exodus of Hispanics/Latinos from the Catholic Church both in Latin America and in the United States will continue. The inroad of Protestant Christianity into historically Catholic Hispanic culture in the United States began as early as 1821 in Texas (see Moises Sandoval, *On the Move: A History of the Hispanic Church in the United States* [Maryknoll, NY: Orbis Books, 2006]) and has intensified with the rise of Pentecostalism in the twentieth century. Compounding the problem is the shortage of Catholic priests that has reached critical proportions in the United States, making it impossible for the most part to create the kind of ethnic community support that Catholicism had made possible for Euro-American immigrants. For a discussion of the continuities and discontinuities of Latino religious traditions within the United States, see David A. Badillo, *Latinos and the New Immigrant Church* (Baltimore: John Hopkins University Press, 2006), and Helen Rose Ebaugh and Janet Saltzman Chafetz, *Religion and the New Immigrants* (Walnut Creek, CA: Alta Mira, 2000).

26. See note 12 for the statistical results of multiple regression analysis demonstrating that identification with Pentecostal/charismatic Christianity is the leading predictor of experiencing divine love.

27. Margaret M. Poloma and Matthew T. Lee, "Postmodernity's Spiritual Renaissance," *On Faith* (a joint venture of the *Washington Post* and *Newsweek*), July 21, 2008, http://newsweek.washingtonpost.com/onfaith/guestvoices/2008/07/post-modernitys_spiritual_renai.html.

28. For more on creedal religion, see Philip Rieff, *Charisma: The Gift of Grace, and How It Has Been Taken Away from Us* (New York: Vintage Books, 2007).

29. Poloma and Lee, "Postmodernity's Spiritual Renaissance."

30. Johns, *The Globalization of Pentecostalism*, 79.

31. For further discussion see Frank D. Macchia, *Baptized in the Spirit: A Global Pentecostal Theology* (Grand Rapids, MI: Zondervan, 2006).

32. Margaret M. Poloma, *Main Street Mystics: The Toronto Blessing and Reviving Pentecostalism* (Walnut Creek, CA: Alta Mira, 2003).

33. In reference to the bombing of his house, King responded, "My religious experi-
ence a few nights before had given me the strength to face it." See Charles Marsh,
*The Beloved Community: How Faith Shapes Social Justice, from the Civil Rights
Movement to Today* (New York: Basic Books, 2005), 37. See also Clayborne Carson,
ed., *The Autobiography of Martin Luther King, Jr.* (New York: Warner Books, 1998);
Eknath Easwaran, *Gandhi, the Man: The Story of His Transformation*, 3rd ed.
(Tomales, CA: Nilgiri, 1997); Eknath Easwaran, *Nonviolent Soldier of Islam:
Badshah Khan, a Man to Match His Mountains* (Tomales, CA: Nilgiri, 1997).

34. John Green presented preliminary findings on the relationship between pentecos-
tal markers, the experience of divine love, and participation in benevolence at a
Flame of Love Project public seminar. See John Green, "Godly Love in the American
Population: Survey Findings," paper presented at the seminar "The Great
Commandment: Theology and Social Science in Dialogue" at Vanguard University
of Southern California in Costa Mesa, CA, October 22, 2010.

35. The questions used in the four benevolence scales are as follows: *familial benevolence* (special effort to be kind to discouraged or upset family members; do all possible to help loved ones; good at figuring out ways to help family members);
neighborly benevolence (visit sick coworkers and friends; enjoy doing favors for people I know; important to be personally helpful to friends and neighbors); *community
benevolence* (assist people in community who are suffering; come to aid of stranger;
provide financial support to local charities); *global benevolence* (important to leave
world a better place; actively support causes around the world that seek to help less
fortunate; seek to help humanity in some way).

36. Evangelical pollster George Barna ("Is American Christianity Turning Charismatic?,"
January 7, 2008, www.barna.org/barna-update/article/18-congregations/52-is-american-
christianity-turning-charismatic) has noted that a growing number of American
Christians are claiming to be charismatic or pentecostal Christians, leading to the question
expressed in his title. After noting that the charismatic orientation "is most popular
among the non-white population," he goes on to state: "Also, the freedom of emotional
and spiritual expression typical of charismatic assemblies, parallels the cultural trend
toward personal expression, accepting diverse emotions and allowing people to interpret
their experiences in ways that make sense to them."

CHAPTER 3

1. For further discussion of this typology and the hybridization of ministries and ser-
vices among the exemplars in the Flame of Love Project see Matthew T. Lee and
Margaret M. Poloma, *A Sociological Study of the Great Commandment in
Pentecostalism: The Practice of Godly Love as Benevolent Service* (New York: Edwin
Mellen, 2009).

2. Heidi Baker, with Shara Pradhan, *Compelled by Love: How to Change the World
through the Simple Power of Love in Action* (Lake Mary, FL: Charisma House, 2008).

3. As this book was going to press, Iris Ministries was changing its name to Iris Global.

4. http://www.irisministries.com/about-our-mission, accessed August 24, 2010.

5. Iris Ministries was founded by Heidi and Rolland Baker in 1980 while they served as missionaries in Asia. In 1995, after both worked in the slums of London while earning PhDs from Kings College London, they answered what they believed was a call to work with the "poorest of the poor" in Mozambique. According to the Iris website, "The highest concentration of activity [of Iris Ministries] is in Mozambique followed by Malawi and then South Africa. The sun never sets on Iris Ministries around the world. Some level of ministry or offices are now located in 25 countries" (www.irisministries.com, accessed August 24, 2010).

6. Heidi Baker professes herself a follower of Mother Teresa's example, of which she writes, "I am forever blessed by the example of Mother Teresa, who blazed a trail of love for all to follow" (Baker, *Compelled by Love*, vi).

7. Rolland Baker, foreword to ibid., x–xi.

8. Paul Alexander, *Peace to War: Shifting Allegiances in the Assemblies of God* (Telford, PA: Cascade, 2009), 19.

9. See Paul Alexander, *Signs and Wonders: Why Pentecostalism Is the World's Fastest Growing Faith* (San Francisco: Jossey-Bass, 2009).

10. Alexander, *Peace to War*, 349.

11. Grant Wacker, *Heaven Below: Early Pentecostals and American Culture* (Cambridge, MA: Harvard University Press, 2001).

12. Bethel Church, Cleveland, is affiliated with a network of churches that have gathered around Bill Johnson's Bethel Church, Redding, California. Johnson's church was a well-established and successful congregation affiliated with the Assemblies of God (AG) when it became an epicenter of the revivals of the 1990s. (For a sociological account of the 1990s revivals, see Margaret M. Poloma, *Main Street Mystics: The Toronto Blessing and Reviving Pentecostalism* [Walnut Creek, CA: Alta Mira, 2003].) In 2008 Bethel withdrew from the AG as Johnson acknowledged the close ties that existed between his church and other revival network churches. Bethel Cleveland had its origins with the Toronto Airport Christian Fellowship (now known as Catch the Fire Toronto), perhaps the best-known revival site of the 1990s. Metro Church South joined the Bethel Redding network of churches in early 2011 and changed the name of its three church locations to Bethel Cleveland.

13. See Poloma, *Main Street Mystics*.

14. For example, in 1998 a prophecy given by Graham Cooke, a minister from Southampton, England, who now resides in northern California, was widely distributed among pentecostals in the Cleveland area and is a prototype of other prophecies given since about the rise of Cleveland. Part of it reads: "[Cleveland] will be a city where the manifest presence of God inhabits. If you will build kingdom, if you will take charge and take the charge of holding my dream in your hearts...then

I will presence myself among you.... Cleveland will no longer be the butt of other people's jokes but it will be a place of wonder that will be spoken in awe. It will become a city set on a hill with a regional presence that will reach out across this state" (*Cleveland: City of God's Dreams* [Cleveland, OH: Metro Church South [Bethel Church], n.d.), 4. Graham Cooke has returned to give conferences at Bethel Cleveland with some regularity, always stoking the fires of the prophetic words offered for Cleveland by him and other prophets.

15. Colette M. Jenkins, "Sacred Heart Building Sold to Expanding Ohio Church," *Akron Beacon Journal*, May 21, 2011.

16. www.gapfamilycenter.org/about us, accessed September 13, 2010.

17. For Anne Beiler's personal story and the account of the founding of Auntie Anne's, see her autobiography *Twist of Faith: The Story of Anne Beiler, Founder of Auntie Anne's Pretzels* (Nashville: Thomas Nelson, 2008).

18. www.thebeilers.com/story.html, accessed September 13, 2010.

19. Beiler, *Twist of Faith*.

20. His church's website includes the following description of some of his activism: "Active in the struggle for integration in the 1950s and community control of schools in the late 1960s, Rev. Daughtry has been involved in protest actions in cooperation with Brooklyn CORE and Operation Breadbasket, the economic arm of Dr. Martin Luther King's Southern Christian Leadership Conference (SCLC). During this period, in addition to serving as co-chairman of Ministers Against Narcotics, he also served as vice chairperson of the board of directors of Bedford Stuyvesant Youth In Action and executive vice chair of Operation Breadbasket's Metropolitan New York Chapter." See www.holnj.org/nationalpresider.html, accessed January 19, 2011.

21. Cornel West, foreword to Herbert D. Daughtry Sr., *No Monopoly on Suffering: Blacks and Jews in Crown Heights (and Elsewhere)* (Trenton, NJ: African World, 1997).

22. Ibid., xv.

23. Daughtry, *No Monopoly on Suffering*, 53.

24. www.youtube.com/watch?v=23Kox5Wt-HY, accessed January 10, 2011.

25. Daughtry, *No Monopoly on Suffering*.

CHAPTER 4

1. Bob Ekblad, "Prophesy and Reconciliation," November 26, 2009, http://bob ekblad.blogspot.com/search?q=Prophesy+and+Reconciliation.

2. Ibid.

3. Ibid.

4. Early research on prayer conducted by Margaret M. Poloma and George H. Gallup Jr. in the late 1980s discovered that of the nearly 90 percent of Americans who said they prayed, over half of them (57 percent) acknowledged that at least on occasion

they "felt divinely inspired or 'led by God' to perform some specific action." For 9 percent of these respondents to a national random sample, such experiences occurred regularly. The corresponding figure for the GLNS conducted some twenty years later is 66 percent of prayers having the experience of a divine leading during prayer, and 11 percent reporting that this is a regular occurrence. See Margaret M. Poloma and George H. Gallup Jr., *Varieties of Prayer: A Survey Report* (Philadelphia: Trinity Press International, 1991).

5. Kenneth I. Pargament, "The Meaning of Spiritual Transformation," in *Spiritual Transformation and Healing*, edited by Joan D. Koss-Chioino and Philip Hefner, 10–24 (Walnut Creek, CA: Alta Mira, 2005), 16.

6. We recognize that spiritual transformations include accounts in which persons abandon a particular spiritual worldview, the belief in a personal God, or even the possibility of a nonmaterial reality. We briefly address this form of spiritual transformation in chapter 5 as we consider the role of spiritual struggles and pain. It is important to note, however, that virtually all of our exemplar interviewees were comfortable with the nomenclature of being "pentecostal Christians." The GLNS permits us to place these interviewees and their stories within the larger context of American Christianity as we seek to explore the relationship between intimacy with God and benevolence that we found in the survey data.

7. Pargament, "The Meaning of Spiritual Transformation," 20.

8. There has been a long-standing bias of the academy against taking religious experience seriously. Although it is lessening, this bias against the empirical study of religious experience has been described as "academic arrogance and limited methodological relevance [that] often too quickly seeks reductive explanations of spiritual phenomena." See Ralph Hood, preface to *Spiritual Transformation and Healing*, edited by Joan D. Koss-Chioino and Philip Hefner, xiv (Walnut Creek, CA: Alta Mira, 2005); see also David J. Hufford and Mary Ann Bucklin, "The Spirit of Spiritual Healing in the United States," in *Spiritual Transformation and Healing*, edited by Joan D. Koss-Chioino and Philip Hefner, 25–44 (Walnut Creek, CA: Alta Mira, 2005).

9. For further discussion of the relationship between spirituality and religion, see Kenneth I. Pargament, "The Psychology of Religion and Spirituality? Yes and No," *International Journal for the Psychology of Religion* 9 (1999): 3–16.

10. Although the theologies of many would insist that one must be born again in order to be a pentecostal Christian, this is more likely to reflect traditional Pentecostal nomenclature than mainline Protestant or Catholic charismatic. Only 64 percent of charismatic Christians report that they consider themselves born again, compared with 93 percent of Pentecostals. Even the most carefully crafted survey questions are riddled with linguistic problems. This became even clearer with the question about "baptism in the Spirit," a common term used by pentecostals to designate a "second blessing" (after salvation) that releases the power of God into the lives of believers. Seventy-eight percent of pentecostals (and a third of the total

sample) claimed they had received "the baptism of the Holy Spirit, also known as the second baptism or second blessing." What we believed to be a specific term turned out to generate affirmative responses from the vast majority of survey respondents, with no clues as to the diverse interpretations this question generated.

11. The bivariate correlation between being born again and the Divine Love scale is $r = .46$.

12. *Existential well-being* is a scale composed of responses to these three questions; the alpha or reliability coefficient for the scale is .66.

13. Interestingly, having a strong sense of meaning, purpose, and destiny was not, for the most part, related to any common demographic descriptors. Existential well-being was not impacted by income, age, education, marital status, race, or ethnicity, although women were slightly more likely than men to indicate higher scores.

14. The bivariate correlation for existential well-being and experiences of divine love is .37. For the benevolence scales and existential well-being the correlations are as follows: family, $r = .42$; friends, $r = .44$; local community, $r = .40$; world/beyond community, $r = .47$.

15. We classified the "medium" range for existential well-being as those who scored either 9 or 10 on our 12-point scale, which accounted for 54 percent of the sample. This gives us a low and high group that roughly corresponds to quartiles: 23 percent scored low (1–8), and 22 percent scored high (11 or 12).

16. Based on multivariate analyses, we would suggest that a prayer item found in our survey (asking the respondent how often they have experienced God asking them to do something specific during prayer) may be a better measure to tap being called by God than the born-again measure. A careful review of our interviews demonstrates that the interviewees rarely used this term to describe their experience of a call unless we introduced it. Furthermore, being born again can be a primarily cognitive decision to "follow Christ," a cognitive decision accompanied by spiritual experiences, or an unexpected spiritual experience that leads to a surrender to do God's bidding.

17. See http://psychology.wikia.com/wiki/Virtuous_circle_and_vicious_circle or http://en.wikipedia.org/wiki/Virtuous_circle (accessed April 26, 2011). Empirical theologian William Kay suggests that a similar kind of virtuous circle may be responsible for the growth of pentecostalism more generally (personal communication with Margaret, May 27, 2012; see also William K. Kay, "Empirical and Historical Perspectives on the Growth of Pentecostal-Style Churches in Malaysia, Singapore, and Hong Kong," paper made available at the International Society of Empirical Research in Theology, Nijmegen, April 19–21, 2012).

18. Multivariate analyses that include the four primary components of the spiritual transformation model in relationship to benevolence—experiencing a divine call to action, experiencing divine love, and existential well-being and benevo-

lence measures (for family, friends, and community separately; then for a composite benevolence scale)—suggest that our model is statistically tenable, especially for a more extensive love that reaches out to the community and beyond. The explained variance for the combined benevolence scale is 18 percent, with existential well-being (beta = .34), experiencing direction from God (beta = .10), and experiencing divine love (beta = .08) all being statistically significant.

19. Rolland Baker and Heidi Baker, *Always Enough: God's Miraculous Provision among the Poorest Children on Earth* (Grand Rapids, MI: Chosen Books, 2003), 24.

20. Baker and Baker, *Always Enough*, 25.

21. For another example from our interviews of embodied religion that, at times, takes the form of dance, see the charismatic Catholic story involving "George" in Matthew T. Lee, "Restorative Justice, Godly Love, and Solutions to the Problem of Crime," in *Godly Love: Impediments and Possibilities*, edited by Matthew T. Lee and Amos Yong, 91–110 (Lanham, MD: Lexington Books, 2012). A shorter version of this narrative appears in chapter 6 of the current book.

22. Baker and Baker, *Always Enough*, 27.

23. These estimates were provided by Heidi's assistant (Ania Noster) in an e-mail to the first author on March 22, 2012. See also www.irismin.org/p/background.php (accessed May 28, 2010). See also Heidi Baker, with Shara Pradhan, *Compelled by Love: How to Change the World through the Simple Power of Love in Action* (Lake Mary, FL: Charisma House, 2008).

24. The quotes are from Barbara Bradley Hagerty, *Fingerprints of God: The Search for the Science of Spirituality* (New York: Riverhead, 2009), 12, 34, 38, 42.

25. Baker and Baker, *Always Enough*, 23.

26. For a sociological account of the so-called Toronto Blessing, see Margaret M. Poloma, *Main Street Mystics: The Toronto Blessing and Reviving Pentecostalism* (Walnut Creek, CA: Alta Mira, 2003).

27. Paul has delivered keynote addresses on religion, peacemaking, and justice in The Hague for the Dutch Ministry of Foreign Affairs; Pune, India, for the United Nations Educational, Scientific, and Cultural Organization (UNESCO); and Bethlehem for Bethlehem Bible College. He cofounded Pentecostals and Charismatics for Peace and Justice and is editor of the book series Pentecostals, Peacemaking, and Social Justice (Wipf & Stock) and the journal *Pax Pneuma: The Journal of Pentecostals and Charismatics for Peace and Justice* (www.palmer seminary.edu/about/faculty, accessed January 24, 2011).

28. Paul Alexander, *Signs and Wonders: Why Pentecostalism Is the World's Fastest Growing Faith* (San Francisco: Jossey-Bass, 2009).

29. Hagerty, *Fingerprints of God*, 33.

30. William Miller, *Quantum Change* (New York: Guilford, 2001).

31. Hagerty, *Fingerprints of God*, 37, 42.

32. See also Matthew 5:12 and Romans 5:3.

CHAPTER 5

1. For further discussion see Keith E. Yandell, *The Epistemology of Religious Experience* (New York: Cambridge University Press, 1993).

2. Brother Lawrence, *The Practice of the Presence of God*, Kindle edition, n.d.

3. Pitirim A. Sorokin, *The Ways and Power of Love: Types, Factors, and Techniques of Moral Transformation* (1952; rpt., Philadelphia: Templeton, 2002).

4. Ibid., 26.

5. Prayer has been increasingly included as a measure of religiosity, but it has been measured mainly by the single-item measure of prayer frequency; see Michael J. Breslin, Christopher Alan Lewis, and Mark Shevlin, "A Psychometric Evaluation of Poloma and Pendleton's (1991) and Ladd and Spilka's (2002, 2006) Measures of Prayer," *Journal for the Scientific Study of Religion* 49 (2010): 710–13. Our analysis of the GLNS goes beyond this limited measure to demonstrate the effects of interactive prayer on benevolent behavior.

6. For further details see George Gallup Jr. and Sarah Jones, *One Hundred Questions and Answers: Religion in America* (Princeton, NJ: Princeton Research Center, 1989), and Margaret M. Poloma and George H. Gallup Jr., *Varieties of Prayer* (Philadelphia: Trinity Press International, 1991).

7. See http://pewforum.org/frequency-of-prayer and www.baylor.edu/artsandsciences/index.php?id=59330, both accessed February 2, 2011.

8. Frequently reported statistics generally fail to note that these demographic variables taken together are relatively weak measures for profiling pray-ers. Using multiple regression analysis that considers the impact of five major demographic variables—gender, age, race, education, and income—we were able to account for only 7 percent (adjusted R^2 = .07) of the explained differences in the frequency of prayer scores. Women (beta = .19), older respondents (beta = –.15), nonwhites (beta = –.13), and those with less education (beta = –.08) and income (beta = –.10) were slightly more likely to pray frequently than were white young men with less education and income.

9. In a regional sample of the Akron, Ohio, area in 1985, Margaret Poloma and Brian Pendleton ("The Effects of Prayer and Prayer Experiences on Measures of Well-Being," *Journal of Psychology and Theology* 19 [1991]: 71–83) reported that the frequency of prayer did not effect scores on subjective perceptions of well-being. The evidence suggested that when other controls were introduced, people who prayed more frequently but did not acknowledge having religious experiences were more likely to be dissatisfied with their lives than those who prayed less often. Adding frequency of prayer to the multiple regression analyses used in this chapter similarly did little to help explain differences reported by survey respondents of knowing God's personal love for them.

10. In the GLNS survey 51 percent of the respondents said they regularly spent time "quietly being in the presence of God." The rest of the 49 percent were divided bet-

ween those who *never or rarely* spent any quiet time in prayer and those indicating that they did so *some of the time.*

11. The three scales measuring prayer activity, divine-human communication, and mystical communion were used in multiple regression analysis to determine which was best able to account for differences in perceiving divine love, the construct and scale that is at the heart of our analysis thus far. All three of the scales proved to be statistically significant for explaining nearly 80 percent of the variance (adjusted $R^2 = .79$) in divine love scores. Those who scored high on experiencing God's love scored high on prayer activity (beta = . 42), mysticism (beta = .39), and prophetic conversational prayer (beta = .17). The Devotional Prayer Activity scale (alpha = .96) included six items ("never" to "more than once a day") asking whether they did the following during prayer: sat quietly in the presence of God, asked for things they need, asked for divine guidance, worshipped and adored, prayed for the needs of others, and thanked God for blessings. The Mysticism scale (alpha = .86) included three items: everything seemed to disappear except consciousness of God, experience of God that no words could express, and feeling unmistakable presence of God during prayer. The Prophetic Conversation scale (alpha = .87) included five items: direct divine call to perform a specific act, hearing divine direction to do something through another, giving a word from God to another person, receiving revelations from God, and seeing future events in dreams and visions.

12. Three multiple regression equations were run to determine the importance of demographics and self-identification as a pentecostal/charismatic Christian on *devotional activity, prophetic conversational prayer,* and *mysticism.* All three equations were statistically significant. The adjusted R^2 for *devotional activity* was .14, with pentecostal identity accounting for the most variance (beta = .27) and women being more likely than men to engage in frequent prayer activity (beta = .16). The adjusted R^2 for prophetic conversational prayer was .12, with pentecostal identity accounting for the most variance (beta = .30). The adjusted R^2 for mysticism was .16, with most of the variance being explained (once again) by pentecostal identity (beta = .30) and with women being more mystical than men (beta = .13).

13. See Michael Wilkinson and Peter Althouse's work on "soaking prayer" for an excellent study of pentecostal prayer that describes in detail the essence of mystical experiences that reportedly are common to the practice of "soaking prayer." Soaking prayer is an innovation in the charismatic renewal that captures other types of prayers and charismatic practices. Soaking prayer cultivates a broad range of charismatic activity including resting, hearing from God, glossolalia, prophecy, dreams and visions, manifestations of the Spirit, impartation, and receiving divine love. Michael Wilkinson and Peter Althouse, "Varieties of Prayer in the Pentecostal Movement," Association for the Sociology of Religion, Atlanta, August 14–15, 2010; Michael Wilkinson and Peter Althouse, "The Place of Soaking Prayer in the Charismatic Renewal," Society for Pentecostal Studies, North Central University, Minneapolis, March 4–6, 2010; Michael Wilkinson and Peter Althouse,

"Charismatic Prayer and Social Engagement," International Society for the Sociology of Religion, Aix-en-Provence, France, July 1–3, 2011; Michael Wilkinson and Peter Althouse, "The Body and Spirit in Charismatic Christianity," Canadian Society for the Study of Religion, Fredericton, NB, May 28–31, 2011.

14. For additional discussion of prophecy in Pentecostal/charismatic traditions, see Margaret M. Poloma, *Main Street Mystics: The Toronto Blessing and Reviving Pentecostalism* (Walnut Creek, CA: Alta Mira, 2003), Margaret M. Poloma and John C. Green, *The Assemblies of God: Godly Love and the Revitalization of American Pentecostalism* (New York: New York University Press, 2010), and Margaret M. Poloma and Matthew T. Lee, "The New Apostolic Reformation: Main Street Mystics and Everyday Prophets," in *Prophecy in the Millennium: When Prophecies Persist*, edited by S. Harvey and S. Newcome (London: Ashgate, 2012).

15. For an anthropological study that explores the relationship with God reflected in prayer for members of an American neo-pentecostal denomination see T. M. Luhrmann's *When God Talks Back: Understanding the American Evangelical Relationship with God* (New York: Alfred A. Knopf, 2012).

16. For a discussion of the abuse, see Tamara Jones, "Auntie's Awakening: She Overcame Heartbreak and Made a Whole Lot of Dough in Pretzels. Now Anne Beiler Serves Life Lessons to Others in Pennsylvania's Amish Country," *Washington Post*, January 2, 2008, www.washingtonpost.com/wp-dyn/content/article/2008/01/01/AR2008010102081 .html.

17. Anne Beiler, *Twist of Faith: The Story of Anne Beiler, Founder of Auntie Anne's Pretzels* (Nashville: Thomas Nelson, 2008), 162.

18. Ibid., 35.

19. Ibid., 41.

20. Ibid.

21. Ibid., 162.

22. Steve Witt, *Voices: Understanding and Responding to the Language of Heaven* (Shippensburg, PA: Destiny Image, 2008), 38.

23. Ibid., 61.

24. Ibid., chap. 7.

25. Although the prophetic was an important component in the establishment of traditional Pentecostal denominations, they are subject to what Margaret has called "the routinization of charisma." Pragmatic actions and programs have replaced primitive spirituality as institutions grew more powerful. This thesis has been explored systematically and in relationship to godly love in Poloma and Green, *The Assemblies of God*.

26. Shane Claiborne and Jonathan Wilson-Hartgrove, *Becoming the Answer to Our Prayers: Prayer for Ordinary Radicals* (Downers Grove, IL: IVP Books, 2008), 11.

27. Ibid., 77. See also Kristen Zimmerman, Neelam Pathikonda, Brenda Salgado, and Taj James, *Out of the Spiritual Closet: Organizers Transforming the Practice of Social Justice* (Oakland, CA: Movement Strategy Center, 2010).

28. One exception to this general trend might be Bob Ekblad, the social activist we introduced in the last chapter. For much of his life, Ekblad was, in the words of one of his blog entries, "estranged from the body of Christ charismatic." In our terminology, this means that he was adverse to the pentecostal worldview. He became "increasingly discontented" with the lack of results of his ministry in fostering the kinds of changes he longed to see in the world. He told Margaret that he was "tired of fruitless ministry." His desperation to see God's power transform lives led him to venture "across the line into an ecumenism broader than I'd ever considered— attending a pastors' and leaders' conference at the infamous Toronto Airport Christian Fellowship." The result of attending this pentecostal center of revival was a spiritual transformation (discussed in the last chapter), enthusiastic utilization of pentecostal-style prayer, and a corresponding increase in effectiveness in his ministry. See Bob Ekblad, "Prophesy and Reconciliation," November 26, 2009, http://bobekblad.blogspot.com/search?q=Prophesy+and+Reconciliation. For more on the Toronto Airport Christian Fellowship, see Poloma, *Main Street Mystics*.

29. Margaret M. Poloma and Matthew T. Lee, "Postmodernity's Spiritual Renaissance," *On Faith* (a joint venture of the *Washington Post* and *Newsweek*), July 21, 2008, http://newsweek.washingtonpost.com/onfaith/guestvoices/2008/07/post modernitys_spiritual_renai.html.

30. Flame of Love Project team member and psychologist Ralph W. Hood Jr. has long used the items contained in the mysticism scale in his own work on religious experience. See Ralph W. Hood Jr., *Dimensions of Mystical Experience: Empirical Studies and Psychological Links* (New York: Rodopi, 2001); Ralph W. Hood Jr., Peter C. Hill, and Bernard Spilka, *The Psychology of Religion: An Empirical Approach*, 4th ed. (New York: Guilford, 2009).

31. See www.tonycampolo.org/media.php, accessed May 27, 2011.

32. Tony Campolo and Mary Albert Darling, *The God of Intimacy and Action: Reconnecting Ancient Spiritual Practices, Evangelism, and Justice* (San Francisco: John Wiley and Sons, 2007).

33. Ibid., 33, 40.

34. The book that came out of the conference bears the same title: Michael A. Edwards and Stephen G. Post, *The Love That Does Justice: Spiritual Activism in Dialogue with Social Science* (Cleveland, OH: Institute for Research on Unlimited Love, 2008).

35. Rolland Baker and Heidi Baker, *Always Enough: God's Miraculous Provision among the Poorest Children on Earth* (Grand Rapids, MI: Chosen Books, 2003), 49–50.

36. Ibid., 52. Margaret has heard a report of "multiplication of food" from a young eyewitness from her church who visited Mozambique recently. Kara described how it was apparent that the boxes of bread they had were not sufficient to feed the crowd, yet they were instructed to give each person an entire loaf. The bread mysteriously multiplied—it just kept coming until everyone in the vast crowd was fed.

37. Ibid., 54.
38. Ibid., 68.
39. Ibid., 69.
40. Ibid., 68.
41. Ibid., 70.
42. Ibid., 55.
43. Ibid.
44. Ibid., 56.
45. Ibid.
46. Eric Velu, producer, *Mama Heidi: The Heroic Story of Heidi and Rolland Baker* (Worcester, PA: Vision Video, 2004).

CHAPTER 6

1. E-mail from Heidi (sent by her assistant, Ania Noster) to the first author on March 22, 2012; see also the cover story of the evangelical publication *Christianity Today* on "Mama Heidi of Mozambique" (Tim Stafford, "Miracles in Mozambique," *Christianity Today*, May 2012, 19–26).
2. www.unitedcaribbean.com/heidibaker-cupofjoyandsuffering, accessed March 9, 2011.
3. For more rituals and the subjunctive, see Adam B. Seligman, Robert P. Weller, Michael J. Puett, and Bennett Simon, *Ritual and Its Consequences* (New York: Oxford University Press, 2008).
4. For further discussion see Matthew T. Lee and Margaret M. Poloma, *A Sociological Study of the Great Commandment in Pentecostalism: The Practice of Godly Love as Benevolent Service* (New York: Edwin Mellen, 2009), 88.
5. Heidi Baker, with Shara Pradhan, *Compelled by Love: How to Change the World through the Simple Power of Love in Action* (Lake Mary, FL: Charisma House, 2008), 43.
6. Ibid.
7. See Lee and Poloma, *A Sociological Study of the Great Commandment*, 88. The idea of seeing beyond circumstances was inspired by grounded theorist Kathy Charmaz's "seeing beyond self." Seeing beyond circumstances can be viewed as a subtype of this more general category. Charmaz studied people living with debilitating physical illnesses and found that some of them learn to "surrender" their hopes and dreams and in the process, paradoxically, they experience a sense of wholeness or unity of self that can be incredibly empowering. By seeing beyond their old self, they discover a new and better self, despite their physical limitations and in some cases their inevitable and untimely deaths. A strong sense of well-being can emerge from this context, just as it has with the exemplars we interviewed who had learned to see beyond their circumstances and follow the call of God without regard for what most of us would consider basic self-interests such as financial security and personal safety.

8. See, for example, our discussion in chapter 1 of Robert D. Putnam and David E. Campbell, *American Grace: How Religion Divides and Unites Us* (New York: Simon & Schuster, 2010).

9. Bill Johnson, "Supernatural by Nature," *Charisma,* June 2011, 51–54. Johnson calls Christians to do the impossible, empowered by God, rather than stopping with that which is humanly possible. He writes, "I'm astonished that the high point of celebration for the church is often when we accomplish something that's humanly possible. We build buildings, organize mission trips, have mass gatherings. But many great service organizations with no faith in God accomplish the same things."

10. Parker Palmer, interviewed on the National Public Radio program *Speaking of Faith,* episode titled "The Soul in Depression," November 16, 2006, http://speakingoffaith.publicradio.org/programs/depression/transcript.shtml. See also Viktor E. Frankl, *Man's Search for Meaning: An Introduction to Logotherapy* (1959; rpt., New York: Simon & Schuster, 1984).

11. The reference to previous work on pentecostals is particularly relevant for our discussion because the pentecostal worldview has been central to the concept of godly love that we are developing. See Margaret M. Poloma and Lynette F. Hoelter, "The 'Toronto Blessing': A Holistic Model of Healing," *Journal for the Scientific Study of Religion* 37 (1998): 258–73.

12. The "anger with God" scale included the following three items, with responses ranging from "never" to "more than once a day": feel anger at God (70 percent "never"), feel as though God is punishing you (76 percent "never") and feel God's actions are unfair (70 percent "never"). Cronbach's alpha for the three-item scale is .75. It is axiomatic in the counseling field that the ability to constructively express emotions like anger in an open and honest way is much more conducive to holistic healing than short-term pseudo-solutions like burying real feelings or trying to stifle anger.

13. Primary demographic measures were used as control measures: age, education, income, race, gender, and pentecostal identity. Women (beta = .12) and accepting a pentecostal identity (beta = .13) were slightly more likely to experience divine love than were men and non-pentecostals. Other demographics were not statistically significant. The healing measures in this equation included anger with God (beta = .23), divine physical healing (beta = .17), and inner or emotional healing (beta = .41). The adjusted R^2 (.52) for this equation explained slightly over half the variance for differences in divine love scores.

14. Lee Strobel, *The Case for Faith* (Grand Rapids, MI: Zondervan, 1998).

15. Julie J. Exline, Kalman Kaplan, and Joshua B. Grubbs, "Anger, Exit, and Assertion: Do People See Protest toward God as Morally Acceptable?," *Psychology of Religion and Spirituality* (forthcoming).

16. Julie J. Exline, Crystal L. Park, Joshua M. Smyth, and Michael P. Carey, "Anger toward God: Social-Cognitive Predictors, Prevalence, and Links with Adjustment to Bereavement and Cancer," *Journal of Personality and Social Psychology* 100 (2011): 129–48.

17. Julie J. Exline and Joshua B. Grubbs, "'If I Tell Others about My Anger toward God, How Will They Respond?': Predictors, Associated Behaviors, and Outcomes in an Adult Sample," *Journal of Psychology and Theology* (forthcoming).

18. Ibid.

19. Ibid.

20. Stephen (Steve) Mory received his MD degree at Jefferson Medical College in Philadelphia and completed his psychiatric residency at the University of Michigan Medical Center in Ann Arbor, Michigan. He has been a practicing physician for over thirty years, his first ten years in family practice and his last twenty in psychiatry. He is board certified by both the American Board of Family Practice and the American Board of Psychiatry and Neurology. He currently practices psychiatry in a community mental health clinic in Nashville, Tennessee. He has served in the Christian Medical and Dental Association as a former member of the house of delegates, as former chair of the marriage commission, and as former president of the psychiatry section.

21. When the three healing measures—anger with God, inner healing, and physical healing—were used in a multiple regression equation (controlling for demographics) to determine the relationship between healing and divine love, inner healing was by far the leading indicant. The results were as follows: anger with God (beta = .23), divine physical healing (beta = .17), and inner or emotional healing (beta = .41). The adjusted R^2 was .52.

22. Margaret M. Poloma, *Main Street Mystics: The Toronto Blessing and Reviving Pentecostalism* (Walnut Creek, CA: Alta Mira, 2003).

23. Ibid., 93.

24. Margaret M. Poloma and John C. Green, *The Assemblies of God: Godly Love and the Revitalization of American Pentecostalism* (New York: New York University Press, 2010).

25. See Matthew T. Lee, "Towards a Nonkilling Society: A Case Study of Individual and Institutional Changes in Social Affinity within a Religious Context," in *Nonkilling Societies*, edited by Joám Evans Pim, 365–87 (Honolulu: Center for Global Nonkilling, 2010).

26. Tamara Jones, "Auntie's Awakening: She Overcame Heartbreak and Made a Whole Lot of Dough in Pretzels. Now Anne Beiler Serves Life Lessons to Others in Pennsylvania's Amish Country," *Washington Post,* January 2, 2008, www.washington post.com/wp-dyn/content/article/2008/01/01/AR2008010102081.html.

27. The incident to which Jonas is referring is the shooting that occurred on October 2, 2006, at the West Nickel Mines School, a one-room Amish school near the Beiler residence in southeastern Pennsylvania. The incident made national headlines when a lone gunman shot ten girls, killing five, before committing suicide. Media coverage of the grisly details of the tragedy was quickly supplanted by the inspirational story of forgiveness and reconciliation shown by the Amish community toward the shooter's family. Jonas was closely involved with the community during

the aftermath, and he tells this story in a recent book: Jonas Beiler, with Shawn Smucker, *Think No Evil: Inside the Story of the Amish Schoolhouse Shooting...and Beyond* (New York: Howard Books, 2009).

28. Linda L. Barnes and Susan S. Sered, eds., *Religion and Healing in America* (New York: Oxford University Press, 2005).

29. Claudia Kalb, "Faith and Healing," *Newsweek*, November 10, 2003, 44–56.

30. John Cole, "Gallup Poll Again Shows Confusion," *NCSE Reports*, Spring 1996, 9.

31. Luis Lugo, *Spirit and Power: A 10-Country Survey of Pentecostals* (Washington, DC: Pew Forum on Religion and Public Life, 2006), http://pewforum.org/Christian/ Evangelical-Protestant-Churches/Spirit-and-Power.aspx, accessed December 28, 2010.

32. Another sample of 1,827 respondents from twenty-one diverse Assemblies of God (AG) congregations, Pentecostals from one of the ten largest denominations in the United States, provides additional support for the widespread belief and practice among Pentecostals. Seventy (70) percent of AG respondents reported having received a divine healing from a physical illness; 75 percent reported personally experiencing a (unspecified) "miraculous healing," and 85 percent said they had "witnessed a miraculous healing in the lives of family members or friends." The Pew Forum survey found that of the Pentecostals surveyed, 62 percent reported witnessing divine healings, compared with 46 percent of the Charismatics and 28 percent of other Christians. The lower figures for witnessing healing in the Pew study when compared with the Assemblies of God sample is in part due to differences in sampling procedures. The AG sample consists of twenty-one purposively selected congregations of a denomination in which divine healing is a "fundamental truth." Moreover, the respondents represent active AG adherents with surveys being distributed immediately following Sunday morning worship services. For further information on AG healing see Poloma and Green, *The Assemblies of God*.

33. The adjusted R square for this multiple regression equation is .16, with statistically significant betas for pentecostal identity (beta = .23), being nonwhite (beta = .23), and age (−.11).

34. E. Josephus Johnson II, *The Eight Ministries of the Holy Spirit* (Emunclaw, WA: Winepress, 2005), 3.

35. Ibid., 7.

36. Bill Johnson, *When Heaven Invades Earth: A Practical Guide to a Life of Miracles* (Shippensburg, PA: Destiny Image, 2003).

37. See www.ibethel.org/, accessed June 5, 2011.

38. Clinical studies of prayer have been especially problematic. While great care has been taken with the physical and medical indicators, the failure to contextualize prayer has led to less-than-satisfying research results. In short, the researchers decide how the pray-ers are to pray, without any regard for what people actually do when they pray. This has been particularly the case for a recent large-scale study that found "prayer" had no effect on sick patients who did not know they were

being prayed for and a slight negative effect if the patients knew they were part of the experimental group who was receiving prayer. See Herbert Benson et al., "Study of the Therapeutic Effects of Intercessory Prayer (STEP) in Cardiac Bypass Patients: A Multicenter Randomized Trial of Uncertainty and Certainty of Receiving Intercessory Prayer," *American Heart Journal* 151 (2006): 934.

39. For a masterful synthesis of empirical research and theological insight using the theoretical model of godly love to discuss religious healing, see Candy Gunther Brown's *Testing Prayer: Science and Healing* (Cambridge, MA: Harvard University Press, 2012).

40. Johnson, *When Heaven Invades Earth*, 25–27.

41. Linda Golz, "Service Honors Judge Unruh," *Akron Beacon Journal*, March 17, 2011.

42. Ibid.

43. Field observations made by Margaret Poloma.

44. Jewel Cardwell and Ed Meyer, "Judge Remembered as Caring Dies of Cancer," *Akron Beacon Journal*, March 14, 2011.

CHAPTER 7

1. E-mail update from Jonathan Wilson Hartgrove titled "Turning Again," received by the first author on December 15, 2011.

2. www.totallivingcenter.org/threefoldministry.htm, accessed December 21, 2011.

3. Ibid.

4. Ibid.

5. December 17, 2011, follow-up interview with Margaret, with additional material provided in a personal e-mail to Margaret on December 26, 2011.

6. Ibid.

7. Follow-up interview with Margaret in June 2011.

8. www.ibethel.org/our-mission, accessed January 19, 2012.

9. www.igloballegacy.org/, accessed January 19, 2012.

10. Partners in Harvest has reorganized into an international organization for "Catch the Fire churches." The Toronto Airport Christian Fellowship recently was renamed Catch the Fire Toronto (www.catchthefire.com/about, accessed December 23, 2011).

11. Bill Johnson had recently made the break from his denominational affiliation to ally with other revival leaders with whom he felt he shared more common ground. Johnson writes in a letter that appeared on the Bethel website (www.ibethel.org/bethel-and-the-assemblies-of-god, accessed May 28, 2012), "Though we haven't yet articulated it very clearly, we feel called to create a network that helps other networks thrive—to be one of many ongoing catalysts in this continuing revival. Our call feels unique enough theologically and practically from the call on the Assemblies of God that this change is appropriate." See also Margaret M. Poloma and John C. Green, *The Assemblies of God: Godly Love and*

the Revitalization of American Pentecostalism (New York: New York University Press, 2010), 201–3.

12. Interview with Margaret and Steve Witt, May 6, 2009.

13. www.bethelcleveland.com/message-the-blessed-life-living-the-epic-life, accessed December 23, 2011.

14. See Margaret M. Poloma, *Main Street Mystics: The Toronto Blessing and Reviving Pentecostalism* (Walnut Creek, CA: Alta Mira, 2003).

15. www.bethelcleveland.com/message-the-blessed-life-living-the-epic-life, accessed December 23, 2011.

16. For more on the Slavic Village Development see http://slavicvillage.org/our neighborhoods, accessed December 12, 2011.

17. See, for example, Forrest Wilder, "Rick Perry's Army of God," *Texas Observer*, July 12, 2011. See also an interview conducted by NPR's Terry Gross with C. Peter Wagner on the Apostolic Reformation: www.npr.org/2011/10/03/140946482/apostolic-leader-weighs-religions-role-in-politics#commentBlock, accessed January 19, 2012.

18. It is worthy of note that there are significant differences between Iris Ministries and some organizations/ministries established by Bethel Redding, particularly with regard to the hierarchy of offices in the so-called fivefold ministries (teacher, evangelist, pastor, prophet, and apostle). Although Heidi and Rolland Baker share with others in the NAR the belief in the power of Spirit-filled revivals to advance global Christianity, they have been less enthusiastic about the restoration of the office of "apostle" as a designated position as taught by Bethel and many other NAR ministries. Iris Ministries is listed in a supportive role as a "partner" of Global Legacy but not as an "affiliate" member. See www.igloballegacy.org/about, accessed May 28, 2012.

19. William K. Kay, *Apostolic Networks in Great Britain: New Ways of Being Church* (Waynesboro, GA: Paternoster, 2007).

20. C. Peter Wagner, foreword to Bill Hamon, *Apostles, Prophets and the Coming Moves of God: God's End-Time Plans for His Church and Planet Earth* (Santa Rosa, FL: Christian International, 1997), xxii.

21. See, for example, Margaret M. Poloma, *The Assemblies of God at the Crossroads: Charisma and Institutional Dilemmas* (Knoxville: University of Tennessee Press, 1989).

22. Robert Welsh and Paul Alexander, "Exemplars of Godly Justice: Peacemaking and Justice Seeking in Dangerous Contexts," *PentecoStudies* (forthcoming).

23. Naim Stifan Ateek, *Justice and Only Justice: A Palestinian Theology of Liberation* (Maryknoll, NY: Orbis, 2001), 96.

24. Ibid., 79.

25. Ibid., 80.

26. Paul Alexander, ed., *Christ at the Checkpoint: Theology in the Service of Justice and Peace* (Eugene, OR: Pickwick, 2012).

27. Ibid., xiii.

28. Matthew T. Lee and Margaret M. Poloma, *A Sociological Study of the Great Commandment in Pentecostalism: The Practice of Godly Love as Benevolent Service* (New York: Edwin Mellen, 2009).

29. For an extended discussion of these possibilities, see the video recording of a presentation by Matthew T. Lee titled "The Diamond Model of Godly Love," given at Vanguard University of Southern California on October 22, 2010. This presentation was part of the public seminar featuring the work of the Flame of Love Project titled "The Great Commandment: Theology and Social Science in Dialogue." This video, along with the rest of the seminar, can be downloaded at iTunes at http://itunes.apple.com/us/podcast/the-great-commandment-theology/id404915128.

30. We have devoted an entire book to this topic. See Matthew T. Lee and Amos Yong, eds., *The Science and Theology of Godly Love* (DeKalb: Northern Illinois University Press, 2012). See also Lee, "The Diamond Model of Godly Love"; Lee and Poloma, *A Sociological Study of the Great Commandment*; and Margaret M. Poloma, John C. Green, and Matthew T. Lee, "Covenants, Contracts, and Godly Love," in *The Assemblies of God: Godly Love and the Revitalization of American Pentecostalism*, 188–206 (New York: New York University Press, 2010).

31. Lee and Poloma, *A Sociological Study of the Great Commandment*, 88.

32. Heidi Baker, with Shara Pradhan, *Compelled by Love: How to Change the World through the Simple Power of Love in Action* (Lake Mary, FL: Charisma House, 2008), 124.

33. C. Dyke, "The Vices of Altruism," *Ethics* 81 (1971): 241–52.

34. Philip Rieff, *Charisma: The Gift of Grace, and How It Has Been Taken away from Us* (New York: Vintage Books, 2007), 242.

35. Pitirim A. Sorokin, *The Ways and Power of Love: Types, Factors, and Techniques of Moral Transformation* (1952; rpt. Philadelphia: Templeton, 2002).

36. Robert D. Putnam and David E. Campbell, *American Grace: How Religion Divides and Unites Us* (New York: Simon & Schuster, 2010).

CHAPTER 8

1. Henry David Thoreau, *Walden and Other Writings* (New York: Bantam Books, 1962), 160.

2. Robert D. Putnam and David E. Campbell, *American Grace: How Religion Divides and Unites Us* (New York: Simon & Schuster, 2010).

3. Instead of exploring what it was about religion that might lead to increased benevolence, Putnam and Campbell focused on social networks. They did include a single variable to tap experiencing divine love, but reported that the measures of social networks were more important in accounting for differences in benevolence.

4. Ibid., 478.

5. Kristen Renwick Monroe, *The Heart of Altruism: Perceptions of a Common Humanity* (Princeton, NJ: Princeton University Press, 1996).

6. Pitirim Sorokin proposed five dimensions of love, one of which is *extensity*: "The extensity of love ranges from the zero point of love of oneself only, up to the love of all mankind, all living creatures, and the whole universe. Between the minimal and maximal degrees lies a vast scale of extensities: love of one's own family, or a few friends, or love of the groups one belongs to—one's own clan, tribe, nationality, nation, religious, occupational, political, and other groups and associations." Sorokin's extensity resonates with the classic Western discussion of the "order of love." How does one balance love for family and friends (the nearest and dearest) with love for the very neediest of all humanity? Pitirim A. Sorokin, *The Ways and Power of Love: Types, Factors, and Techniques of Moral Transformation* (1952; rpt., Philadelphia: Templeton, 2002), 16.

7. These Weberian concepts have been widely applied. For example, Lee and Gailey discuss how the focus on technical rationality (net profits) in the corporate sector can interfere with substantive goals like consumer or worker safety. See Matthew T. Lee and Jeannine A. Gailey, "Who Is to Blame for Deviance in Organizations? The Role of Scholarly Worldviews," *Sociology Compass* 1 (2007): 536–51.

8. This is not to suggest that only the religious pursue the path of substantive rationality. However, our survey findings and interview data both suggest that religion has important implications for the content of this rationality.

9. For more on Paul's conflict with his denomination, see Matthew T. Lee, "Towards a Nonkilling Society: A Case Study of Individual and Institutional Changes in Social Affinity within a Religious Context," in *Nonkilling Societies*, edited by Joám Evans Pim, 365–87 (Honolulu: Center for Global Nonkilling, 2010).

10. See Matthew T. Lee and Margaret M. Poloma, *A Sociological Study of the Great Commandment in Pentecostalism: The Practice of Godly Love as Benevolent Service* (New York: Edwin Mellen, 2009).

11. Adjusted R^2 for the equation in which "giving time" was the dependent variable was .20. The betas for the significant independent variables are as follows: divine love (beta = .22); political liberal (beta = .17); age (beta = .14); religious network (beta = .12); income (beta = −.10); and male (beta = −.09).

12. Adjusted R^2 for the equation in which "giving money" was the dependent variable was .12. The betas for the significant independent variables are as follows: income (beta = .21); education (beta = .19); age (beta = −.09); being male (beta = −.09); divine love (beta = .15); and religious network (beta =.10).

13. Adjusted R^2 for familial benevolence was .12. The betas for the significant independent variables are as follows: being female (beta = .12); income (beta = .19); spiritual affinity (beta = .12); and divine love (beta = .12).

14. Adjusted R^2 for benevolence toward friends and neighbors was .11. The betas for the significant independent variables are as follows: spiritual affinity with all humanity (beta = .26); divine love (beta = .17); and being female (beta = .09).

15. Adjusted R^2 for community benevolence was .16. The betas for the significant independent variables are as follows: spiritual affinity with all humanity (beta = .18); divine love (beta = .12); and age (beta = −.12).

16. Adjusted R^2 for global benevolence was .13. The betas for the significant independent variables are as follows: spiritual affinity (beta = .21); divine love (beta = .19); and liberal ideology (beta = .12).

17. Monroe, *The Heart of Altruism*, 122.

18. Ibid., 248.

19. Unlike our study, Monroe's findings were not based on a nationally representative survey. A bigger limitation is her narrow focus on some select forms of benevolence (e.g., heroic rescue of Jews during the Holocaust), and she may have missed other forms where religion might have mattered.

20. Sorokin, *The Ways and Power of Love*, 36.

21. Ibid.

22. Ibid., 26.

23. Ibid.

24. Caitlin Flanagan, "The Madness of Cesar Chavez: Cesar Chavez's Story Shows That Saints Should be Judged Guilty until Proved Innocent," *Atlantic*, July/August 2011, 128–35. See also Christopher Hitchens, *The Missionary Position: Mother Teresa in Theory and Practice* (London: Verso, 1995), and "Gandhi's Pride: Did His Asceticism Make Him a Friend of the Poor—or of Poverty?" *Atlantic*, July/August 2011, 136–42.

25. Ann Taves, *Fits, Trances, and Visions: Experiencing Religion and Explaining Experience from Wesley to James* (Princeton, NJ: Princeton University Press, 1999), 350.

26. Stanley Eugene Fish, *Is There a Text in This Class? The Authority of Interpretive Communities* (Cambridge, MA: Harvard University Press, 1980).

27. This episode was discussed in our interview, as well as in the television series *One Punk under God*, first broadcast on the Sundance Channel and now available on DVD.

28. We are continuing our practice of only identifying by name exemplars who have taken a public stand.

29. www.bridges-across.org/ba/campolo.htm, accessed September 8, 2011. Some years ago, when Tony Campolo and Margaret were both on the campus of Lee University as invited speakers, Tony tried to divert his luncheon talk away from the controversial topic of gay marriage by addressing the issue in his opening comments. Margaret remembers him saying, "I know many of you are upset with me because of what my wife Peggy is doing to promote gay marriage. Well, Peggy hears from God. She came up to me one day saying, 'Tony, you are not going to like this, but God told me to work for gay marriage.'" Tony, with a dry humor that he uses well in such presentations, went on to say that God hadn't told him anything about whether gay marriage was right or wrong, so he decided

to go to the New Testament to find out what Jesus had to say. "Well, I couldn't find Jesus saying anything about homosexuality. But while I was there, I did find out what he said about divorce. Oh, I know you evangelicals—Jesus didn't really mean what he said about divorce." No one in the audience raised the issue about gay marriage in the Q&A after Tony's talk.

30. Kris Vallotton, *Developing a Supernatural Lifestyle: A Practical Guide to a Life of Signs, Wonders, and Miracles* (Shippensburg, PA: Destiny Image, 2007), 106–9.

31. See also Margaret M. Poloma and Ralph W. Hood Jr., *Blood and Fire: Godly Love in a Pentecostal Emerging Church* (New York: New York University Press, 2008). The classic anthropological distinction between emic and etic accounts of behavior are relevant here, with the former referring to the insider's view and the latter the perspective of an "outside," ostensibly more objective observer.

32. Philip Rieff, *Charisma: The Gift of Grace, and How It Has Been Taken away from Us* (New York: Vintage Books, 2007).

33. Ibid., 21.

34. Ibid., 228.

35. Ibid., 5. Rieff's language is fluid and often imprecise, with meanings that seem to shift throughout his works. For our purposes, we accept the following definitions. *Interdicts* represent a "renunciation of 'instinct'" (36), or those behaviors that might otherwise naturally occur in the absence of cultural constraint, and are "the fundamental motivational form of all culture by which men [*sic*] feel what it is they are not to do, the very basis for the conduct of their lives" (7). *Faith* is "the general term of obedience to particular interdictory contents" (15). Faith is often "identical with obedience" (70). *Guilt* is "disobedience to…interdictory commands" that prompts genuine remorse. Rieff refers to this as "saving guilt" (36) to indicate its centrality to the experience of divine grace and personal salvation. The power of guilt is reduced or eliminated in a therapeutic culture that Rieff claims has over-turned the possibility of transgression itself. *Charisma* is a "derivation from [divine] authority" (69), a "particular and individual practice of faith, within and only within the cultic organization" (80), with "cultic" referring to a religious tradition that makes interdictory demands on its adherents, not to the deviant "cults" in the modern sense of the word. Charisma is therefore a "practice of the interdictory form" (81) involving the "intensification and resolution of…tension of the faith/guilt complex" (60) and "the task of the charismatic [is] to remind [people] of the eternal presence of authority" (69). *Charisms* are "spiritual" gifts of "God's grace" (80) and represent a "gift or capacity for right action" (81). *Grace* is a "freely given" gift of divine love that results in the bestowal of charisms, and "forgiveness for transgression" (79) in the context of a faith/guilt complex.

36. See Margaret M. Poloma, "Sociology, Philosophy, and the Empirical Study of Godly Love," in *The Science and Theology of Godly Love*, edited by Matthew T. Lee and Amos Yong (DeKalb: Northern Illinois University Press, 2012).

37. See Hitchens, *The Missionary Position*, and Hitchens, "Gandhi's Pride."

38. Poloma, "Sociology, Philosophy."

39. Jim Hill and Rand Cheadle, *The Bible Tells Me So: Uses and Abuses of Holy Scripture* (New York: Anchor, 1996).

40. See http://en.wikipedia.org/wiki/Rhema, accessed September 2, 2011; see also Lee, "Towards a Nonkilling Society," on the "Christocentric hermeneutic."

41. Lee and Poloma, *A Sociological Study of the Great Commandment.*

42. See, for example, Forrest Wilder, "Rick Perry's Army of God," *Texas Observer*, July 12, 2011. Wilder describes the New Apostolic Reformation as "a little-known movement of radical Christians and self-proclaimed prophets" who want "to infiltrate government."

43. William K. Kay (*Apostolic Networks in Great Britain: New Ways of Being Church* [Waynesboro, GA: Paternoster, 2007]) provides some history that is relevant not only for the United Kingdom but also for the United States.

44. C. Peter Wagner, foreword to Bill Hamon, *Apostles, Prophets and the Coming Moves of God: God's End-Time Plans for His Church and Planet Earth* (Santa Rosa, FL: Christian International, 1997), xxii.

45. As we were writing this chapter, National Public Radio ran the headline "Rick Perry's Religious Revival Sparks a Holy War" to describe an upcoming event associated with some NAR leaders and the governor of Texas (see www.npr. org/2011/08/05/138995325/rick-perrys-religious-revival-sparks-a-holy-war, accessed August 5, 2011). The reference to "holy war" seems appropriate given the contentiousness of the topic; for one example of Christian-based criticism of NAR, see www.deceptioninthechurch.com/newapostolic.html, accessed August 5, 2011. One observer notes, "There is a lot of cross-pollination and sharing and borrowing (and in some cases, plagiarizing) of ideas and strategies" among the NAR and other religious movements such as Word of Faith (see www.religiondispatches.org/dispatches/sarahposner/4874/rick_perry_and_the_new_apostolic_reformation/, accessed August 5, 2011).

46. Wilder, "Rick Perry's Army of God."

47. For further discussion see Bill Johnson, *When Heaven Invades Earth: A Practical Guide to a Life of Miracles* (Shippensburg, PA: Destiny Image, 2003).

48. The members of the NAR network and its American leaders reflect a loosely structured group that is subject to change. One list identifies the leaders as the "Revival Alliance," consisting of Bill Johnson (Bethel Church, Redding), Ché and Sue Ahn (H-Rock Church, Pasadena), Georgian Banov (Global Celebration), Randy Clark (Global Awakening), Rolland and Heidi Baker (Iris Ministries), and John and Carol Arnott (former pastor of the Toronto Airport Christian Fellowship—now Catch the Fire Toronto). We were able to interview all of these leaders for this project (www.globalawakening.com/Groups/1000015990/Global_Awakening/Global/Directory/Revival_Alliance/, accessed September 5, 2011).

49. Bentley, who was initially considered for inclusion in our study, is discussed in Lee and Poloma, *A Sociological Study of the Great Commandment*, 136–38. His partici-

pation in an extramarital affair while leading a revival in Lakeland, Florida, was revealed in the media while Margaret and Matt attended the GA conference.

50. See Bentley's website: www.freshfireusa.com/, accessed January 19, 2012. For a letter of endorsement from Bill Johnson detailing the restoration process, see www .freshfireusa.com/index.php/articles/view/216, accessed December 10, 2011.

51. See www.freshfireusa.com/index.php/articles/view/216, accessed December 10, 2011.

52. For further discussion of NAR church government by a leader at Bethel Church Redding see Danny Silk, *Culture of Honor: Sustaining a Supernatural Environment* (Shippensburg, PA: Destiny Image, 2009), esp. chap. 2.

53. See www.ibethel.org/our-mission and www.bethelcleveland.com/, both accessed September 5, 2011.

54. www.rightwingwatch.org/content/ahn-america-needs-confront-gay-marriage-we-confronted-slavery, accessed August 5, 2011.

55. Especially noteworthy as Ahn's longtime colleague is the controversial Lou Engle, cofounder with Ahn of The Call solemn assemblies. See www.louengle.com/, accessed August 5, 2011. Ahn regards Engle as the prophet for his (Ahn's) apostolic ministry.

56. Herbert D. Daughtry Sr., *No Monopoly on Suffering: Blacks and Jews in Crown Heights (and Elsewhere)* (Trenton, NJ: African World, 1997), 53.

57. www.youtube.com/watch?v=23Kox5Wt-HY, accessed January 10, 2011.

58. J. Kameron Carter, *Race: A Theological Account* (New York: Oxford University Press, 2008), 230.

59. Daughtry, *No Monopoly on Suffering*, 114–15.

60. Ibid., 40.

61. Ibid., 38.

62. Ibid.

63. Ibid., 32.

64. A. G. Miller. "From Prison to the White House: Herbert D. Daughtry and the Making of a Black Nationalist Pentecostal Leader," paper presented on March 3 at the annual meetings of the Society for Pentecostal Studies, 2012, 5.

65. Herbert Daughtry, "Unnamed 1957 Lewisburg Prison Document," 2, quoted in ibid., 10.

66. Ibid., 11.

67. Herbert Daughtry, *My Beloved Community: Sermons, Speeches and Lectures* (Trenton, NJ: Africa World, 2001), 133, quoted in ibid., 23.

68. Quoted in ibid., 24.

69. Video of this event is archived on YouTube; see www.youtube.com/watch?v=KYWDJfGUkh8, accessed May 31, 2010.

70. See www.pcpj.org/, accessed May 31, 2010.

71. In their study of the Assemblies of God, Paul's denomination, Poloma and Green found that most congregants support Israel over Palestinians in the Middle East

crisis, and two-thirds agreed with the U.S. prerogative for preemptive military action against other countries. Margaret M. Poloma and John C. Green, *The Assemblies of God: Godly Love and the Revitalization of American Pentecostalism* (New York: New York University Press, 2010).

72. For more on the importance of staying centered on Jesus for benevolent service, see Stephen G. Post, "Godly Love: Why We Cannot Endure without It," in *The Science and Theology of Godly Love,* edited by Matthew T. Lee and Amos Yong (DeKalb: Northern Illinois University Press, 2012). For more on Paul Alexander's peace and justice work, see Lee, "Towards a Nonkilling Society."

73. Paul Alexander, *Peace to War: Shifting Allegiances in the Assemblies of God* (Scottdale, PA: Cascadia, 2009).

74. Ibid., 346.

75. Quotes in this paragraph are from ibid., 347–49.

76. Lee, "Towards a Nonkilling Society."

77. See www.pcpj.org/index.php/resources-topmenu-45/125-sermons/409-paul-alexander-preaches-to-6000-at-mennonite-church-usa-biennial-convention-july-4-2007, accessed August 5, 2011.

78. Founded by Ché Ahn, Harvest International Ministries (HIM) is an apostolic network of churches, ministries, missions organizations, church networks, and marketplace ministers "committed to loving and helping each other fulfill the Great Commission." The "heart" of HIM is Mercy Ministries, in which churches "reach out across the globe with the message of hope and the hand of mercy," in which they service "the broken and the abandoned" (http://harvestim.org/, accessed September 7, 2011).

79. See www.youtube.com/watch?v=L8_GXfFqY3k, accessed August 17, 2011.

CONCLUSION

1. Audio of a sermon on file with the first author; details omitted to protect anonymity. For additional discussion of similar incidents, see Arlene Sanchez Walsh, "Toward a Grounded Theory of Godly Love: Latino/a Pentecostals," in *The Science and Theology of Godly Love*, edited by Matthew T. Lee and Amos Yong, 200–215 (DeKalb: Northern Illinois University Press, 2012), see especially 207 and 215, n. 22.

2. Craig Cable, "Author of *The Shack* Reveals Its Meaning, and Where Real Hope and Healing Come From," March 24, 2011, www.breakingchristiannews.com/articles/display_art.html?ID=8778.

3. Stephen G. Post, "Works of Love: A Newsletter from the Institute for Research on Unlimited Love," November 27, 2011.

4. Margaret M. Poloma and Ralph W. Hood Jr., *Blood and Fire: Godly Love in a Pentecostal Emerging Church* (New York: New York University Press, 2008).

5. Matthew T. Lee and Margaret M. Poloma, *A Sociological Study of the Great Commandment in Pentecostalism: The Practice of Godly Love as Benevolent Service* (New York: Edwin Mellen, 2009), 15.

6. H. Richard Niebuhr, *Christ and Culture* (New York: Harper Torchbooks, 1951), 13, 15. For recent assessments of Niebuhr's classic, see Craig A. Carter, *Rethinking "Christ and Culture": A Post-Christendom Perspective* (Grand Rapids, MI: Brazos, 2006); D. A. Carson, *"Christ and Culture" Revisited* (Grand Rapids, MI: William B. Eerdmans, 2008).

7. Niebuhr, *Christ and Culture*, 19, 27.

8. Ibid., 2.

9. As a result of Tolstoy's partial renunciation of wealth, "responsibility for the management of the [Tolstoy] estate fell on his wife, who was poorly equipped for the task. Under her inadequate supervision, incompetent or dishonest stewards allowed the property to fall into general disorder. A horrible accident occurred as a result of the maladministration—a peasant was buried alive in a neglected sandpit. 'I seldom saw father so upset,' writes his daughter." Niebuhr, *Christ and Culture*, 75.

10. We have classified our interviewees according to these types in Lee and Poloma, *A Sociological Study of the Great Commandment*, 153–54.

11. The bivariate relationship between the Divine Love scale and the Existential Well-Being scale is .36. Causation, however, is always difficult to determine in statistical tests, so we proceed to multivariate analysis only with caution. Assuming that experiences of divine love are the "cause" of an increased sense of meaning and purpose in life, the latter became the dependent variable and five demographic measures were added to the Divine Love scale as independent variables. The adjusted R^2 for this equation testing for the effects of divine love on existential well-being is .17, with divine love explaining most of the variance (beta = .36). Smaller positive effects were found for women (beta = .11) and for those with higher incomes (beta = .09).

12. Robert Welsh and Paul Alexander, "Exemplars of Godly Justice Peacemaking and Justice Seeking in Dangerous Contexts," *PentecoStudies* (forthcoming).

13. www.sojo.net/index.cfm?action=about_us.home, accessed August 11, 2011.

14. See Poloma and Hood, *Blood and Fire*.

15. We distinguish the classic Pentecostal denominations from the broader pentecostal worldview by capitalizing the former (see chapter 2).

16. http://ag.org/top/Press/organization.cfm, accessed May 28, 2012.

17. For further discussion see Margaret M. Poloma, *The Assemblies of God at the Crossroads* (Knoxville: University of Tennessee Press, 1989); Margaret M. Poloma and John C. Green, *The Assemblies of God: Godly Love and the Revitalization of American Pentecostalism* (New York: New York University Press, 2010).

18. See "David DuPlessis Talks about Wigglesworth Prophecy," www.youtube.com/watch?v=s-pB6xtWqUE, accessed January 9, 2012.

19. Cited in Poloma, *The Assemblies of God at the Crossroads*, 132.
20. We have respected Mel's wishes that the details about this issue not be publicized.
21. E-mail from Mel Robeck to Margaret Poloma, January 6, 2012. Two documents were attached: an undated "Christmas Letter" and untitled letter to "Friends and Family," dated October 29, 2011.
22. Carson, *Christ and Culture Revisited*, 219, approvingly cites Carter, *Rethinking Christ and Culture,* on this point.
23. "Jonas Beiler on WJTL," www.youtube.com/watch?v=4DCD9t0CQgI, accessed December 11, 2012.
24. www.gapfamilycenter.org/aboutus.php, accessed December 11, 2012.
25. Grant Wacker, *Heaven Below: Early Pentecostals and American Culture* (Cambridge, MA: Harvard University Press, 2001).
26. Margaret M. Poloma, *Main Street Mystics: The Toronto Blessing and Reviving Pentecostalism* (Walnut Creek, CA: Alta Mira, 2003). See also Margaret M. Poloma and Matthew T. Lee, "The New Apostolic Reformation: Main Street Mystics and Everyday Prophets," in *Prophecy in the New Millennium: When Prophecies Persist*, edited by Sarah Harvey and Suzanne Newcombe (Farnham, UK: Ashgate, forthcoming).
27. www.irismin.org/news/newsletters, March 1, 2001, accessed January 12, 2012.
28. This notion of relying on God's power and love was a common theme in many of the narratives that we collected. As Anne Belier explained to Matt, God was able to find a way forward for her when she could not: "And in the middle of my despair…on that plane ride when the Lord spoke to me, not audibly, but I'm telling you I heard it like I hear that waterfall out there [referring to a nearby waterfall]. He said to me, 'I will make a way for you.' It so interrupted my thoughts. It was so abrupt and so powerful.…Lord, okay, I heard you. But what I heard you say is that you will make a way for me. Okay, if that's true, then you will do that. I can't."
29. www.youtube.com/watch?v=L8_GXfFqY3k, accessed August 17, 2011.
30. "Heidi Baker Testimony," www.YouTube.com/watch?v=0836Bq44a61, accessed December 29, 2011.
31. See Margaret M. Poloma, "Sociology, Philosophy, and the Empirical Study of Godly Love," in *The Science and Theology of Godly Love*, 157–82.
32. www.irisministries.com/about-our-mission, accessed August 24, 2010.
33. Ibid.
34. William James, *The Varieties of Religious Experience: A Study in Human Nature* (1902; rpt., Cambridge, MA: Harvard University Press, 1985).
35. 1 Corinthians 13:13.

Author Index

Salgado, Brenda, 266
Sandoval, Moises, 257
Schoenrade, Patricia, 256
Seligman, Adam B., 254, 268
Sered, Susan S., 271
Shakespeare, William, 251
Shevlin, Mark, 264
Silk, Danny, 279
Simon, Bennett, 254, 268
Smucker, Shawn, 271
Smyth, Joshua M., 269
Sorokin, Pitirim, 247, 264, 274, 275, 276
Stafford, Tim, 268
Strobel, Lee, 269

Taves, Ann, 276
Thoreau, Henry David, 274
Tolstoy, Leo, 250, 251, 281

Underwood, Lynn G., 252

Vallotton, Kris, 277
Varacalli, Joseph, 257

Velu, Eric, 268
Ventis, W. Larry, 256

Wacker, Grant, 253, 259
Wagner, C. Peter, 273, 278
Walsh, Arlene Sanchez, 280
Weber, Max, 275
Wedam, Elfriede, 256
Weems, Renita J., 257
Weller, Robert P., 254, 268
Welsh, Robert, 249, 273, 281
West, Cornel, 260
Wilder, Forrest, 273, 278
Wilkinson, Michael, 254, 265, 266
Wilson-Hartgrove, Jonathan, 266
Witt, Steve, 266, 273
Woolever, Cynthia, 255, 256
Wuthnow, Robert, 248

Yamamori, Tetsunao, 254
Yandell, Keith E., 264
Yong, Amos, 249, 263, 274, 280

Zimmerman, Kristen, 266

Subject Index

The Will